Faithful Persuasion

Winner of the 1990 Bross Prize

David Cunningham's book, *Faithful Persuasion: In Aid of a Rhetoric of Christian Theology,* was awarded the $15,000 first prize in the 1990 Bross Prize competition. Since 1880, an endowment established by William R. Bross, a charter trustee of Lake Forest College, has provided prizes approximately once a decade for the best unpublished manuscript on the relation between any discipline and the Christian religion. Cunningham's study of rhetoric and contemporary theology now joins this distinguished library of Bross Prize books that has accumulated over the past century:

1880   *Evidences of Christianity,* Mark Hopkins. Published 1909, T. R. Marvin and Son.

1905   *The Problem of the Old Testament,* James Orr. Published 1922, Scribner's.

1915   *The Mystical Interpretation of the Gospels,* Thomas J. Thoburn. Published 1916, Scribner's.

1925   *The Reasonableness of Christianity,* Douglas Clyde MacIntosh. Published 1928, Scribner's.

1940   *Christianity,* Harris Franklin Rall. Published 1940, Scribner's.

1950   *Modern Poetry and the Christian Tradition,* Amos N. Wilder. Published 1952, Scribner's.

1960   *Language and Faith: Studies in Sign, Symbol, and Meaning,* John A. Hutchison. Published 1960, Westminster Press.

1970   *Revolution in Theology,* Dean Claude Welch. Published 1972, Yale University Press, under the title *Protestant Thought in the Nineteenth Century.*

1980   *Beyond the Burning Plain: A Study of Matthew Arnold's Religious Criticism and Belief,* James C. Livingston. Published 1986, University of South Carolina Press, under the title, *Matthew Arnold and Christianity: His Religious Prose Writings.*

Faithful Persuasion

In Aid of a Rhetoric of Christian Theology

DAVID S. CUNNINGHAM

University of Notre Dame Press
Notre Dame and London

Some Sections of this book have appeared in a different form
in "Theology as Rhetoric," *Theological Studies* 52/3
(September 1991): 407–430.

All citations and quotations of Scripture are according to the
New Revised Standard Version of the Bible

Library of Congress Cataloging-in-Publication Data

Cunningham, David S., 1961–
    Faithful persuasion : in aid of a rhetoric of Christian theology
    David S. Cunningham.
        p.   cm.
    Includes index.
    ISBN 0-268-00984-8
    1. Language and languages—Religious aspects—Christianity
I. Title.
BR115.L25C86   1991
230'.014—dc20   91-50565
                                                            CIP

To my parents
Donald and Patsy Cunningham

sine quibus nihil

For since by means of the art of rhetoric both truth and false-hood are urged, who would dare to say that truth should stand in the person of its defenders unarmed against lying, so that they who wish to urge falsehoods may know how to make their listeners benevolent, or attentive, or docile in their presentation, while the defenders of truth are ignorant of that art?

While the faculty of eloquence, which is of great value in urging either evil or justice, is in itself indifferent, why should it not be obtained for the uses of the good in the service of truth, if the evil usurp it for the winning of perverse and vain causes in defense of iniquity and error?

St. Augustine of Hippo
De doctrina Christiana 4.2

Contents

Preface

Theology is language *(logos)* about God *(theos)*. Whenever people attempt to communicate through language, they will eventually find themselves disagreeing with one another; and, when their language concerns God, they may find themselves disagreeing quite frequently. At its very core, then, theology is concerned with disagreements (and agreements) about God and about things related to God. Hence, the enterprise of theology necessarily involves the construction and the dissection of arguments and argumentative strategies. And because many people hold particularly strong opinions about religious belief, efforts at persuasion can become strident or even lead to violence. The highly-charged nature of religious discourse helps to account for the passionate responses that theological argument has sometimes provoked. It has led to strife, schism, and war.

And if this is an adequate description of religious thought in general, it applies with even greater force to Christianity. Unlike faiths that regard themselves as essentially closed to outsiders, Christianity frequently seeks to engage the rest of the world. Christians have actively sought to defend their faith—in the political arena, in the academy, and in the "squares and avenues." Christians have preached the Gospel to both the converted and the unconverted, and have entered upon disputations concerning Christianity's theological import, its socio-political role, and its general intellectual muster.

But despite the obviously confrontational posture of much Christian theological discourse, few of its practitioners have been willing to admit that it is, in fact, composed of arguments. After all, the word *argument* implies at least two possible positions; this, in turn, implies multiplicity and contingency, for if argument is possible, then everything could be otherwise. To many observers, such contingency seems alien to Christianity, which often makes quite absolute claims that seem not to admit of alternatives—in turn suggesting little room for argument. And indeed, many theologians attempt to disguise the inherently argumentative character of their claims, precisely in order to make them more effective as arguments. An argument assigned a different label—say, *proposition* or *command* or *prophecy*—seems less contingent and more normative. Theologians who thus disguise their arguments can dispense with specific warrants and concrete examples in support of their claims.

Or so they may think. They may discover, however, that such absolute claims—initially effective as they may be—do not have the lasting impact for which the claimant might have hoped. As soon as the audience has left the comfortable surroundings in which the claims are made, its members may discover a number of competing claims—and may then realize that what had appeared to be definitive statements were actually *arguments* for a particular position. But because the arguments were put forward without warrants and examples, they suddenly seem bereft of support.

In other words, even though Christian theology has often refused to acknowledge its own reliance on argumentative discourse, it still competes with other worldviews and philosophies for the hearts and minds of those who hear its message. An audience exposed to the Christian Gospel will typically be exposed to other gospels as well—be they faiths, philosophies, political platforms, or economic systems. These alternative perspectives are often supported with carefully fashioned arguments, making a much more self-conscious effort to win the audience's favor. Thus, Christianity has frequently placed itself at a disadvantage. Audiences have judged the Christian Gospel against more powerfully focused messages, and have made their choices accordingly.

In this book, I propose an alternative. I believe that Christian theologians should frankly acknowledge the radical contingency of the language they use to talk about God. "No one has ever seen God" (John 1:18); and no one, least of all the Christian theologian, is competent to act as the expert on the nature and purposes of God. Far from the absolute enterprise that it is often assumed to be, Christian theology is a fragile and uncertain endeavor. Its claims can be only tentative, and the truth of its assertions are known only to God. In the field of Christian theology, even the most brilliant scholar can do no more than creep along, "amid th' encircling gloom," aware only that a "kindly light" seems to shine somewhere in the distance.

This vision of theology—traditionally called the *negative way*—lends itself to a very different understanding of theological language. Theology cannot rely on descriptions of the absolute and the necessary, for it is not privy to any inside information concerning the ways of God. Instead, theology must employ language that takes account of contingency and uncertainty. Composed neither of propositions, nor of directives, nor even primarily of narratives, exhortations, or prophecies, Christian theology is instead—and above all—a form of persuasive argument.

If we are willing to recognize the persuasive function of Christian theology, then we will better serve the interests of all participants in the theological conversation. Arguments are constructed by human beings, not by God. Even if some assertions are thought to come directly from God, they can be expressed only in human language. They are developed by particular individuals and communities, for specific audiences, in concrete contexts. They can thus be analyzed with the same tools that are used to analyze other attempts at persuasion. The most important tool for this enterprise is the ancient faculty of rhetoric.

The purpose of this book, then, is to present a sustained account of the relationship between Christian theology and the classical rhetorical tradition. The recent widespread revival of rhetoric—increasingly evident among scholars of contemporary philosophy, communication theory, and literary criticism—can provide an excellent opportunity for theologians to reevaluate their own methodological assumptions. By applying the insights of classical rhetoric to Christian thought, some perennial (and seemingly intractable) theological debates can be seen in a new light.

This book is written not by a rhetorical theorist but by a theologian who is also trained in communication studies. I have done my best to keep up with the ever-expanding literature in argumentation theory, but I make no claim to be on the cutting edge of rhetorical scholarship. Rather, I write for theologians, for clergy, and for laypeople with an interest in theology—and for all others who are interested in the Christian faith. I write in order to introduce to these colleagues and fellow travelers the richness of the rhetorical tradition, as well as its important implications for the discipline of Christian theology.

Because this study brings together two academic fields, I find myself indebted to more than the usual number of teachers, colleagues, and friends. My interest in both rhetoric and theology began during my undergraduate days at Northwestern University; I owe thanks to Michael Hyde, Richard Kieckhefer, Edmund Perry, and David Zarefsky for putting me on course. My vocation as a theologian was decisively shaped by my teachers at Cambridge and at Duke—Thomas Langford, Nicholas Lash, Ken Surin, John Sweet, and especially Geoffrey Wainwright and Rowan Williams. Their passion for theology and their devotion to the mystery of the Triune God continue to inspire my work.

Thanks are also due to many other scholars who helped shape this book. Although scattered all across the country, they have made a special effort to keep in contact with me as I wrote and rewrote successive versions. They read significant parts of the work in draft and provided much-needed comment and correction. They also helped keep me abreast of new material that pertained to my project. For their many kindnesses, I offer my thanks to Michael Cartwright of Allegheny College; to Roy Melugin of Austin College; to Teresa Berger, Michael Gillespie, Stanley Hauerwas, and Phil Kenneson of Duke University; to Andrew Adam and Margaret Adam of Eckerd College; to Jim Buckley and Greg Jones of Loyola College in Maryland; to Dan Sack of Princeton University; to Gary Atkinson and Joe Hallman of the University of St. Thomas; and to Jonathan Wilson of Westmont College.

I also want to thank the president and trustees of Lake Forest College and everyone associated with the Bross Foundation, who judged this work worthy of their decennial prize. Special acknowledgment is due to Dan Cole, who coordinated the program, and to the internal and external judges, who read the fifty-one book-length manuscripts that were submitted. Similarly, everyone at Notre Dame Press has been tremendously helpful—especially my editor, Dr. Jeannette Morgenroth Sheerin, who has corrected the manuscript with expert attention to detail while maintaining a sincere respect for the integrity of the book as a whole.

Finally, this volume would never have come into being without the unfailing devotion of my wife, Teresa Hittner. She read many drafts of the text, helped organize the bibliographic material, and offered much helpful advice and support. More importantly, she has always been a source of inspiration—both through her strong commitment to education and through her moral, intellectual, and financial support for my scholarly vocation. By her words and deeds she has encouraged me to do my very best work and has given me hope and strength: she is truly a remarkable example of "faithful persuasion."

I want to conclude by acknowledging my debt to all those whom I cannot here mention by name. Over the years, many people have sought diligently to persuade me of the truth of the Gospel. Some of them still make their abode on this earth; others now dwell in more comfortable surroundings. Together they constitute the communion of saints: friends and family, teachers and pastors, apostles, martyrs, and theologians. They all earnestly sought to argue the case for the Christian faith, and they persuaded me to belief and action. These saints have made me who I am; my debt to them is incalculable. They all partake in the qualities of two of the greatest exemplars of faithful persuasion, whose feasts are celebrated—one in the East and one in the West—on this day.

Feast of St. Gregory of Nazianzus, the Theologian
Feast of the Conversion of St. Paul the Apostle
Anno Domini 1991

Introduction

Speaking about the
Unknowable

"The human being is a rational animal"—or so we are told, in the common translation of this famous Greek dictum. But given the typical modern connotations of the word *rational*, this translation obscures a very interesting emphasis in the Greek. The human being is a *zōon logon echon*—a living and *speaking* being, a living thing that is capable of speech. Human beings are creatures who communicate with one another by means of language. We speak, we write, we listen, we read.

Moreover, our communication is purposeful: we often expect that by means of speech something particular will be brought to pass. Occasionally, we may speak simply for the pleasure of hearing our own voices. Typically, however, our words have a goal: we explain, demand, ask, answer, praise, blame, amuse, and plead. Often we speak in order to get someone else to think or act in a particular way. Yet the words that we use seem so ordinary to us that we rarely consider them in detail; we rarely give them our careful, undivided attention.

Sometimes we speak from a position of security and certain knowledge. For example, we do not hesitate when teaching arithmetic and the alphabet to small children; we are quite certain of what we know and what we say. But more often—indeed, most of the time—we speak of things about which our

1

knowledge is incomplete. We make predictions; we operate according to assumptions; we offer the best explanation we can muster. Only rarely do we know beyond all doubt, and even then concerning only the most trivial matters. Our access to the realm of rock-solid certainty is limited at best.

Yet despite the incompleteness of our knowledge, we continue to speak. We speak about what we cannot know (and will never learn with final certainty). This aspect of the human condition has been quite gracefully described by Kenneth Burke:

> Imagine that you enter a parlor. You come late. When you arrive, others have long preceded you, and they are engaged in a heated discussion, a discussion too heated for them to pause and tell you exactly what it is about. In fact, the discussion had already begun long before any of them got there, so that no one present is qualified to retrace for you all the steps that had gone before. You listen for a while, until you decide that you have caught the tenor of the argument; then you put in your oar. Someone answers; you answer him; another comes to your defense; another aligns himself against you, to either the embarrassment or gratification of your opponent, depending upon the quality of your ally's assistance. However, the discussion is interminable. The hour grows late, you must depart. And you do depart, with the discussion vigorously in progress.[1]

We may as well put in our oars like everyone else. We are all participants in a discussion that began long before we arrived, and will continue long after we have departed.

But note carefully: the participants in this discussion are not simply having a pleasant conversation. They are not seeking mutual edification; nor are they expecting to arrive at the final, definitive, ultimate truth. Instead, they are *arguing:* most of them have been around for long enough to have developed a particular point of view, and they are actively seeking to persuade others to endorse that view. No one has the final, definitive proof; no one can retrace every winding track of thought in order to reduce the discussion to a complete and coherent logical demonstration. In short, no one can close the disputation by revealing the final answer.

Moreover, the discussion takes place on uneven ground. Most participants have been disputing long enough to know the ropes; some have just arrived. Some deploy their arguments from positions of power and influence; others speak from weakness. Some attract a large number of allies and apologists; others fight their battles alone. Burke's "parlor scene" depicts the world of human discourse: uneven, unfair, uncertain, unresolved, and never coming to a close.

If these comments accurately describe human discourse in general, then they apply with even greater force to the enterprise of theology. Theology is language about God—which is to say that, while the subject matter of theology is God, its vehicle is human language. Necessarily operating in that ill-defined space between God and humanity, theology attempts to speak of God and divine things in language that is comprehensible to human beings. Theology dwells *in media res*—sometimes a highly unstable and insecure abode.

Indeed, the attempt to talk about God is often considered the most difficult of human undertakings. This was certainly the view of Plato, who considered God to be far beyond the range of human contemplation. Yet even Plato's skepticism was considered far too optimistic by St. Gregory of Nazianzus, who offered a more radical version of the famous Platonic dictum.

> It is difficult to conceive God, but to define him in words is an impossibility, as one of the Greek teachers of divinity taught, not unskillfully, as it appears to me. . . . But in my opinion it is impossible to express God, and yet more impossible to conceive God. For that which may be conceived may perhaps be made clear by language, if not fairly well, at any rate imperfectly, to anyone who is not quite deprived of his hearing, or slothful of understanding. But to comprehend the whole of so great a subject as this is quite impossible and impracticable, not merely to the utterly careless and ignorant, but even to those who are highly exalted, and who love God.[2]

God cannot be fully discovered through human power alone. This principle, frequently obscured in the Western theological and philosophical traditions, might nevertheless be called *the* fundamental assumption of Christian theology. "God makes His dwelling there where our understanding and our concepts can gain no admittance."[3]

And yet Christian theology continues to talk about God, to speak about what it cannot prove or discover on its own. Hence, Christian theology should not be understood as a set of propositions that can be decisively proved to be true. The theologian longs for truth, but also recognizes that the fullness of truth belongs to God rather than to human language about God. Any theology claiming to speak *the truth* is speaking a word that God alone can speak. For human beings, the knowledge of truth is an eschatological reality: "For now we see in a mirror, dimly, but then we will see face to face. Now I know only in part; then I will know fully, even as I have been fully known" (1 Cor. 13:12; all quotations and citations of Scripture are given according to the NRSV).

Meanwhile, in this "time between the times," Christian theology can only speak about what *seems* to be true. Following the *via negativa*, theology gains its greatest insights when it leaves matters of truth to God and strives, rather, toward verisimilitude—toward what appears to be true. And this is no discredit to theology, for verisimilitude is all we can expect to achieve; the truth subsists in God alone.

This change in focus may help us understand why the essence of Christianity must remain an "essentially contested concept."[4] Yet theology must still continue to speak—even about what cannot yet be fully known. Our lack of complete knowledge does not prevent us from speaking, nor indeed, from acting. This is why Burke's parable of the parlor is so appropriate: it reminds us that we continue to engage in passionate argument, even concerning matters about which—in this world, at any rate—we can never expect to learn the whole truth.

Christian theology, then, is necessarily a tentative and fragile enterprise. It claims to speak about a truth to which, by its own admission, it has no definitive access. It thus must operate under the assumption that all its formulations concerning belief and practice are necessarily open to revision: That Christian theology refers to the absolute, but does so within the vicissitudes of history, accounts for what Ray Hart has called the "tentativity" of the theological enterprise.[5]

If these observations are accurate, then we must revise radically our common assumptions about the nature and function of theological language. In this book, I offer a vision of Christian theology that can account for our willingness to continue to speak about and act upon the Christian faith—even in the midst of uncertainty.

Specifically, I want to claim that Christian theology is best understood as *persuasive argument*. Theologians are involved not in the exchange of propositions, nor even in edifying "conversations," but in debates, disputes, and arguments. Theologians are always seeking to persuade others—and to persuade themselves—of a particular understanding of the Christian faith. The goal of Christian theology, then, is *faithful persuasion:* to speak the word that theology must speak, in ways that are faithful to the God of Jesus Christ and persuasive to the world that God has always loved. This has been the goal of Christian theology since the days of one of its earliest practitioners, St. Paul. "Therefore, knowing the fear of the Lord, we try to persuade others" (2 Cor. 5:11).

The most appropriate tool for analyzing theological language, then, will be able to account for the variety of ways in which persuasion occurs. This was precisely the role of the ancient faculty of *rhetoric.* The classical rhetorical tradition provides a wellspring of insights into the functions and effects of theological language. These insights will be developed and examined throughout the present volume, which is itself an extended persuasive argument—specifically, an attempt to persuade its audience of the rhetorical nature of Christian theology. Thus, like all rhetorical treatises, this work is already intimately involved in the practices and procedures that it seeks to demonstrate. Admittedly, then, any attempt to speak or write about rhetoric is necessarily a circular endeavor; circularity, however, can be a virtue, for a rhetorical treatise can hope to exemplify the method which it advocates.

While classical rhetoric was originally concerned primarily with the spoken word, it later came to give significant attention to written as well as oral modes of communication. Thus, both spoken and written forms of persuasion are examined in the present work. The differences between speech and writing, however significant, cannot be explored in detail here. In avoiding this issue, I recognize that I am eliding a number of important distinctions.[6] Nevertheless, I must postpone any full consideration on the grounds that, had I addressed this issue, I would have written two volumes instead of one. Instead, I have taken care to specify those instances in which the differences between writing and speech seem decisive. Otherwise I use terms for written discourse interchangeably with those for spoken discourse.

Rhetoric has had a long and distinguished career, which will be explored in detail in chapter 1. The rhetorical tradition intersects with Christian theology in a number of ways. The New Testament, the patristic era, the Reformation: all influenced, and were influenced by, the rhetorical tradition. Not surprisingly, then, we will discover that classical rhetoric and Christian theology share a number of historical, methodological, and structural similarities.

The activity of persuasion has three identifiable features: a rhetor, an audience, and some form of communication (which can be discursive, nondiscursive, or both). The three constituent rhetorical elements cannot be understood in isolation from one another. Nevertheless, they provide a convenient way of organizing and structuring an investigation into how persuasion occurs; and so they provide the basis, respectively, for the three central chapters of this book. Chapter 2 discusses the audience to which theology speaks; chapter 3 examines the speaker or writer, inquiring into the character with which theology speaks; and chapter 4 investigates the arguments themselves: the word which theology speaks.

In practice, these three elements of persuasion work in concert. Thus, the final chapter explores their symbiotic relationship as manifested in three particular theological practices: doctrinal formulation, biblical exegesis, and Church historiography. This chapter provides a more concrete description of the reasons why Christian theology can best be characterized as faithful persuasion.

A complete rhetoric of Christian theology would attempt to catalogue the wide variety of appeals that are employed in order to persuade others to faithfulness. Clearly, the compilation of such a catalogue would be a project of enormous scope. Consequently, the present volume offers only an initial pointer toward such an enterprise; it describes some of the sources, methods, and structures of a rhetorical approach to Christian theology. It seeks to suggest a point of entry, in the hope that others might be willing to carry the project further.

A rhetorical approach to Christian theology can shed light on the process of argumentation and may thereby have some impact on debates which have proved intractable and have divided Christians, one from another. I can only hope that the approach suggested here might help to clarify these debates and to reconcile the disputants. Of course, the argument will continue—long after I have left the parlor. But the fragility and incompleteness of this process should not diminish the eschatological hope on which all Christian theology is grounded: "that they may all be one" (John 17:21).

1

Theōria

Theology and Rhetoric

The present chapter examines the ancient faculty of rhetoric and its implications for Christian theology. But rather than developing a *theory* of this relationship, I want to offer what the Greeks called *theōria*—a looking at, a beholding. The word *theōria* named a particular attitude, a way of approaching the world; it was relatively free of the modern baggage carried by the word *theory*, which typically connotes the abstract, the hypothetical, and the rigidly systematic.[1] For the Greeks, *theōria* was simply an attempt to behold, to "see with the mind's eye"—in essence, to think in a serious and disciplined way. This chapter, then, is an essay in thinking about rhetoric and about theology as a rhetorical activity.

I begin by offering a brief historical survey of the classical rhetorical tradition. This account is certainly not exhaustive; I simply try to describe the features of rhetoric that are most important for the present work. Then I discuss the degeneration of the rhetorical tradition during the modern period and the methodological implications of its recent revival. Finally, I turn to the discipline of Christian theology, showing why I believe it to be a thoroughly rhetorical enterprise.

THE VARIETIES OF
CLASSICAL RHETORIC

In popular usage, the term *rhetoric* has attained an almost entirely negative connotation. The word usually suggests either empty speech (as in the well-worn phrase "mere rhetoric") or something considerably worse: outright lies and deception, passed off as truth. This understanding of rhetoric is so pervasive that the standard textbooks usually take pains to repudiate the negative connotations. One such text begins discussing "four myths which have contributed significantly to the contemporary practice of relegating the idea of rhetoric to the level of a pejorative concept."[2] These four false conceptions are: (1) rhetoric as flowery, excessively ornamental language; (2) rhetoric as mere appearance, as opposed to reality; (3) rhetoric as concerned only with style and delivery; and (4) rhetoric as inclusive of every possible form of communication. While the fourth definition is so broad as to be useless, the first three are clearly meant to restrict the scope of rhetoric to a range much smaller than was enjoyed by the classical rhetorical tradition. Indeed, for the ancients, rhetoric was broadly concerned with all speech designed to persuade—that is, with speech designed to change someone's heart, or mind, or words, or deeds.

The orientation of ancient rhetoric toward the goals of *praxis* and persuasion will be developed in detail in this section. The presentation is more or less chronological, except that the treatment of Aristotle is postponed to the end of the section. As we shall discover, the Aristotelian view of rhetoric will set the agenda for its methodological application to other disciplines.

EARLIEST MANIFESTATIONS

We begin with the Sophists, for whom our evidence is scant at best. We know of them primarily through the writings of Plato and Aristotle, who were among their chief detractors. They apparently claimed to practice rhetoric as a political art (*politikē technē*),[3] which could teach the virtue of excellence in the *polis*. Their primary contribution was an ability to recognize that, for a great many fields of inquiry, people can justifiably hold widely varying opinions. Because of this insight, the Sophists constitute "the first big event in the history of rhetoric," because "rhetoric finds fertile ground only in a situation in which one doubts that truth may exist as a given outside the interaction of human beings, their exchange and comparison of opinions that necessarily occur through language."[4] In other words, the pre-Socratic insistence on the conflictive nature of human existence[5] provided a philosophical environment in which rhetoric could develop. Rhetoric was valuable for deliberating about matters that could be otherwise—matters about which we have some choice. "Only insofar as men are potentially free," notes Kenneth Burke, "must the spellbinder seek to persuade them. Insofar as they *must* do something, rhetoric is unnecessary."[6]

The Sophists recognized that most of our judgments are made, not on the basis of incontrovertible evidence, but on the basis of probability (*eikos*) or opinion (*doxa*). Today, we tend to think of probability and opinion as unreliable; although sometimes statistically measurable, we assume that they should never be accepted if more dependable evidence can be found. But the terms were used by the Sophists in a more positive way—an emphasis obscured by translation. Both words suggest that something seems a certain way; that is, that its nature or function is apparent, almost obvious.[7] Either word might be used to imply something like, "I see things this way; and anyone with whom I could expect to have an intelligible conversation can certainly be expected to see things this way as well."

In other words, we can rely on opinion and probability because of their broad, general appeal among those with whom we would be likely to converse. Thus, the Sophists seem to have had a well-developed sense of the significance of community in the process of communication. Far from being the despicable scoundrels that they are often depicted to be, the Sophists placed great faith in common opinion—in whatever most people believe to be the case.

Thus, the connection between the Sophists and the current negative connotations of the word *sophistry* are tenuous at best. As a number of commentators have noted, the techniques of the Sophists were no different from those employed by the later, more "respectable" rhetoricians.[8] The later rhetorical tradition judged the Sophists harshly, not because of their techniques, but because of their lack of concern for the moral implications of persuasive discourse. In other words: although the Sophists recognized that communication is facilitated by what binds a community together, they did not have much to say about the moral and political norms of such communities. Their amoralism generated many of the negative connotations of "sophistic" speech and, by association, lent a pejorative sense to *rhetoric* as well.

One of the first rhetoricians to reject the explicitly amoral character of sophistic rhetoric was Isocrates (436–338 B.C.). His work *Against the Sophists* attempts to distinguish his own views from the argumentative "trickery" of his predecessors. He argues that the orator must be trained in philosophy, by which he apparently means practical wisdom. But more importantly, he contends that the good orator is a person of good moral character.[9]

Despite its emphasis on the good, however, Isocrates' approach to rhetoric was explicitly rejected by Plato.[10] Plato argued that, whether self-consciously moral or not, rhetoric relied upon the opinion of the many; and his opposition to "mere opinion" entailed a negative verdict on rhetoric, or at least on all contemporary forms of rhetorical practice.[11] The differences among various rhetoricians—Isocrates, Protagoras, Gorgias—mattered less to Plato than their general insistence on the *particularity* and *fragility* of truth. Rather than relying on mere opinions, Plato sought true knowledge or science (*epistēmē*)—a knowledge attainable only through philosophy. Because Plato's judgment against *doxa* has had such a profound influence on the subsequent reception of rhetoric, his writings deserve our close attention.

Plato's dialogues do not develop a theory of rhetoric. The *Gorgias* and the *Phaedrus* deal with rhetoric explicitly; but here, as often, Plato does not treat the matter systematically. Instead, the dialogues show a supposed expert—a teacher of rhetoric—being frustrated by the simple questions posed by Socrates. From time to time, a more definitive statement slips through the dialectic:

> Well then, to me, Gorgias, rhetoric seems not to be an artistic pursuit at all, but that of a shrewd, courageous spirit which is naturally clever at dealing with men; and I call the chief part of it flattery. It seems to me to have many branches and one of the them is cookery, which is thought to be an art, but according to my notion it is no art at all, but a knack and a routine.[12]

This flattery of the mere opinions of the audience Plato simply cannot accept.

As we shall observe shortly, Plato's sharp distinction between "mere opinion" and "true knowledge" has been called into serious question. More importantly, though, the relationship between truth and opinion becomes blurred even in Plato's own work. For example, Plato expels the poets from his *Republic*; but the *Republic* itself is certainly the work of a poet. And similarly, Plato's works that oppose rhetoric are clearly the products of a master rhetorician.[13] In all the dialogues, Plato clearly seeks to persuade: to make the reader believe that Socrates employed speech for the sake of truth, while the Sophists employed it for the sake of flattery. Plato uses heavily loaded (and rhetorically effective) labels when describing these positions. His own method, he claims, is not a quest for mere comfort and security; it is a quest for truth. Similarly, he views his opponents' method not as an admission of the fragility and instability of human life, but as mere flattery.

Certainly, Plato succeeded in persuading generations of philosophers, politicians, and educators that his view was the truth; the very success of his argumentative strategies underscores his rhetorical prowess. And indeed, in the *Phaedrus*, Plato seemed to "envisage a true philosophical rhetoric which worked by means of 'disputation' and 'deception' and yet was useful in leading men to knowledge of the Forms."[14] Plato believed that this "true rhetoric" was to be found in the enterprise that he called *dialectic*.

But the notion of a rhetoric that could be *true* (in the strong sense in which Plato uses that word) is generally at odds with the rhetorical tradition. In fact, a true rhetoric (Plato's dialectic) would be useless for reasoning about the practical affairs with which most people are concerned. Why? Because if the truth could be known for certain and agreed on by all parties, disputation would be unnecessary. For this very reason, Isocrates argued that no one could ever achieve the kind of absolute knowledge that Plato sought. "In pursuing such knowledge the 'disputers' pursue a phantom and their results are useless to the community."[15]

Today, the battle between these two positions hardly seems a contest; no one speaks of the history of Western thought as "footnotes to Isocrates." But in the ancient world, Plato's victory was rather more hollow. Rhetoric continued to thrive alongside enterprises such as ethics, politics, and the general education of citizens. "Plato's works were continuously read throughout antiquity, but his views on rhetoric exercised relatively little direct influence on classical rhetoricians."[16]

LATER SYSTEMATIZATION

In sharp contrast to the *ad hoc* considerations of rhetoric in the Platonic dialogues, rhetoric eventually developed into a codified and formal system. This is most obvious in Roman rhetoricians such as Cicero, Quintilian, and the anonymous author of the *Rhetorica ad Herennium*. In Cicero, rhetoric is especially connected with law and politics. But in Quintilian, the political implications have faded; rhetoric is a means for the education of the Roman gentleman and is chiefly practiced in the schools (not in the law courts). The significance of persuasion is less obvious; rhetoric is defined as *bene dicendi scientia*—a special knowledge about speaking well.[17]

Admittedly, Quintilian shows an intense interest in the relationship between rhetoric and morality. His work can thus provide a number of insights into the role of character in the process of persuasion; we shall return to these matters in chapter 3. More negatively, Quintilian marks a dramatic shift in the history of rhetoric: a shift from the creation of fresh insights to the mere compilation of past insights. Quintilian wrote the first

encyclopedic guide to rhetoric, documenting a great variety
of opinions and cataloguing a seemingly infinite number of
rhetorical commonplaces (*topoi*). After Quintilian, the primary goal of rhetoric was to construct the perfect handbook
rather than to explore the process of persuasion; and this
remained the case well into the modern age. "To Hugh Blair,
in the second half of the eighteenth century, the authoritative
statement of classical rhetoric was still that in Quintilian."[18]
The *Institutio oratoria* thus became not so much a summary
of the classical rhetorical tradition as its epitaph.

Nevertheless, the Roman rhetorical systems have profoundly
influenced both popular and scholarly conceptions of rhetoric.
The Romans bequeathed to us the five chief categories of
rhetoric: the invention and/or discovery of various means of
persuasion (*inventio*); the arrangement of these arguments in a
specific order (*dispositio*); ornamental elements of style (*elocu-
tio*); memorization of the speech (*memoria*); and appropriate
delivery through voice and gesture (*pronunciatio*). This five-
fold division places considerably more emphasis on the outward appearance of the speech than on the development of the
argument (which is more or less exhausted by the first part,
inventio). Nevertheless, this schema is often assumed to constitute the essence of classical rhetoric.[19]

For the Romans, then, rhetoric was primarily a technique for
expressing one's thoughts in language, rather than an investigation into how form and content can combine with synergistic
effects. As Gerhard Ebeling has noted, Roman rhetoricians took
this distinction of form and content as primary; they assumed that

> the words, as the outward form, were to a considerable degree
> autonomous, or could even be dismissed with indifference by
> comparison with the *res* as the content of the speech. A typical
> conception is that the content of the speech has first to be worked
> out and structured, while the form of the language is mere addi-
> tional clothing and ornamentation.[20]

Indeed, this separation of form and content is obvious in the
five so-called chief divisions of rhetoric. First, the content is
determined (*inventio*); then, the ideas are arranged, orna-
mented, memorized, and delivered.

Finally, the Roman systems of rhetoric, and especially that of Quintilian, emphasize the system itself. In fact, the system has become so important that the artistic component of the faculty is almost lost. The claim of the early rhetoricians—that language and ideas work together in concert to achieve a persuasive effect—seems foreign to the Romans. Thus, Roman rhetoric is significant primarily as a means of analyzing the cultural history of the period, especially because of its role in the schools. But its usefulness as a methodological tool is more limited, due to its narrow focus on structure, style, and order.

THE PHILOSOPHER

In the middle of this long and variegated history stands the imposing figure of Aristotle. His treatise on rhetoric remains perhaps the definitive work on the subject—the point from which all other studies take their departure. For example, in 1968, when the modern revival of rhetoric led to the creation of a new journal (*Philosophy and Rhetoric*), Aristotle's treatise was the very first book to be reviewed. Because his approach to rhetoric will be so important for the present work, its philosophical context demands our attention. We thus postpone our discussion of rhetoric for a few pages, turning first to Aristotle's more general comments on method.

Aristotle divided method into two categories: analytic and dialectic. Analytic method operates from an agreed-upon set of first principles and is thus able to claim finality for its results. Because its principles are conventional, however, its claims cannot be novel; its finality is based on a tautological closure of the system. For Aristotle, analytic method plays an important role in physics, metaphysics, and logic.

Dialectic, on the other hand, begins not with first principles alone but with common opinion (*endoxa*)—that is, with whatever most people consider to be the case. But because common opinion is often wrong and never univocal, dialectic cannot claim absolute finality for its results. Nevertheless, its ambiguity makes it able to achieve genuinely new (nontautological) insights. The domain of dialectic is politics, ethics, and poetics.[21]

Aristotle's work in analytic method became a point of reference for formal logic. As a result, his discussions of logical reasoning and the rules for formal inference are often considered his primary contribution to the theory of argumentation. But as Chaïm Perelman has noted, "modern logicians have failed to see that Aristotle studied dialectical reasoning in the *Topics*, the *Rhetoric*, and the *Sophistical Refutations*."[22] These are the works in which Aristotle develops an appropriate mode of investigation for *contingent* matters, just as he developed an approach to *necessary* matters in the *Prior Analytics*.

Unfortunately, however, Aristotle's division of reasoning into analytic and dialectic modes is often interpreted as an attempt to build a hierarchy of method. Due to the prevailing philosophical tendencies of the modern period, the definitive finality of an analytic approach is often privileged over the flux of dialectic. But "in antiquity, the two approaches lived side by side, in complete synergy and synchronicity. To resort to one or the other depended on the compatibility of the subjects treated and on the audiences one was addressing, but they always remained joint tools."[23]

In other words, neither analytic nor dialectic has the greater claim to methodological superiority; their difference lies in their applications. Analytic methods are clearly preferable when the first principles of a particular inquiry are clear and undisputed. But when first principles are in some dispute, dialectic is clearly more appropriate; for analytic cannot examine its own first principles.[24] Thus, in turning to analytic over dialectic (or *vice versa*), we are simply choosing the more appropriate method in a given case.

These musings on the status of dialectic and analytic in Aristotle's method are central to our investigation, because dialectic forms the basis for Aristotle's understanding of rhetoric. "Rhetoric," says Aristotle, "is the counterpart of dialectic."[25] A counterpart is not merely an opposite; rather, rhetoric and dialectic are two sides of the same coin. Aristotle's word for "counterpart" is *antistrophē*—suggesting, by allusion to the role of the chorus in Greek tragedy, something of equal importance and purpose but moving in the opposite direction.[26] Like dialectic, rhetoric begins with the "common opinions" (*endoxa*) about any problem presented.[27] Moreover, because these opinions are malleable and highly specific to place and time, they cannot be universalized or even generalized. Again, like dialectic, rhetoric calls for attention to concrete, historical reality—idiosyncratic and antisystematic as it may be. And also like dialectic, rhetoric cannot guarantee tautological finality. For what would be the use of deliberating about something which could never be otherwise? "Nothing would be gained by it."[28]

But although similar to dialectic, rhetoric is not identical with it; the two enterprises, like *strophē* and *antistrophē*, move in opposite directions. More specifically, Aristotle understands dialectic as most appropriate for purely *theoretical* inquiry; when the discussion turns to *practical* matters—especially in the realms of politics and ethics—the faculty of dialectic is insufficient. Dialectic may move a person's intellect, but it does not necessarily bring about fundamental changes in a person's attitudes and actions.[29] People are induced to such thoroughgoing changes not by dialectical arguments but by rhetorical ones; for only rhetorical arguments are able to attend to the concrete specificity of speaker, audience, and argument.

Aristotle's permanent place in the history of rhetoric is assured not only by his systematic and concise (yet wide-ranging) treatise, but also by the unique category through which he understands rhetoric. For the Sophists, rhetoric was an art; for Plato, it was a knack; for Cicero, it was a name for the speech itself; for Quintilian, it was a pedagogical system. For Aristotle, rhetoric was, instead, a "faculty" (*dunamis*). Rhetoric was a capacity, an ability, a way of organizing and making sense of the practical exigencies of the world. Today, it might be called a "method"—though without the connotations that have become attached to this word as a result of the rise of the natural sciences.

Aristotle divides rhetoric into three components. The first, rhetoric proper, is concerned with the preparation for the speech. He defines this part as "the faculty of discovering, in the particular case, the available means of persuasion."[30] This involves the discovery and actual construction of arguments that will be appropriate in a given situation. The second part is style, which includes language and diction and which pays attention to meter and emphasis. The third part, organization, is treated with great brevity. The latter two aspects of the faculty of rhetoric—style and order—were taken up much more avidly by the Romans.

The first of the three aspects will concern us most here, because it describes the way in which an argument is constructed—the process that the Romans called *inventio*. While style and organization are of great importance, they are also the most variable elements of rhetoric: they depend more heavily on a specific language, specific cultural assumptions, and the restrictions of format and genre. Moreover, while the treatment of style and arrangement in ancient rhetoric concentrated primarily on the spoken word, its insights into the process of invention can frequently be applied to both speech and writing. Thus, Aristotle's definition of *rhetoric proper* will become the working definition for rhetoric in the present work: "the faculty of discovering, in the particular case, the available means of persuasion."

Aristotle offers a further subdivision of rhetoric proper into three parts: *pathos*, which is concerned with the audience (its emotions and tendencies); *ēthos*, which is concerned with the character of the speaker; and *logos*, which deals with the arguments themselves. These divisions are not isolated categories; they overlap and cross-refer. Rhetoric, after all, admits the dynamic relationship between language and its users—the interrelationship among speakers, hearers, and the language through which they communicate. The three divisions of rhetoric do not enable us to divide discourse in order to conquer it; nevertheless, the threefold structure can give us a starting point for analyzing arguments. But the three modes of persuasion in Aristotelian rhetoric will not be treated in detail now, for they will form the structure of chapters 2 through 4. For the present: having traced some features of classical rhetoric, we need to examine why it faded to near extinction in the modern period—and why it is presently experiencing a renaissance.

THE DEATH AND
RESURRECTION OF RHETORIC

From the time of Quintilian until the Renaissance, rhetoric continued to be marked primarily by the compilation and memorization of argumentative appeals. Admittedly, it played a significant role in the schools; and certainly, enough material may be gathered on the medieval period to form a solid chapter in any standard history of rhetoric—or, for that matter, enough for an entire book.[31] Nevertheless, rhetoric's role in this period was essentially static; at best, it was viewed as a benign tool of pedagogy. Its more profound implications for philosophical inquiry were not explored in detail.

After a brief revival during the Renaissance (to which we will return shortly), rhetorical modes of thought came into sharp conflict with modern rationalism and did not survive intact. In order to understand how and why these two approaches were so sharply opposed, we need to explore their features and their relationship in some detail.

THE FALL OF RHETORIC

The demise of rhetorical thought over the past three centuries can be charted against the rise of rationalism and empiricism in that same period. Despite minor interruptions in these tendencies, the large picture is one in which philosophical assumptions shifted from primarily rhetorical and poetic modes to primarily rationalistic and empirical modes.

The *locus classicus* for the development of modern rationalism is the philosophy of René Descartes.[32] Descartes's work encapsulates and symbolizes the effort to overthrow a worldview dominated by church and state, and to allow the mind to operate unrestrained. For this reason, Descartes is justly esteemed as the herald of the Age of Reason; his philosophy helped to bring down a great variety of tyrants. His approach shifts the ground of authority from external forces to the self: that is, to the thinking *I* of the *cogito*.

But Descartes was motivated by more than antiauthoritarianism. As Richard J. Bernstein has noted, Descartes's *Meditations* are not simply an exercise in skepticism; they are also a reflection on the transitory and finite nature of human existence. "The specter that hovers in the background of" Descartes's "journey is not just radical epistemological skepticism but the dread of madness and chaos where nothing is fixed, where we can neither touch bottom nor support ourselves on the surface."[33]

On Bernstein's interpretation (which is supported by other commentators),[34] Descartes can avoid madness and chaos only by means of a *deus ex machina*. Specifically, he attempts to base all certainty on the human understanding of God. In order to eliminate doubt, Descartes says, "I ought at the first opportunity to inquire if there is a God, and, if there is, whether or not he can be a deceiver. If I am ignorant in these matters, I do not think I can ever be certain of anything else."[35] He goes on to demonstrate that because God is good, his postulated "evil deceiver" can be no god at all. Certainty is thus made to rely on the perfection of God; and at the same time, God is made to seem a static and impersonal force. The Cartesian understanding of God bears little resemblance to the dynamic, mysterious, personal being whom believers had worshiped for centuries.

Descartes is thus a twofold archetype of Enlightenment thought. On the one hand, he celebrates skepticism by focusing on the ability of the human ego to think, and to think independently of institutions and preestablished moral codes. On the other hand, he insists on the need for absolutely certain knowledge and creates a harmless God to provide this certainty. The only alternative would have been to take a path with no fixed bearings; to submit to the dark night of the soul, to chaos, and to madness: to what a later generation of philosophers would call *nihilism*.

But Descartes's reaction situated him not only against anarchy and authoritarianism, but also against what should have been a less frightening specter—we might call it the Ghost of Rhetoric Past. Concomitant with the rise of rationalism was the fall of rhetoric—and this despite the fact that rhetoric had experienced a miniature revival during the Renaissance.[36] For example, Leonardo Bruni (1360–1442) and Lorenzo Valla (1407–1457) had emphasized the specificity and concreteness of language. In almost diametrical opposition to the later rise of rationalism, they saw language as an organic endeavor, inextricably imbedded in history. For Bruni and Valla,

> rhetorical thought is always bound to context and has the task of showing the way things are in and through the historicity of speech. Rhetoric assumes primacy for the Humanists over the truth conceived as something universal, abstract, and logical. This philological, "tropological" attitude provides a new kind of philosophizing that is completely different from traditional, metaphysical thought. It is fundamentally historical, bound to the here and now, and hence, "rhetorical." Yet it is concerned with the problem of showing the way things are, the revelation of beings; such truth is not abstract nor logically deducible.[37]

As familiar as these words might sound to postmodern ears, they represented precisely what Descartes feared: uncertainty, context-dependence, and, ultimately, chaos and madness.

Descartes's rejection of the rhetorical tradition is foreshadowed in the work of Peter Ramus (1515–1572).[38] Ramus reduced rhetoric to the elements of style and delivery, and separated these ornamental pleasures from True Reason. For Ramus, rhetoric and grammar "become cosmetic arts, and speech—and of course writing—along with them. Reason breaks free of speech and takes on a Platonic self-standing freedom."[39] Like Descartes after him, Ramus was opposed to the shifting, perhaps tragic, uncertainties of life, and so proposed to ignore them; in his view, "arts ought to consist of subjects that are constant, perpetual, and unchanging, and they should consider only those concepts which Plato says are archetypal and eternal."[40] This view was in direct opposition to the broad rhetorical tradition, which recognized that real life did not fit into such tidy categories. Ramus believed that it did, and so had little use for persuasive discourse. Thus, although Ramus is often classified as a rhetorician, his major contribution was to define rhetoric as such a narrow and pedantic enterprise that the rationalism of Descartes seemed to offer a genuine relief.

The last major advocate of rhetoric in the early modern period was Giambattista Vico (1668–1744). Vico strenuously opposed Descartes's rationalism, claiming that the vicissitudes of practical life need not be denied their own appropriate methodological foundation. According to Vico, not all truths are reducible to mathematical propositions (though mathematics is the field in which our knowledge can be most complete— because it is conventional). Certain aspects of human knowledge are best understood through an appeal to the *sensus communis*— not merely common sense, but the sense that forms and nurtures community.[41]

But this call for a wider notion of knowledge fell on deaf ears. "Vico's insights into the practical situational and interactional aspects of language and knowledge were drowned in the rising tide of positivism."[42] Moreover, Vico was already so formed by the rationalism (and Baconian empiricism) of his day that his own arguments bear a surprisingly rationalistic stamp. In his sharp differentiation of "clear and precise" matters from those that are "confused and obscure," Vico tended to solidify the subordinate position of rhetoric and poetics. Thus, even the staunchest advocates of rhetoric contributed to its demise.[43]

Vico receives scant attention in the intellectual history of the modern age; instead, Cartesian skepticism and rationalism became the basis for the most far-reaching implications of Enlightenment thought. For example, some thinkers supplemented Descartes's rationalism with an emphasis on the priority of the natural world, which could be observed with the senses. This view not only generated the avowedly empiricist philosophy of Locke, Berkeley, and Hume; it also served as a primary assumption for Immanuel Kant. All four philosophers devalued the role of the traditional tools for producing knowledge—tools such as the *sensus communis* and the ancient notion of Wisdom.[44] Throughout the eighteenth and nineteenth centuries, these tools were increasingly considered subjective and inferior, incapable of producing the "hard" knowledge offered by empirical observation.

The empirical world, so the argument goes, is not subject to the whim of the individual subject but is inert; it cannot impinge differently on different knowing subjects. It will be perceived identically by all people who have the opportunity to sense it. Of course, empiricism was a two-edged sword; in order to objectify the natural world, that world had to be deprived of its moral and spiritual meaning. This objectivism constituted, simultaneously, "an intellectual coming-of-age with respect to natural science, and a painful loss of the former conviction of moral meaning or unity in nature."[45] Yet despite the loss it entailed, empiricism was widely embraced. It was seen as a way of overthrowing the subjective interpretation of the world that had been imposed by established institutions for centuries.

Like Cartesian rationalism, empiricism was understood as a means of subverting the supposedly subjective and ornamental qualities of rhetoric. John Locke "described traditional rhetoric as 'an art of deceit and errour' and wanted to exclude figures of speech and other rhetorical devices from serious discourse."[46] Hume's short treatise, though praising the ancients for their oratorical skills, still sought to contrast rhetoric's artifice and emotionalism to modern "superior good sense."[47] Finally, Immanuel Kant also contributed to the general demise of rhetoric; for him, persuasion named an entirely subjective phenomenon, illusory and private. "Persuasion is a mere illusion, because the ground of the judgment, which lies solely in the subject, is regarded as objective. Such a judgment has only private validity, and the holding of it to be true does not allow of being communicated."[48]

The intuitive appeal of the discourse of empiricism had a tremendous effect on learning. The predictability that it claimed to guarantee was especially appealing in a world that had been resigned to instability and tragedy. The newly discovered methods of the natural sciences were adopted by most fields of inquiry and had an especially large impact in historiography and hermeneutics.[49]

As rationalism and empiricism became standard arbiters of judgment, so the role of rhetoric diminished or even vanished altogether. Even in those sheltered academic enclaves where the rhetorical tradition still held some sway, its approach had become formalized and stylized to the point of ridicule. George Campbell's *Philosophy of Rhetoric* (1776) was primarily an attempt to rework classical rhetorical insights into a form that could be accepted by empiricist devotees of Hume. Finally,

Richard Whately's *Elements of Rhetoric* (1828; 7th edition, 1846), completely in the thrall of the rationalist tradition, became a textbook for generations of British and American students of "eloquence." But by this point, any similarities to the classical rhetorical tradition were in name only; the ancient faculty of rhetoric was moribund.

THE REVIVAL OF ANCIENT RHETORIC

Most commentators place the *terminus a quo* for the current revival of classical rhetoric firmly in the twentieth century. But in doing so, they omit a very significant nineteenth-century thinker who, while an undergraduate at Oxford, was introduced to rhetoric by Richard Whately himself. In later years, his interests changed, and so he is not normally associated with the rhetorical tradition. However, he *is* associated— significantly for the argument of this book—with the tradition of Christian theology. Whately's most famous pupil was John Henry Newman.

Newman's contribution to this chronology is twofold. First, he argues for reducing the emphasis on rationalism and empiricism as modes of thinking. In the *University Sermons*,[50] and more systematically in the *Grammar of Assent*,[51] Newman balked at the notion that all certitude must depend upon formal inference and logical deduction. Second, as a recent study has clearly demonstrated,[52] Newman was steeped in the classical rhetorical tradition; indeed, he may have been a more significant rhetorician than was his mentor. "Later Whately was to say that, if he were given three wishes, they would all be for a mind like Newman's."[53]

Newman attempted to rehabilitate informal modes of argument—specifically, those which did not bear the marks of logic (which had been so central to the rationalist perspective).

The crux of the matter as Newman saw it was "informal inference," an exercise of personal interpretation and induction from particulars. . . . For Newman the method of reasoning in the concrete, in matters of human conduct and choice, is at once more living, "delicate," and "effective" than those of science or logic, and more ambiguous, dynamic, and difficult to assess.[54]

So Newman sought to reappropriate the classical formulation, in which a person's assent to rhetorical/dialectical matters is at least on a par with, and in some ways superior to, one's assent to analytical matters.

Newman's effort to rehabilitate the classical rhetorical tradition never gained a widespread following. The full-scale revival of rhetoric would have to wait until the twentieth century, when it could be aided by a critical reaction against the hegemony of modern rationalism and empiricism. If Cartesian certainty is no longer considered the foundational starting point of all investigation, then other forms of reasoning once again become viable.

This change in philosophical perspective was the point of departure for one of the most important rhetorical treatises of this century, entitled, appropriately, *The New Rhetoric*. Its authors, Chaïm Perelman and Lucie Olbrechts-Tyteca, saw their work as a radical departure from Descartes and from the entire Western philosophical tradition that followed him.[55]

The authors argue further that the fascination with Descartes hinges primarily on an addiction to self-evident, axiomatic truths at the expense of deliberative reason. Despite having failed to solve all the problems that its devotees had hoped it might solve, Cartesian rationalism still dominates our understanding of argument. Richard Bernstein calls it "the Cartesian anxiety": "the belief that there are or must be some fixed, permanent constraints to which we can appeal and which are secure and stable."[56] In an effort to overcome this anxiety, many Enlightenment thinkers found it necessary to place narrow restrictions on what could pass as human reason. As the authors of *The New Rhetoric* suggest, these restrictions amount to "a perfectly unjustified and unwarranted limitation of the domain of action of our faculty of reasoning and proving."[57] The return to rhetoric, they believe, will rehabilitate those dialectical proofs which Aristotle thought so essential to the process of deliberation. The significance of *The New Rhetoric*, supplemented by Chaïm Perelman's many books and articles

on argumentation theory, make him perhaps the most important rhetorician of this century.

But that appellation might just as easily be assigned to the
American critic Kenneth Burke. Burke's *oeuvre* defies description: it is simultaneously literary criticism, philosophy, rhetoric,
political analysis, and high drama. Influenced heavily by Marx
and by Freud (yet unwilling to become attached to any particular school), Burke moves effortlessly from one piece of speech
or writing to another. He analyzes, criticizes, summarizes,
explicates, describes.

Burke speaks of human beings as "symbol-using animals."
He describes language as *symbolic action*—a term that has
tempted some commentators to describe him as an idealist. But
Burke's notion of language is more nuanced; he emphasizes
not only the first word of the term, but the second as well (not
merely *symbolic* action, but symbolic *action*). The term thus
comprises, in Frank Lentricchia's words, "very wide-ranging
representational force, rooted in the personal (even the biolog-
ical) but reaching out through the familial into the large structures of society."[58] According to Burke, the use of symbols as a
means of interpreting and provoking action is a quite fundamental human activity.

Burke's notion of language as symbolic action offers a new
perspective on rhetoric which appropriates and expands the
classical tradition, in that his version of rhetoric takes an
overtly political stance.

> Rhetoric remains an art or method of expression, argument, and
> "persuasion." But Burke expands this art so that it becomes a
> method not only of persuasion but of "identification," including all
> unconscious as well as conscious attribution and analysis of
> motives. Hence it contains a *critique* of unconscious motives—of
> "ideology," political or otherwise—that went unthematized in the
> ancients.[59]

The political and representational qualities of rhetoric will become more significant as the argument of the present work
unfolds.

As a result of the pioneering efforts of theorists like
Perelman and Burke, a new rhetoric is flourishing—both as a

scholarly discipline and as a means of understanding the persuasive appeal of texts and speeches. This renaissance has
been energized by the work of a wide range of rhetoricians and
communication theorists. In addition, rhetoric has captured the
interest of literary critics, who have produced an additional
body of literature on the relationship between theories of interpretation and the classical rhetorical tradition. Finally, rhetoric
also plays a role in contemporary efforts to question the fundamental presuppositions of rationalism and empiricism which
have steered the course of Western thought for centuries. I do
not wish to suggest that the revival of rhetoric needs to be
labeled yet another postmodern phenomenon. Nevertheless,
the inverse movements of rhetorical thought and Enlightenment rationalism seem to lend support to a general thesis:
Rhetoric can provide a worthy alternative to some of the most
sacrosanct assumptions of modernity.

RHETORIC AS A
METHODOLOGICAL TOOL

According to Aristotle, rhetoric is not so much an art or science as a *faculty*. This makes rhetoric an excellent candidate
for application to other fields. Of course, the examples that fill
the classical handbooks are specific to certain periods of history, to specific political and economic systems, and even to
particular categories of speech and writing. But the insights
that I wish to draw from the rhetorical tradition are largely
methodological rather than substantial. I want to show that
rhetoric has a bright future as a critical tool by indicating four
specific methodological advantages of rhetorical analysis.

Epistemic function

Over twenty years ago, Robert L. Scott published a short but
influential article entitled "On Viewing Rhetoric as Epistemic."[60]
Scott notes that rhetoric usually tends to be considered episte-
mologically empty. It is interested in action: in "mere" activity, as
opposed to knowledge; in unpredictable practices, rather than
absolute truths. Such characterizations of rhetoric, however,

assume that people first know what they will do, and then do it. In practice, Scott argues, the order is reversed: "One may act assuming that the truth is fixed and that his persuasion, for example, is simply carrying out the dictates of that truth, but he will be deceiving himself."[61] We do not wait until we have gained complete knowledge in order to act to speak; in fact, we only gain knowledge through the process of acting and speaking. This suggests not only an epistemological priority for action but also a considerably more complicated ethical picture than we usually suppose. We still act (and speak, and write) when we face incomplete knowledge, or even irreconcilable conflict.[62]

More often than not, our knowledge is the nontautological, synthetic variety with which rhetoric is concerned. In fact, as Stephen Toulmin concluded in his classic study of argumentation, very few fields of inquiry can depend on analytic knowledge alone.[63] But if we stop insisting on the analytic ideal and instead admit that our knowledge is formed in the midst of argument (rather than prior to it), then radical skepticism becomes unnecessary. In other words, rhetoric helps to fill the epistemological void left by the limitations of an analytic method. In fact, the ubiquitous role of rhetoric seems to justify an even stronger claim: "not only that rhetoric is epistemic, but also that epistemology and ontology are themselves rhetorical."[64]

Concreteness

Rhetorical analysis all but eliminates abstract appeals to the mental constructs of philosophical idealism, forcing us to deal with particular speakers, in particular settings, addressing particular audiences, with particular arguments. Rhetoric directs our attention toward concrete, historical categories: it requires us to consider the context in which an argument is presented. This concreteness should not be confused with empiricism; unlike empiricism, it does not claim to be radically free from presuppositions, nor to stand as a pure perceiver of discourse and action. Rather, it admits its perspective as one among many—one that seeks to describe the life process in a more concrete way.

Rhetoric can be employed in such a way that it consciously attempts to remain aware of its own modes of social production and reproduction. It can examine the motives that direct an audience or a speaker, aware that the actual interests and motives of a particular discourse will not always be identical to its asserted interests. Thus, a political appropriation of rhetoric resonates well with certain aspects of Marxist critical theory. As Kenneth Burke has indicated, the terminology of Marxism "is not a neutral 'preparation for action' but 'inducement to action.' In this sense, it is unsleepingly rhetorical."[65]

Linguistic sophistication

Rhetorical analysis recognizes the epistemological priority of language. For too long, language was considered to be an instrument with which the mind, already endowed with rational concepts, expressed itself to a wholly external world. But people are often shaped by the very language they claim to use—an inversion discussed throughout the later work of Ludwig Wittgenstein. Wittgenstein argued, for example, that if we showed no outward signs of pain, we could not even learn the meaning of the word. And if we were not pedagogically formed by language, naming our pain would make no sense.[66] Only within the context of language do our concepts and our sensations become related to the external world. Language is thus itself a presupposition of thought—not its aftermath.

Consequently, if we hope to gain a better understanding of human thought and action, we could do worse than to begin with human language. And while this might be so for any field of inquiry, it is especially relevant for Christian theology (as we shall discover later on in this chapter). If language is central to theological understanding, then the study of language through the faculty of rhetoric will be an extremely valuable investigative approach.

Hermeneutical awareness

A final advantage may be attributed to rhetorical analysis: it recognizes the complex relationship between reader and text, between auditor and speech. Such analysis does not seek to posit a one-to-one relationship between words and meanings. Every utterance is capable of a wide variety of interpretations; attempts to claim one particular interpretation as always and everywhere normative have met with failure.[67] Because rhetorical analysis attends to the particular situation in which communication occurs—the audience, the speaker, the general context—it does not tempt us to universalize interpretations across time and space. In both hermeneutics and rhetoric, "theory is subsequent to that out of which it is abstracted, that is, praxis. . . . Reflection in rhetoric, like that in hermeneutics, is a meditation about a praxis that is in itself already a natural and sophisticated one."[68]

The grounding of rhetoric in *praxis* manifests a common theme that runs throughout my comments on the methodological advantages of rhetorical analysis: its refusal to understand itself apart from the particular world in which it exists. Thus, when these methodological insights are brought to a specific field of inquiry, the method of application must be carefully delineated. Rhetoric will take on different emphases when it is put to different tasks. In fact, it gains its strength from its unique application to specific contexts. As Aristotle observed, "the more one tries to trump up either dialectic or rhetoric, not into what they really are—practical faculties—but into exact sciences, the more one shall inadvertently be destroying their nature."[69] Accordingly, I now want to leave the realm of rhetoric in general and turn to its specific application to theology.

THE RHETORICAL
NATURE OF THEOLOGY

Rhetorical analysis has been gaining prominence in recent theological reflection. Indeed, the revival of interest in rhetoric within the human sciences generally, and in literary criticism in particular, has made some mention of the subject *de rigueur* for many theologians. Unfortunately, however, the long and rich tradition of ancient rhetoric is usually mentioned only in passing.[70] More thoroughgoing applications of rhetoric to theology have thus far been limited to what communication theorists would normally call *rhetorical criticism*—the use of rhetorical categories in the analysis of texts.[71] Indeed, hundreds of articles and dissertations explore "The Rhetoric of X," where X is a theologian, a type of theology, a theological text, or (very often) a passage of Scripture. But these studies analyze only discrete rhetorical categories (usually the tropes), applying them selectively to a wide range of theological texts.[72] In at least one work, rhetoric has been employed in the treatment of a specific theological *locus*—namely Christology.[73] But few theologians have been "persuaded" to turn to rhetoric as a fundamental methodological category.

On the other hand, theologians should be wary of adopting every new method that arrives on the scene. Many new methodologies promise to be important or useful, or at least interesting; but the final product frequently fails to live up to expectations. Moreover, Christian theologians have sometimes unwittingly adopted methods that contain hidden theological or antitheological assumptions.[74] Thus, any new method should be required to present a *prima facie* case for its theological relevance. This is the goal of the present section, which argues that the classical rhetorical tradition is both compatible with, and complementary to, the enterprise of Christian theology. In support of the claim that theological method should make a rhetorical turn, I offer three interrelated appeals: a historical argument, a methodological argument, and a structural argument.

THE HISTORICAL ARGUMENT FOR
A RHETORICAL THEOLOGY

Christian theology's basic features developed during the first four to five centuries after the birth of Jesus, in the areas surrounding the Mediterranean Sea. As has often been noted, the philosophical currents of that time and place (primarily middle- and neo-Platonism) left a definitive stamp on the methods and norms of theology. But only rarely have commentators observed that during the same period and in the same place, the rhetorical tradition had become firmly fixed in the curriculum of the schools. Thus, throughout the entire formative period of Christian theology, rhetorical categories pervaded the world of thought—perhaps to a greater extent than did Platonic categories.

The influence of the rhetorical tradition on the Bible has been generally recognized. Even the Old Testament (the writing of which predates the development of classical rhetoric) often speaks in language designed to persuade. It also emphasizes the power of the spoken word: "And God said, 'Let there be light'; and there was light" (Gen. 1:3). Moreover, as George Kennedy has noted, "the essential rhetorical quality of the Old Testament is [its] assertion of authority. God has given his law to his people. They are convinced because of who he is, what he has done for them, and how this is revealed to them."[75] The Old Testament describes events in which persuasion occurs and also has its own persuasive function.

The New Testament is even more overtly rhetorical, appealing to the authority embodied in the *ēthos* of a particular person: for example, Jesus, Mary, Peter, or Paul. It is often directed to a specific audience; it employs the standard tropes and topics categorized by Greek and Roman rhetoricians; and it seeks to persuade the reader. In fact, the New Testament appears to be so thoroughly formed by these categories that it has recently become the object of extensive rhetorical analysis.[76]

Not only is Scripture itself rhetorical; it is also employed rhetorically by Christian believers. The texts are read aloud; they become the basis for persuasive preaching; and they are read for personal and communal edification. Scripture thus emphasizes the rhetorical nature of theology through its role in the traditional theological categories of revelation and proclamation.[77]

Rhetorical criticism of the Bible is not the focus of my argument; nevertheless, I will often allude to rhetorically suggestive passages in Scripture and to the rhetorical purposes for which they are employed. I do so because the relationship between the biblical text and Aristotelian rhetorical categories is a close and complementary one, and helps make the case for understanding theology in rhetorical terms. Only because of this close interconnection do we find such humor in the attribution to the Reverend William A. Spooner of that most famous

Spoonerism: "In the sermon which I have just completed, wherever I said Aristotle, I meant Saint Paul."[78]

Rhetorical influences on Christianity did not stop with the closing of the biblical canon. For example, a thorough rhetorical training clearly informs the writings of Tertullian. He pays attention to the specificity of the audience; he appeals to his own moral authority as a speaker, castigating the arguments of those who speak without such authority; and he develops specific modes of argumentation that are drawn from the rhetorical training he received. According to Robert Sider, Tertullian's "uniqueness as a second-century exegete was made possible by the special skill through which he was able to adapt his training in classical rhetoric to Biblical materials and thus sharpen and improve the tools he inherited from the tradition."[79]

Similarly, rhetorical categories pervade the work of St. Gregory of Nazianzus;[80] indeed, among Gregory's best-known works are five sermons called *theological orations.* The oration is perhaps the most overtly rhetorical genre of communication; moreover, the context of Gregory's theological orations—in the midst of the late Arian controversy and with certain intractable theological disputes especially prominent—makes these speeches very important in assessing the relationship between theology and rhetoric. They will receive further treatment in the discussion of character in chapter 3.

Perhaps the most important early rhetor-theologian is St. Augustine. His masterful use of the tropes and his remarkable style have been a continuing object of study for classicists and rhetoricians alike.[81] Trained as a lawyer, Augustine was well acquainted with the art of persuasion. In fact, in Augustine's own words, the primary focus of his education was "to learn the art of words, to acquire that eloquence that is essential to persuade men of your case, to unroll your opinions before them."[82] Not surprisingly, then, Augustine is a major figure not just in Christian theology but in classical rhetoric as well.

Specifically, the fourth book of Augustine's *De doctrina Christiana* influenced not only Christian appropriations of rhetoric but also the rhetorical tradition generally.[83] Augustine encourages Christian preachers to equip themselves with as many rhetorical devices as possible. After all, preachers might as well be armed appropriately against the enemy (who will doubtless also be well equipped!). Moreover, Augustine emphasizes another important focus of the rhetorical tradition: its role in inducing action. The Christian orator should seek to persuade others, "not that they may *know* what is to be done, but that they may *do* what they *already* know should be done."[84] As Kenneth Burke points out, Augustine justified his appropriation of pagan rhetoric by endowing it with a theological purpose; he "held that every last embellishment should be brought to the service of God, for the glory and power of the new doctrine."[85]

My narrative here offers only a small sample of early Christian thinkers who show evidence of having been profoundly influenced by the classical rhetorical tradition. Nor does this influence stop in the fifth century. Other theologians whose rhetorical sophistication has been studied and documented include Eusebius of Caesarea, St. Basil the Great, St. Gregory of Nyssa, St. John Chrysostom, John Calvin, Søren Kierkegaard, and John Henry Newman.[86]

This historical argument for the rhetorical nature of theology clearly makes no logical demonstration but, rather, suggests that Christian theology, especially in its early formative period, was influenced by the broad tradition of classical rhetoric. We should not be surprised, then, to discover rhetorical categories built into the very structure of Christian thought.

THE METHODOLOGICAL ARGUMENT FOR
A RHETORICAL THEOLOGY

From the Enlightenment through the first half of this century, theological and ethical reflection was dominated by a method that may be called *analytic* (following the Aristotelian distinction articulated earlier in this chapter). Inspired by the quest for a firm foundation, theologians and ethicists found solace in philosophers of certitude: Descartes, Hegel (on some interpretations), Frege, Russell. More recently, this quest for a totalizing system has been abandoned in deference to the concrete variety of religious belief. The new touchstones of theological method are the philosophy of language, literary criticism, and the sociology of knowledge. Representing a change from finality to tentativity, from univocity to polysemy, this transition may be characterized as a methodological shift from analytic to dialectic.

Here we have the perfect context for the appropriation of the classical rhetorical tradition as a methodological tool. With rhetoric's attention to common opinion and its willingness to abandon the quest for definitional finality, a rhetorical method is unlikely to repeat the mistakes wrought by theology's modern preoccupation with analytic method. But because rhetoric accents the practical and attends to the concrete location of arguments in time and space, a rhetorical approach cannot ignore issues of politics and ethics.

The methodological compatibility between theology and rhetoric has been recognized by Elisabeth Schüssler Fiorenza, who has advocated a similar approach for the field of biblical interpretation:

> A rhetorical hermeneutic does not assume that the text is a window to historical reality, nor does it operate with a correspondence theory of truth. It does not understand historical sources as data and evidence but sees them as perspectival discourse constructing their worlds and symbolic universes. . . . Not detached value-neutrality but an explicit articulation of one's rhetorical strategies, interested perspectives, ethical criteria, theoretical frameworks, religious presuppositions, and sociopolitical locations for critical public discussion are appropriate in such a rhetorical paradigm of biblical scholarship.[87]

This is precisely the sort of paradigm shift which I am advocating for theological method in general.

The need for a rhetorical turn in theology has been further specified by Rebecca Chopp, who points out that any notion of authority "is concerned with persuasive discourse in relationship to matters of deliberation in the polis."[88] As such, she argues, the authority of theology is rhetorical—determined by the assent of the community it addresses. The task of theology is to persuade others to thought and action. Such persuasion will be unable to operate in a value free, individualistic mode;

it must take account of the moral presuppositions of both speaker and audience, as well as the "material concerns, resources, and strategies in the present situation."[89]

The methodological intersection of theology and rhetoric can be defined even more precisely: like rhetoric, Christian theology affirms and celebrates the power of language, and especially the power of the spoken word. Language is the medium through which we relate to one another and to God. But the Christian tradition also recognizes the ambiguity of speech, which can be used for good or for ill. These currents run deeply through the history of Christianity, and they deserve further investigation.

Christianity has traditionally placed great emphasis on the category of *logos*. Few other words are as rich in theological connotations as *the Word*. From its earliest connection to Spirit (as the breath of God's mouth, Gen. 1:1–2), to the spoken words of God in the Covenant (Exod. 20:2), to the Word who became flesh and lived among us (John 1:14), to the Word that Christ spoke and that the Church continues to speak today—Christian theology can hardly extricate itself from involvement in language, in speaking, in the Word. With its many metaphors of light and darkness, and its connections between seeing and knowing, Christianity is often considered a primarily ocular faith; but from its beginnings and throughout its history, it has also been a faith of the spoken word. Even in the midst of a society where printing and video technology are in the ascendancy, some of the most important activities of Christian worship continue to be aural: the reading of the Gospel, the prayers of the people, the preaching of the Word, and the eucharistic prayers of anamnesis and epiclesis.

Moreover, Christianity has always recognized the importance of speaking well—of coming together for worship around a common form of words, of speaking of doctrine rightly, and of lifting voices in praise and thanksgiving in a manner befitting the God of Jesus Christ. This is not to suggest that the efficacy of a prayer or a sacrament depends on a precise verbal formula—or that a hymn's value depends upon a well-tuned choir! Nevertheless, the significance of the category of *word* means that Christians are called to "watch their language in the presence of God."[90] And in fact, Christians have traditionally ended their worship gatherings with an act of *bene dicendi*: a benediction.

A biblical *locus classicus* for the relationship between Christianity and the power of language is James 3:5–10a.[91] The passage reveals the capacity for both great good and great evil that always attends human speech.

> So also the tongue is a small member, yet it boasts of great exploits. How great a forest is set ablaze by a small fire! And the tongue is a fire. The tongue is placed among our members as a world of iniquity; it stains the whole body, sets on fire the cycle of nature, and is itself set on fire by hell. For every species of beast and bird, of reptile and sea creature, can be tamed and has been tamed by the human species, but no one can tame the tongue—a restless evil, full of deadly poison. With it we bless the Lord and Father, and with it we curse those who are made in the likeness of God. From the same mouth come blessing and cursing.

Clearly, this passage recognizes the power of language to do as much harm as good. Nevertheless, James does not argue for silence. In fact, he urges his fellow Christians to "fight the odds" and use the gift of speech for good (James 3:13; 3:17–18; 4:11–12; 5:13–18).

Christianity understands language as a gift from God that is powerful, yet highly ambiguous. And it is precisely the ambiguous power of language that necessitates rhetoric. If we are to distinguish the blessings from the cursings, the good from the evil, we must pay extraordinarily close attention to our language. As Augustine notes,[92] the faculty of rhetoric is itself indifferent; since it is often employed for evil purposes, why should it not also be employed for the sake of the good?

I would highlight three important methodological arguments for a rhetorical theology. First, because rhetoric operates within the framework of dialectic rather than analytic, it can remind us that Christian theology should emphasize its own uncertainty and the incompleteness of its knowledge. Second, because rhetoric emphasizes how argument can move audiences to both thought and action, a rhetorical approach to theology requires attention to the concrete *praxis* of the Christian community.

And third, because rhetoric focuses on the power of spoken and written words, it can provide an excellent paradigm for analyzing the theological categories of revelation, proclamation, and hermeneutics.

The theological significance of language, however, should not be taken as a denial of the simultaneous importance of silence in Christian theology. Indeed, silence is a fundamental feature of the *via negativa*, the importance of which I have repeatedly emphasized. Silence provides theology with a certain receptivity, a willingness to hear even those voices which do not speak. As St. Ignatius of Antioch comments, a person "who has truly mastered the utterances of Jesus will also be able to apprehend His silence, and thus reach full spiritual maturity, so that his own words have the force of actions and his silences the significance of speech."[93] We are persuaded not through language alone but also through the presence of the "other." Thus, chapter 3 of this book is devoted to persuasion by character, or *ēthos*. There I shall consider further the theological significance of silence.

THE STRUCTURAL ARGUMENT FOR A RHETORICAL THEOLOGY

This final appeal for the appropriation of rhetoric in Christian theology is a potpourri of several structural commonalities between the two fields. Some of these points of contact will strike the reader as coincidental at best, contrived at worst; and certainly, they are not meant to function as conclusive proofs. Rather, these observations are offered simply to provoke the reader to continue to later chapters, where the relationship between rhetoric and theology will be taken up in greater detail. Three specific structural similarities are worth emphasizing: those based on etymology, on triadic structure, and on tentativity.[94]

Etymology

Rhetoric and Christian theology are related etymologically.[95] One of the most basic terms in Christianity, "faith" translates

the Greek word *pistis*, which is also the word for "persuasion."
This interesting connection was made at least as early as
Bauer's *Lexicon* (1920); but it was probably observed much
earlier. It is described in detail by Kenneth Burke:

> The Greek word [for persuasion], *peithō*, comes from the same root
> as the Latin word for faith. Accordingly, Aristotle's term for rhetori-
> cal "proof" is the related word, *pistis* . . . the word which, in Greek
> ecclesiastical literature, came to designate the highest order of
> Christian knowledge, "faith" or "belief" as contrasted with "rea-
> son." While the active form of *peithō* means to persuade, its middle
> and passive forms mean "to obey."[96]

This connection has recently been pursued in much greater detail. James L. Kinneavy has argued[97] that the Christian notion of
faith, which has always been thought to differ from its Greek and
Hebrew predecessors, actually has roots in the Greek rhetorical
tradition.

Triadic structure

The threefold nature of rhetorical analysis has specific theological connotations as well. For example: interesting parallels
can be drawn between the triad of speaker–audience–speech
and Augustine's lover–beloved–love. Each triad is composed of
one who acts, one who is acted upon, and an action that mys-
teriously connects them. Even more suggestive is John Milbank's
recent attempt to offer a fuller account of the nature of communication in the Trinity.

> The Spirit which proceeds from the paternal-filial difference is gen-
> uinely a "second difference" whose situation is that of a listener to
> a rhetorical plea of one upon behalf of the other. As the Father is
> not immediately available, the Spirit must listen to, judge and inter-
> pret the testimony of the Son—a testimony in which "personal
> integrity" *is* the content of witness to reality.[98]

In Milbank's account, the Spirit is the audience that judges the
testimony of the Son, whose character *(ēthos)* is an integral part
of the argument.

While we need not claim to have discovered in rhetoric a *ves-
tigium trinitatis*, we should not lightly dismiss the connection.

The mystery of the Trinity has provoked significant and far-reaching philosophical inquiry;[99] and some of the most profound investigations of theology have borne a threefold architectonic structure.[100] Perhaps such "triangles" can provide us with alternatives to Cartesian dualism. As one such triadic structure, the faculty of rhetoric can point a possible way forward; it can stress the dynamic, destabilizing, and subversive character of discourse, rather than operating within the more typical modern pattern of polar oppositions.

Needless to say, not all theological speech will be worthy of an analogy to the divine communication that occurs within the Godhead. Nevertheless, theology should strive to speak with an appropriate character—it should seek to be, not simply persuasion, but *faithful* persuasion. If it does so, it can become a sign for the threeness-in-unity which Christians confess as the most fundamental truth about God.

Tentativity

Theology and rhetoric are both tentative, permanently unfinished, and essentially unstable and destabilizing endeavors. Both must admit the inherent revisability of their own assumptions and conclusions. Rhetoric concerns matters that might be otherwise; and theology concerns matters to which, this side of the beatific vision, human beings can gain no final and definitive access. Both theology and rhetoric can concentrate only on what is given—the *phainomena*, the *doxa*. Like the Sophists, theologians must rely on "whatever most people take to be the case" in order to justify their claims. Yet they do so with just as much integrity and rigor as do their colleagues in mathematics or psychology or philosophy.

This position challenges the Enlightenment's negative verdict on the possibility of justifying theological claims. Neither rhetoric nor theology need accept abstract theories of verification in order to assess the truthfulness of their assertions. Think of Wittgenstein's remark: "Is our confidence justified? What people accept as justification is shewn by how they think and live."[101]

A rhetorical theology, then, will be a theology that operates under a radicalized notion of *truth*. This notion is best understood by returning once again to ancient Greece, where the word for truth was *alētheia*—a word that, as Heidegger and others have noted, suggests an unconcealment, an unveiling, a revealing—even, perhaps, a revelation. This notion of truth can have a significant role in both rhetoric and theology: truth can once again be recognized as abiding, not in human beings, but in God. In other words, truth can once again become something that *comes to us*—rather than something that we grasp and manipulate how we will.

This radicalized understanding of truth will be especially appropriate for Christian theology; for one of the fundamental acts of Christian worship is the prayer for the Holy Spirit (the Spirit of *Truth*) to come to us, to come down upon the created order. This prayer of *epiclesis* (from the Greek word meaning "invocation" or "appeal") is a frank admission that, in the created order, truth abides only as a shadow or image. In its final, definitive, and archetypal form, truth rests with God alone. This recognition leads John Zizioulas to suggest that "Christians must learn not to lean on objective 'truths' as securities for truth, but to live in an *epicletic* way—i.e., leaning on the communion-event in which the structure of the Church involves them. Truth liberates by placing beings in communion."[102] Indeed, when developing a specifically Christian notion of truth, we are called to turn not to a theory, nor even to a practice, but to a *person* who speaks a particular *word:* "I am the Way, the Truth, and the Life" (John 14:6).

The argumentative appeals offered in these last few pages offer few firm guarantees. In that sense, they reflect the Christian life as a whole, which has always been lived in an "insecure security"—a confidence and hope that abide, despite the perilous and radically contingent nature of human existence.[103] Christians dwell with certainty in the midst of uncertainty; they are a people who have come to the conclusion that, "with no new houses in prospect, we have to learn to live in tents."[104] This may be unsettling in a world where permanent, pleasant homes are valued so highly and where those who are homeless are thought to deserve little more than pity. But perhaps the unsettled, nomadic existence of homelessness is the way of true obedience to One who, according to the Greek text of John 1:14, "pitched his tent among us."

2
Pathos
The World to Which
Theology Speaks

According to Aristotle, one of the three means of persuasion is *pathos*, or "putting the hearer into an appropriate frame of mind."[1] He explains that persuasion occurs "by means of the hearers, when they are aroused to emotion [*pathos*] by the speech; for the judgments we deliver are not the same when we are influenced by joy or sorrow, love or hate."[2] This literal sense of the word *pathos* (emotion) is certainly one of its primary senses for Aristotle. In book 2 of the *Rhetoric*, he will discuss a variety of emotions: anger and placability, love and hate, fear and confidence, shame and shamelessness, benevolence, pity, indignation, envy, and emulation. Such appeals to the emotions, however, do not exhaust the ways in which persuasion occurs "by means of the hearers."

In fact, too much attention to the emotions has led some commentators astray. For example, the work of Kenneth Burke—which relies, in part, on a phenomenological analysis of the emotions—sometimes drifts toward abstraction and vague generality.[3] For example, Burke can speak of "patterns of emotion" that he "characterizes variously as 'natural,' as 'racial appetites,' as 'innate forms of the mind'—all inherent 'in the very germ plasm of man.'"[4] Such wide-ranging, abstract accounts of the emotions do little to explain how audiences are actually persuaded.

Moreover, the isolation of *emotion* as one category of persuasion tends to reinforce a popular misconception of rhetoric. By emphasizing a speech's emotional appeal in radical opposition to so-called rational discourse, persuasion would seem to become a tool of irrationalism, flattery, and even outright deception. This false dualism of reason versus emotion is sharply opposed by the Aristotelian view of rhetoric, "which is capable of combining reason and emotion in premises that address the concrete affairs of daily life."[5]

In order to avoid reifying the emotions and setting them against reason, I use the word *pathos* in a wider sense—a sense also found in Aristotle—to refer more generally to the audience's state or condition: everything that the audience brings to the rhetorical situation. Persuasion with reference to the *pathos* of the audience concerns not only the emotions, but also the wide variety of ways in which the state or condition of the audience affects the persuasive appeal of the speech.

Any appeal that hinges on the attitude of the audience must always be relative to a *particular* audience. In fact, when Aristotle lists the emotions in book 2 of the *Rhetoric*—as when he lists the virtues in the *Nicomachean Ethics*—he frequently reminds us that the concrete examples he employs are appropriate only under particular circumstances. For example, in discussing the emotion of shame, he notes that "it is a cause of shame not to have any part in the honorable things in which all men, or all or most persons like ourselves, participate. By 'persons like ourselves' I mean those of the same race, or city, or age, or kin, or in general terms, those who are on our own level."[6] Consequently, persuasion by means of *pathos* will depend on judgments about whether, or to what degree, the members of the particular audience are "persons like ourselves."

Thus, if we hope to develop a rhetoric of Christian theology, we must examine the state, condition, and experience of the audience(s) for which theological arguments are developed and deployed. The classical rhetorical tradition recognized that the audience plays a central role in determining the success of persuasive appeals—an insight that was transparently obvious to the earliest Christians. But in the modern period, the general neglect of rhetoric has allowed the audience to disappear from most theological discourse. The audience's role needs to be reconstructed in a rhetorically sophisticated way; this new perspective can, in turn, have a significant impact on the practice of theological argumentation.

PERSUASION BY MEANS OF THE AUDIENCE

"Now the object of rhetoric," says Aristotle, "is judgment."[7] Rhetoric differs from logic, which can appeal to the rules of logical inference as the ultimate arbiter of truth. Rhetorical arguments must have access to a much wider range of appeals because of the variations among those who will sit in judgment. If the audience to which an argument is directed judges it to be a failure, it fails—however logically coherent it may be. By rhetorical standards, an argument succeeds only when the audience is persuaded.

This apparently whimsical standard of arbitration has played an important role in the intentional subversion of rhetoric since the Renaissance.[8] Modern thought has tended to assume that the success or failure of an argument could be determined by examining it in isolation. On this view, if the argument could be demonstrated to be logically coherent, or "valid," it was deemed a success; if not, a failure. This objectifying view would claim that the decision of any audience to the contrary would simply speak against the intelligence or good will of those sitting in judgment.

These assumptions were taken to their extreme in the philosophy of logical positivism. Thinkers such as G. E. Moore and Bertrand Russell believed that human language was as atomistic and mechanistic as mathematics; therefore, argumentative truth could be distilled into propositions or symbol sets. In logical positivism, the Cartesian anxiety was at work with a vengeance: here was a renewed search for absolute, fundamental certainties, beyond which no analysis could penetrate.

To the analytically trained mind such theories were very attractive; for example, Ludwig Wittgenstein fell under the influence of logical positivism in the early part of his career.

Eventually, though, he noticed a severe drawback: just when these atomistic theories attempted to explain the most basic activities of human life and thought, they were mute. They could not even describe a shopper's simple request for five red apples; and when linguistic activity became more complex and differentiated, atomistic theories failed miserably.[9]

Wittgenstein's own "linguistic turn"[10] provides a paradigm for the shift to a rhetorical mode of criticism; for rhetoric insists that the logical construction of an argument is only one of many factors determining its potential for success. When we go out into the world and make arguments, we are not faced with people holding small books containing the rules of logical inference and language use. Instead, we encounter people whose emotions, biases, and presuppositions will be the primary forces that shape how they evaluate arguments. By recognizing the importance of these factors, Wittgenstein contributed to the modern rehabilitation of a tradition that finds its point of departure in Aristotle's *Rhetoric.*

Yet in most fields of inquiry today, writers and speakers still wrongly assume that argumentation consists of making clearly demonstrable statements. "This attitude," claim the authors of *The New Rhetoric,* "rests on the illusion, widespread in certain rationalistic and scientific circles, that facts speak for themselves and make such an indelible imprint on any human mind that the latter is forced to give its adherence regardless of its inclination."[11] But in fact, arguments do not always affect their audiences as intended, even when the logic is flawless and the language clear and comprehensible. In order to persuade, an argument must "move" (*suadeo*: to impel) its audience from one place to another. That is, the audience must come to accept or to recognize certain conclusions (or premises) that it had not previously accepted or recognized.

THE RELATIONSHIP BETWEEN
AUDIENCE AND SPEAKER

Persuasion is the attempt to evoke action by changing the attitude of another person, usually bringing another's attitude into alignment with one's own. A speaker constructs an argument in

order to move an audience from point A (the audience's attitudes or beliefs) to point B (the speaker's attitudes or beliefs).
But in order to move the members of one's audience, one must
first gain their interest and attention, which usually requires the
speaker to argue that the audience's beliefs are already very
similar to the speaker's own beliefs. Persuasion is thus paradoxical and circular; it moves from disagreement to agreement,
yet all disagreement presupposes some level of agreement.[12]

The less that the speaker and the audience hold in common,
the more difficult persuasion will be. Unless the members of
the audience are unusually eager to have their opinions
altered, they are unlikely even to listen to an orator whom they
know to be hostile to their entire worldview. So the process of
persuasion must begin with common ground, requiring what
Kenneth Burke calls *identification*; we persuade others by
speaking their language, identifying our ways with theirs.[13]
Although the rhetor may be trying to change the opinions of
the audience, this task will be impossible unless the members
of the audience agree with the speaker on at least a few points.
"Some of their opinions are needed to support the fulcrum by
which" the orator "would move other opinions."[14]

The process of identification, says Burke, can be substantive
or formal. A substantive approach would pay particular attention to the emotional appeals that Aristotle outlines; the
speaker would magnify or reduce a particular aspect of the
audience's state or experience in order to bring the audience
closer to her or his own position. A formal appeal, on the other
hand, would make use of Aristotle's *topoi*; the audience would
come to identify with the speaker through a shared appreciation for a formal device (among these are oppositions, climax,
homoeoteleuton [consecutive words with similar endings] and
asyndeton [omission of connectives]). Formal appeals might
seem at first to be less effective in truly moving the audience to
identify with speaker; yet as Burke notes, audiences often find
the mutual recognition of these devices quite attractive.
Listening to a rhythmic list of opposites, for example, "you will
find yourself swinging along with the succession of antitheses,
even though you may not agree with the proposition that is
being presented in this form."[15] By getting the audience to

appreciate the form in which a statement is cast, the speaker or writer will be better poised to interest the audience in identifying with the content of that statement.

But might not this desire for identification begin to take precedence over the speaker's interest in changing the audience's attitude? As modern political oratory has often shown, an obsession with the presuppositions of one's audience can lead the speaker to make the speech pleasing at any cost. On the other hand, a speech that does nothing but reinforce the audience's presuppositions is not persuasion at all; for persuasion suggests a movement, a realignment. How can we move someone to thought and action without simply pandering to that person's every whim?

The need to appeal to the audience's presuppositions was recognized by the Sophists; this is why they honored *doxa* as the starting point of argument (and thereby incurred Plato's wrath). Yet Plato, too, was aware that any argument that remained completely oblivious to the audience would fail. Of course, such flattery can be taken to an extreme; but the audience must have a good reason to listen, if the speaker hopes to persuade. Plato employed some flattery in his own writing; he often has Socrates build up the ego of an interlocutor, just before deflating it. In just the first few pages of the *Republic*, for example, Socrates flatters as often as he can. To offer but four instances from among many:

> "What you say is very fine indeed, Cephalus."

> "Well, it certainly isn't easy to disbelieve a Simonides. . . . He is a wise and divine man."

> "Surely it's far more fitting for us to be pitied by you clever men than to be treated harshly."

> "It's more fitting for you to speak; for you are the one who says he knows and can tell."[16]

If Plato's Socrates had failed to gain the attention of his audience, his entire argument would have failed, because an argument that fails to flatter is often simply ignored. Indeed, such an argument might very well have the opposite of its intended effect: the hearers might decide that if a hostile individual is trying to persuade them to take one action, then they probably should take the exact opposite action. Only by beginning with some initial level of agreement does persuasion become possible.

A similar point is made by the American philosopher Donald Davidson when he speaks of the "principle of charity" with which we interpret the language of others. This principle is not merely an *option* for interpretation, but a necessity; if we did not assume that our interlocutors were right about most matters, we would not even have a language by means of which to communicate. This approach, Davidson suggests, "is not designed to eliminate disagreement, nor can it; its purpose is to make meaningful disagreement possible, and this depends entirely on a foundation—*some* foundation—in agreement."[17] So while arguments are based on disagreement, certain assumptions must be held in common. Otherwise, the audience may not even recognize the speaker's argument as *argument*— and perhaps not even as language at all.

The challenge for rhetoric, then, is to tread a fine line between a desire for sheer identification (which simply panders to the audience's assumptions and thus fails to effect a change) and an absolute demand for instant movement and realignment (which may alienate the audience completely). When the argument unfolds between the limits of these two extremes, persuasion is possible.

The activity of persuading others to belief and action played a central role in the spread of the Christian Gospel during its first four centuries. Thus, early Christian theology was quite rightly preoccupied with its various audiences.

THE ROLE OF THE AUDIENCE IN
EARLY CHRISTIAN THEOLOGY

We begin with the gospels, and two observations: (1) the canonical gospels are four in number; and (2) many other gospels were written that did not achieve canonical status. Apparently, this "good news" could be preached in many different ways to many different audiences; these variations were accepted not only by those who wrote the narratives but also by those who authorized them. In one of the earliest attempts to define the canon of Christian Scripture, for example, the gospels are admitted to be several in number, yet one in Spirit:

> Though various ideas are taught in the several books of the Gospels, yet it makes no difference to the faith of believers, since by one sovereign Spirit all things are declared in all of them concerning the Nativity, the Passion, the Resurrection, [Jesus'] conversation with his disciples and his two comings, the first in lowliness and contempt, which has come to pass, the second glorious with royal power, which is to come.[18]

Early attempts to synthesize the gospels into a single voice, in works such as Tatian's *Diatessaron*, were not well received.[19]

In advocating multiple perspectives on the story of Jesus, early Christians were simply recognizing that people evaluate an argument in a variety of ways. Not everyone would be persuaded to faith as a result of hearing quotations of the Torah, or by manipulating complex theological distinctions, or even by listening to straightforward narration. Differing in argument, style, and arrangement, the gospels remind us of the multiplicity of rhetorical contexts for which they were written.

The variation among the audiences of biblical texts is hardly a recent discovery; biblical scholars have been attempting to describe the *Sitze im Leben* of the gospels for decades. Moreover, despite intensive study, no consensus has been built concerning the precise specification of the various audiences of the gospels. (For example, the attempt by Kennedy[20] to specify the precise rhetorical concerns of the different evangelists would seem overly simplistic to many biblical scholars.) But for the purposes of my argument here, the *specification* of the various audiences of the gospels matters far less than the *recognition* that audiences do vary—and, thus, that the story of Jesus Christ would need to be told in differing ways, according to the circumstances of the particular audience.

The gospels are not the only New Testament books to display a rhetorical character. For example, Acts is composed largely of speeches, and these can be analyzed with attention to their rhetorical technique.[21] But they also show how early Christian preaching self-consciously attempted to adapt itself to varying audiences. For example, St. Paul's speech before Agrippa (Acts 26:2–23) narrates a story very similar to the one in his speech before the Jews in Jerusalem (Acts 22:3–22) yet in a very different form. The formal differences between the two speeches can be attributed primarily to their differing audiences. Before the Jews, Paul appeals (unsuccessfully) to his own Jewishness; before Agrippa, he chooses arguments that are more likely to appeal to a hellenized king.

St. Paul quite willingly admitted that he changed his message for different audiences: "I have become all things to all people, that I might by all means save some" (1 Cor. 9:22b). He adjusts his message to his audience as he identifies himself, by turns, with Jews and with Gentiles. He does not claim that the Gospel is infinitely malleable; in that case, it would have no power to change lives. Nevertheless, the various emphases of the Christian faith allow it to shift its weight when necessary. For example, Paul argues that the Gospel does not require adherence to the Law; nevertheless, one may subject oneself to the Law. On the other hand, the Gospel does not eliminate the Law—although one may place oneself outside it, if a particular instance of proclamation so requires (1 Cor. 9:20–21). Paul has not altered the Christian faith simply in order to flatter his audience into agreement; but he has rewoven and tailored the story of "Christ Crucified and Risen" in order that it might gain adherence among whatever particular group of people he was addressing.

Paul's extant writings are in the form of epistles, a genre that appears frequently among early Christian writings, both canonical and otherwise. The genre lends itself naturally to a conscious specification of the audience: an epistle is written by a particular author or authors, in a concrete time and place, and is typically addressed—formally, at least—to a particular person or group of people. Among the New Testament epistles, the initial audience normally seems to be a single *ekklēsia* or a particular group of such communities. Even in the case of the catholic epistles, where no particular audience is specified, the very detailed exhortation and proclamation suggest that, at least initially, the writer's attention may have been fixed upon a certain audience.

Attention to the particularities of an audience continued into the early history of the Church. Consider, for example, the highly effective rhetorical skills of Tertullian. His success as a rhetor did not simply result from the sharpness of his language; he also knew how to address the people for whom he was writing. Here, as Hans von Campenhausen has noted, "we come across the living language of the Christians of that time, the Latin of the growing Latin church. . . . It observes and adopts at the same time even in grammatical details the language actually spoken by the society of Carthage, and by the people whom Tertullian knew, observed and sought out."[22] The ability to write in a style and grammar acceptable to the audience marks the "rhetorically sophisticated theologian."

Such an appellation would certainly fit St. Augustine of Hippo, one of the most overtly rhetorical thinkers in the early Church. He considered the audience of great importance, because he recognized that the truth of the Gospel would not be obvious to everyone. Thus, the theologian must frame the argument in ways which the members of audience will appreciate, even while they are being persuaded to change their minds. "Because of those whose fastidiousness is not pleased by truth if it is stated in any other way except in that way in which the words are also pleasing, delight has no small place in the art of eloquence."[23] This insight can certainly be attributed to Augustine's training in rhetoric; but he may also have realized that his view was not without scriptural warrant: "The wise of heart is called perceptive, and pleasant speech increases persuasiveness" (Prov. 16:21).

Christian theology has traditionally been a rhetorical enterprise, insofar as it maintained an interest in the presuppositions of the audience it addressed. Theology has sought to make use of these presuppositions in order to make its message more persuasive. Such attention to varying audiences could also be documented in the works of the Cappadocians, St. Anselm, St. Thomas, Luther, and Calvin. In the modern period, however, the story is very different.

THE DISAPPEARANCE OF THE AUDIENCE
IN MODERN THEOLOGY

In the modern period, Christian theologians have very rarely elaborated on their notion of the audience. This reticence can be attributed to a number of factors. First, given the rise of rationalism and the simultaneous demise of rhetoric in the modern period, the specificity and uniqueness of the audience has gradually been replaced by the assumption that arguments are universal and self-evident. Second, the modern emphasis on pluralism and diversity rebels against the imposition of a single point of view—even one brought about by persuading an audience of its merits.

Later in this book, I shall argue that both these tendencies are inappropriate. But a third concern about excessive attention to the audience has a greater claim to our attention: that it gives the speaker immense power in determining what sorts of arguments are appropriate for particular audiences, thereby turning the theologian into a censor. In *On Christian Doctrine*, for example, Augustine speaks of matters that "should never, or only rarely on account of some necessity, be set before a popular audience."[24] This raises larger questions of power, authority, and control. Are power structures perhaps magnified, even enforced, by rhetoric? After all, classical rhetoric developed when the typical audience was carefully restricted according to age, gender, race, and socioeconomic status. Was Christian theology persuasive only because it operated through structures of hegemony, carefully withholding from its audience its rather less persuasive features? Such self-legitimating power structures were subjected to a thorough critique by Enlightenment philosophy, and this critique remains one of its permanent contributions.[25]

Nevertheless, this very concern would seem to argue for *confronting* the audience's role and for carefully unpacking its implications. Instead, theologians have usually chosen simply to ignore the audience—much to the detriment of Christian theology. This choice has led to ambiguity about the audience of theology; it has allowed theologians to mask their interests and purposes; and it has created confusion among theological interlocutors.

These deleterious effects will become more evident as we examine and critique the ways in which various theologians have unconsciously appropriated one of four modern perspectives on the audience. Nor can these difficulties be resolved simply by investigating the "addressees" of theology more explicitly—an approach exemplified in the work of one of this country's foremost philosophical theologians, David Tracy. Tracy's approach, as we will discover, combines all four modern perspectives in a way that unfortunately fails to transcend their inadequacies.

FOUR MODERN PERSPECTIVES
ON THE AUDIENCE

Because modern theologians have operated without much attention to the rhetorical tradition, their understanding of their audiences has been ambiguous at best. Very rarely do theologians speak about the audience explicitly; usually, their assumptions can only be inferred. Such inferences form the substance of the present section, in which I describe four of the most common perspectives on the audience.[26] In each case, I begin with a very general description; I then present a brief critique, and offer an example from modern theological discourse.

The intentionalist perspective

We sometimes believe the audience to consist of only those persons whom the speaker or writer wishes to persuade. In *The New Rhetoric*, for example, the audience is provisionally defined as *"the ensemble of those whom the speaker wishes to influence by his argumentation.* Every speaker thinks, more or less consciously, of those he is seeking to persuade; these people form the audience to whom his speech is addressed."[27] In theology, the speaker might choose to address only those who consider themselves believers, or only nonbelievers, or some combination of the two; this choice will typically identify a theology as dogmatic, apologetic, or constructive.

The intentionalist perspective is not restricted to the spoken word but is also common in written discourse. At one time, writers could sculpt their audiences by the very language in which they chose to write. (Consider Luther's treatises, of which some were in Latin, others in German; or the differences between Descartes's *Discours de la méthode* and his *Meditationes de Prima Philosophia*.) With the decline in the number of people able to write well in two languages and the increased availability of translations, differentiation by language occurs less commonly (though it has not vanished).[28] In addition to the choice of a natural language, writers also shape their audiences by diction and style, prefatory comments ("This book is not intended for . . ."), and even the choice of a publisher.[29]

However, the rhetor can completely control neither who receives the argument, nor how it is received. Even when an audience is perfectly specified (as in a closed meeting of a committee, for instance), details may be leaked to the press or passed along in private conversations. With the advent of broadcast media, speeches or portions of speeches are often seen and/or heard (perhaps in an altered form) by a much wider audience. A speech may receive less (or more!) media coverage than the speaker had hoped; similarly, a book may be poorly publicized, or overmarketed, or simply neglected. Works may be translated and disseminated to a degree far beyond what the author could have imagined. Finally, because speeches can be stored on audiotape and videotape, and because printed matter can easily be reproduced, the audience may be extended across wide variations in time and place. No matter how diligently an author labors to sculpt the contours of the audience for a particular work, it will often be encountered by a very different group of people. As a result, the work's persuasive appeal may differ markedly from what was expected.

Despite these difficulties, the intentionalist perspective is very common in Christian theology (as it undoubtedly is in other fields), because it seems to allow speakers and writers to exclude from their audiences those persons least likely to be persuaded by the argument. Thus, when Karl Barth seeks to address his *Church Dogmatics* primarily to the *Evangelische Kirche*, he does so by specifying his audience.

We must be consistent here and confess that it is not possible for us suddenly to speak undogmatically about the confessional attitude of dogmatics, instead of standing ourselves within the confessional attitude. Negatively, the confessional point of view undeniably means this at least, that other confessional positions are excluded with a final seriousness, i.e., as heretical.[30]

Barth thus seems to exclude from his audience those who would take up an alternative confessional position, such as Roman Catholicism. But not quite; as he later suggests, a theologian's confessional stance may become the basis of productive discussion with adherents of other confessions.

Even on this very "intolerant" presupposition, with an attitude which is actually and not merely verbally confessional, it is still possible to conduct the controversy between Roman Catholicism and Protestantism in a way which is not merely worthy of the participants but of the matter which both sides confess to be indisputably at stake, and therefore in a way which is Christian in a unity even in disunity.[31]

These observations have been at least partially vindicated; Barth's work has been taken very seriously by a number of Roman Catholic theologians.[32]

We might conjecture that Barth intended his audience to include all those who believe that theology should be done from a particular confessional stance. Consequently, he seems to exclude from his audience anyone who did not agree, and would not be persuaded, that Christian theology must necessarily be confessional theology. Nevertheless, his inattention to this category of potential auditors did not prevent them from reading and reacting. They often responded with hostility or dismissal, even though their theological positions were sometimes more closely aligned with Barth's than were those of the Roman Catholics who took him so seriously. In much English-speaking theology, for example, Barth was quickly dismissed as a narrow-minded reactionary. And even when it became obvious that he was a theologian of stature, the die had already been cast.[33] Barth's attempt to specify an audience was not wholly successful because his arguments were evaluated by those whom he had not originally intended to address.

The misalignment of intentions and readers can have quite disastrous consequences—as in the infamous case of Martin Luther's *Against the Murderous and Thieving Hordes of Peasants.* Luther was upset because radicals were threatening the whole reform movement, and he wanted them stopped. But the effect of his pamphlet went well beyond his intention.

> Unhappily Luther's savage tract was late in leaving the press and appeared just at the time when the peasants were being butchered. He tried to counteract the effect by another pamphlet. . . . But this tract was not noticed, and that one sentence of Luther's, "smite, slay, and stab," brought him obloquy never to be forgotten. He was reproached by the peasants as a traitor to their cause, though he never ceased to be held responsible by the Catholic princes for the entire conflagration.[34]

Luther intended a more limited audience; accordingly, he did not account for the effect that his rhetorical choices might have on those who were only too willing to use his words to justify the ongoing massacre.

While the intentionalist perspective seems quite natural, it fails to describe the complex relationship between speaker and audience. Those who actually hear a speech (or read a text) may not be those intended by the rhetor; and this may have a number of unforeseen consequences. Furthermore, we are only able to *infer* the intended audience from the author's work; we can never have unencumbered access to a rhetor's intentions.[35] The inadequacies of the intentionalist perspective have led some writers and speakers to adopt a very different view of the audience.

The empiricist perspective

The audience is sometimes assumed to comprise all people who actually hear or read an argument, regardless of what the rhetor intended. This empiricist perspective demands a much more specific accounting of the audience. Although some information on the composition of an audience may be gained simply through hearsay, the rhetor may also employ sophisticated techniques of polling and audience analysis. The empiricist perspective is frequently used in marketing, where it becomes a tool for assessing and shaping the audience's appetites and desires.

This sort of empirical analysis, however, is unavailable in less trivial rhetorical situations. We may know how many copies of a particular book were purchased, but the number of people who actually read it may be much greater (if frequently lent) or much smaller (if gathering dust). Similarly, an audience may listen to a speech diligently or distractedly. This problem did not escape the authors of *The New Rhetoric*, who note "how difficult it is to determine by purely material criteria what constitutes a speaker's audience. The difficulty is even greater in the case of a writer's audience."[36]

Even were such empirical information available, its usefulness would not be altogether obvious. Surveys and opinion polls offer only broad, general descriptions of the tastes and responses of audiences: enough information for Madison Avenue, perhaps, but of little use to the Christian theologian, who usually attempts to persuade a more particular audience about a more complex reality. Simply put, the members of the audience will differ; and this may be especially true concerning their religious beliefs.

Attempts to discover the empirical audience of Christian theology may provide interesting insights, but speakers may be disappointed in the limited usefulness of such assessments. One recent attempt at empirical description is *Habits of the Heart*,[37] which sought to describe the ethical and religious commitments of people living in the United States. Among other observations, the authors noted that in this country, human existence—religious and otherwise—is dominated by privatization and individualism.

But of course, this sort of generalized conclusion is of little value in determining which persons will constitute the audience in some future rhetorical situation. At best, *Habits of the Heart* presents a very abstract portrait of American religious

life. For example, we learn that people who consider themselves "religious individualists" are critical of the institutions of
religious faith.

> "Hypocrisy" is one of the most frequent charges against organized
> religion. Churchgoers do not practice what they preach. Either they
> are not loving enough or they do not practice the moral injunctions
> they espouse. As one person said, "It's not religion or the church you
> go to that's going to save you." Rather it is your "personal relation-
> ship" with God. Christ will "come into your heart" if you ask, without
> any church at all.[38]

An interesting perspective, and doubtless very useful information for those seeking to persuade "religious individualists."
But in the same chapter of *Habits of the Heart*, we learn that 40
percent of people living in the United States attend religious
services regularly, and that 60 percent are church members.[39]
In any particular rhetorical context, the speaker will not know
if the audience comprises mostly attenders or mostly detractors. Indeed, many people may belong in both categories!
    Moreover, an empirical analysis of this sort is likely to over-
look significant subgroups within the audience and thus skew
the results. For example, *Habits of the Heart* has been criticized
for completely failing to consider the role of the Church among
African-Americans.[40] Audiences are frequently diverse and
sometimes unpredictable; and this fact directs us toward a third
possibility.

The pluralist perspective

Audiences are rarely homogeneous; they are typically composed of people with widely varying presuppositions. Arguments that effectively persuade one individual or subgroup
may be ineffective, or even counterproductive, with another.
Each member of the audience will bring, to any event of hearing or reading, particular assumptions, attitudes, and practices.
These factors will often differ in important ways among members of the audience.
    How can a composite audience be addressed? Some rhetors
might revert to the intentionalist perspective: by addressing the

presuppositions held only by certain members of an audience, at least some people may be persuaded. Or, one might choose to divide and conquer: by expanding the range of arguments employed, perhaps most members of the audience will be persuaded by at least one of the arguments. Finally, the speaker or writer may attempt to divide the audience physically: for example, by offering two lectures at different times, one for specialists and one for nonspecialists; or by writing two or more versions of an essay, on varying levels or in different genres.

Unfortunately, these ways of addressing the audience have their drawbacks. First, they meet problems similar to those encountered by the intentionalist perspective: while the speech or text may be aimed at particular audiences, the rhetor has no way of insuring that the arguments will arrive at their intended destination. In addition, this strategy may reduce the overall effectiveness of the argumentative appeal; in seeking to identify with so many different audiences, the rhetor's own identity (and argumentative position) may become unclear. And as audiences learn of the pluralist's tactics, they may come to believe that the speaker is being inconsistent or even underhanded. These are the very difficulties that have contributed to rhetoric's reputation as a means for making "the weaker argument appear the stronger."

In its attempt to divide the audience into discrete groups, a pluralist perspective tends to diminish the significance of the results of persuasion, namely, judgment and action. After all, the members of the audience must still decide—even if they decide not to decide.

> The magic moment of transmutation, what drives the system, is the need to *reach a decision.* Chaïm Perelman is fond of citing Article 4 of the Napoleonic Code in this connection, the article which says that *the judge is required to make up his mind and render a verdict in every case.* As York says in *Richard II*, when he has to decide whether to join Bolingbroke or not, "Somewhat we must do."[41]

Not all persuasive arguments have the urgency of a jury trial, of course; but jurisprudence and theology are similar in that neither is a purely theoretical endeavor. Both eventually seek to induce others to act in a certain way; and in order to act, people must make cautious decisions and come to temporary conclusions, even though they cannot know all the details with certainty. The need to come to at least a tentative decision is not diminished simply by the articulation of a wide variety of choices.

The pluralist perspective on the audience has been employed by theologians who are highly conscious of the diversity of their audiences. It has been used, for example, by Avery Dulles, whose arguments in books such as *Models of the Church* and *Models of Revelation*[42] assume that the members of the reading audience will hold widely varying views of the subject under discussion. In *Models of the Church*, for instance, different chapters describe the Church as "Institution," "Mystical Communion," "Sacrament," "Herald," and "Servant." In the final chapter, Dulles evaluates these five models, but he concludes that none of them is completely adequate; one must simply attempt to harmonize them "in such a way that their differences become complementary rather than mutually repugnant."[43]

This approach seems to overcome the problem that we discovered in our example from the work of Karl Barth; the pluralist can make room for a wide variety of viewpoints within the audience. No potential listener is alienated from the outset; everyone should find something here to appreciate. But this universality is only apparent, for in his pluralism, Dulles has weakened his persuasive appeal among those who would insist that only one of his models can be the right model of the Church. Moreover, the attempt to harmonize all five models tends to blur the distinctions that Dulles has so painstakingly constructed. In its very attempt at fairness and balance, *Models of the Church* may leave the reader wondering: What is the Church, *really?*

These difficulties might not be terribly important if the reader were simply contemplating the Church as an idea; but they become urgent when practical considerations come into view. One may *think* about a plurality of models; but one cannot *act* in five different directions simultaneously.[44] Those who read *Models of the Church* from within a well-established ecclesiological framework can rest comfortably with the final

conclusion—namely, that the Church is a mystery that tran-
scends all our models. But what of readers who must live and
act in a rather less stable environment? What of those who, having become disillusioned with the ecclesial setting in which
they were formed, are seeking direction and guidance? While
the pluralist perspective may win praise from the disinterested
intellectual, it may be of little value to those who are faced with
a fork in the road: "Somewhat we must do."

The idealist perspective

Finally, the goal of specifying an audience is sometimes considered so elusive that the rhetor simply addresses the argument to a *universal audience*—an audience whose members
need not be differentiated or accurately described. The concept
of a universal audience has been given sustained attention in
the work of Chaïm Perelman; however, his views admit of a
number of differing interpretations. On a first reading, he
seems to understand a universal audience as one comprising
the entire human race. In this case, the rhetorical notion of persuasion directed toward a universal audience would be identical to the rationalistic notion that arguments can be evaluated
independently of their context. Yet this seems odd, for such
rationalistic abstraction was the very target at which Perelman
had taken aim in *The New Rhetoric*.

On closer inspection, Perelman's description of the universal
audience appears more nuanced. The term refers "not to an
experimentally proven fact, but to a universality and unanimity
imagined by the speaker, to the agreement of an audience which
should be universal, since, for legitimate reasons, we need not
take into consideration those which are not part of it."[45] In this
definition, the words *should* and *imagined* suggest that the universal audience is not simply the entire human race. But other
questions are now raised: what could count as a "legitimate" reason for excluding certain people from the audience? Did Karl
Barth, for example, legitimately exclude pluralists from his audience? Did Dulles legitimately exclude particularists?

On this point, the authors of *The New Rhetoric* are not clear;
and the ensuing confusion among argumentation theorists has

still not dissipated.[46] In fact, Perelman and Olbrechts-Tyteca
magnified the confusion by their use of *philosophers* as an
example of a class of speakers who address a universal audience. Philosophers, they suggest, "think that all who understand
the reasons they give will have to accept their conclusions."[47]
But now we appear to be back with the idealist notion that all
people of good sense will necessarily believe the truth of the
statement. Regardless of how Perelman and Olbrechts-Tyteca
might have intended this notion of universality, their empirical
audience seems to have taken it—at least initially—in an idealist sense.[48] (I shall return to an alternative interpretation of
Perelman's universal audience below.)

Clearly the idealist perspective does not operate under the illusion of some transhistorical idealism, for one could imagine a
universal audience that was redefined over the course of time.
But the notion of universality does, at minimum, suggest that a
very large group of people (if not all people of "good sense")
may be addressed at once, with arguments that are supposed to
be (at least contextually) self-evident.

Such a perspective on the audience is difficult to sustain
except in the most abstract cases. And yet, Perelman explicitly
recognizes rhetoric as a faculty that treats cases of particularized and practical decision making. A universal audience thus
seems at odds with the very argumentative contexts for which it
was created. Just to the extent that the universal audience can
overcome the inadequacies of other perspectives on the audience, it loses any ability to treat matters of practical concern.[49]
In fact, a universal audience faces many of the same critiques
as the notion, developed by Jürgen Habermas, of an (admittedly counterfactual) "ideal speech situation."[50] Habermas has
more recently admitted that conversations only approach the
character of an "ideal speech situation" when their actual content is of little significance to the participants.[51]

In Christian theology, this idealist perspective is well exemplified in the work of Paul Tillich. Tillich opens his systematic
theology with a discussion of the "situation" to which theology
speaks. After arguing against a psychological or sociological
understanding of this term, he defines it as

the scientific and artistic, the economic, political, and ethical forms in which [individuals or groups] express their interpretations of existence. . . . The "situation" theology must consider is the creative interpretation of existence, an interpretation which is carried on in every period of history under all kinds of psychological and sociological conditions. . . . The "situation" to which theology must respond is the totality of man's creative self-interpretation in a special period.[52]

While not suggesting that one theology could be universal for all historical periods, Tillich nevertheless implies that the situation to which theology speaks at any one time will be a singular, total, universal one. Again, this fails to describe the audience addressed by Christian theology. To speak of "the totality of man's creative self-interpretation" is to ignore the tremendous gulfs between one person and another. Such language veils significant differences in material conditions, narrative structures, and practical experiences.

Significantly, Tillich chooses the term *situation* to describe the world to which theology speaks. To name something a situation is to lend it a character of distance, stability, and determinacy; the word is related to *situs*, a fixed location. (This is why political candidates like to refer to "the *situation* in the Middle East." The term not only masks the instability and violence under which Arabs and Jews live their lives; it also prevents that instability from impinging on comfortable people elsewhere.)[53] Through the use of this term, the audience of Christian theology—an inherently diffuse group of people—is reified into a "situation" to which theology can be (rather more straightforwardly!) addressed.

The intentionalist, empiricist, pluralist, and idealist perspectives describe the four most common ways in which the audience is understood, both for persuasive argumentation generally and for Christian theology in particular. The perspectives are not usually adopted explicitly; in most cases, we have only been able to infer a particular theologian's notion of the audience. Now, however, we turn to the work of David Tracy, who has wrestled with the problem of audiences in a more self-conscious way. Even though Tracy does not employ the term *audience*, he grapples quite seriously with the question of "the world to which theology speaks."

THE "PUBLICS" OF THEOLOGY

In seeking to define "the addressee of the theologian's reflections,"[54] David Tracy develops a notion of the three "publics" of theology: society, the academy, and the Church. Tracy argues that, while theologians are usually not wholly determined by the particular public that they choose to address, there will be times when "clear or obscured elective affinities exist between the distinct publics and distinct plausibility structures of particular theologies."[55] Thus, in a seminary setting, the public of the Church may have a more determining influence on the theologian than it would in the setting of a secular university.

Tracy's discussion of the addressees of theology is marked by rigorous specificity. Nevertheless, an analysis of theology's publics cannot substitute for a rhetorical analysis of the audience, primarily because the word *public* has connotations which are too abstract to account for the complex relationships between the theologian and those to whom theology is addressed. As a result, Tracy's own understanding of the audience of theology can be difficult to determine. At various points in his discussion, he seems to advocate all four of the perspectives described above.

At the outset, Tracy seems to be speaking from what I have called the pluralist perspective. He realizes that not everyone will approach Christian theology with the same assumptions. Therefore, he recommends a strategy of divide and conquer: by apportioning the audience of theology into three different publics, the theologian can specify his or her arguments to be applicable to various audiences under differing circumstances. "Some one of these publics will be a principal, yet rarely exclusive, addressee. The reality of a particular social locus will, to be sure, affect the choice of emphasis."[56]

Tracy's pluralism may be persuasive to those for whom theology is a primarily contemplative endeavor. And in fact, Tracy's choice of the category of *dialectic* to characterize his own theology accords well with his reservations about the primacy of *praxis*.[57] But if theology is to move its auditors to action, it cannot demand an endless suspension of judgment for the sake of negotiating differences among its various publics. Indeed, most members of the audience of Christian theology would probably find it difficult to sift themselves into one or another of Tracy's three publics. Is not every member of the public of the Church also a member of the public of society? Should not all members of the public of society have an interest—a political interest—in what flows from room to room within the academy? Tracy's three publics do not merely overlap; they each potentially include everyone who might care to listen to the argument.

Yet Tracy is not wholly committed to the pluralist perspective; he also speaks of the publics of theology as if they were empirical audiences that could be specified and known. Through a sociological investigation, Tracy claims to be able to identify these publics, such that each can be addressed in an argumentatively meaningful way. "In studying each [public], I have chosen to use certain relatively non–theory-laden analyses. We first need a more descriptive account of the 'publics' of the theologian rather than another strictly prescriptive account."[58] But in claiming to offer this descriptive account, Tracy obscures the power structures and other institutional factors that distort a theologian's perceptions of the (ostensibly) empirical audience. Moreover, Tracy's analysis is hardly specific enough to be of concern in any particular rhetorical situation.[59]

At other points, Tracy seems to operate from the perspective of the intentionalist: he seems to assume that a theologian can aim arguments in such a way as to be relatively certain of their reception. He insists that the public character of theology demands an adherence to predetermined criteria of judgment; thus, it addresses itself only to those who are willing to abide by such criteria. For example, in discussing "The Public of the Academy," Tracy specifies this "demand for publicness" as a demand for "criteria, evidence, warrants, [and] disciplinary status."[60] Indeed, such specifications of criteria for judgment characterize much of Tracy's own methodological work.[61]

But from a rhetorical viewpoint, such efforts are in vain. The intended audience will rarely be identical to the empirically hearing (or reading) audience, because the speaker has no control over how the argument is received. Arguments are mediated by too many specificities of reception; the audience will make judgments according to the variations that its individual members will bring to the particular rhetorical situation. The simple specification of criteria cannot overcome the widely varying standards of judgment that the audience will employ in order to evaluate the argument.

Finally, Tracy also employs the notion of an idealistically conceived universal audience. By his very choice of the word *public*, he suggests that theological arguments are characterized primarily by universality, rationality, and continuity. When speaking of the public of society, for example, Tracy claims that

> In the realm of polity, the one realm where all the citizens of the polis presumably meet, civic discourse and a genuinely public philosophy grounded in comprehensive notions of rationality and the demands of practical reason are imperative. . . . [A] public discussion of polity issues appealing to all intelligent, reasonable and responsible persons is a necessity, not a luxury, for any humane polity.[62]

If this statement were accurate, then the outlook for "humane polity" would be grim indeed, for the sorts of "comprehensive notions of rationality" to which Tracy appeals are illusory at best. More often, in fact, they tend to mask serious disparities in the distribution of power, wealth, socioeconomic status, and symbolic capital.[63]

Moreover, Tracy's universalism is not restricted to his comments on the public of society. He also argues that theologians must essentially address all people, regardless of their membership in a particular public. "However personally committed to a single public (society, academy or church) a particular theologian may be, each strives, in principle and in fact, for a genuine publicness and thereby implicitly addresses all three publics."[64] Or again: "Insofar as theologians must render explicit the major claims and counterclaims of each of the three publics, they aid the cause of clarity for the wider public."[65] Given the difficulties of describing even a *particular* audience, any universal claims about the wider public must be viewed with considerable suspicion.

This diversity and confusion among Tracy's perspectives on the theological audience will frequently escape his readers' notice, not only because of Tracy's own persuasive skills (which are indeed significant), but also because of his choice of terminology. By discussing the *public* to which theology speaks, rather than its *audience*, Tracy's work deploys a notion similar to Tillich's *situation*, and thus operates at a level which is sufficiently abstract not to raise many eyebrows. Nevertheless, in simply assuming that the addressees of Christian theology already form a public, Tracy unconsciously reifies the audience. He transforms a highly diverse, discontinuous, and dispersed group of people into a specified object on which criteria may then be imposed.

Interestingly enough, Tracy's own work does not appear to address *any* of the three publics which he describes. Rather, it seems to address a much more specific audience. In order to be persuaded by Tracy's work, an audience would need to hold certain assumptions about matters that remain unarticulated in the text: assumptions about rights, responsibilities, democracy, rationality, empirical evidence, warrants, the University of Chicago, the Roman Catholic magisterium, and the citation of academic authorities. Indeed, Tracy's audience includes those who believe, or can be persuaded to believe, that theology addresses the three different publics he hypothesizes.

But wait a moment. Why this sudden judgment on "Tracy's audience," after a long discussion about the enormous difficulties of specifying a writer's audience? How can anyone claim to be able to describe, in a single paragraph, the composition of someone else's audience? Am I not taxing the patience of a different audience—namely, the one composed of all those still willing to plow through this book?

Patience, gentle reader. These difficulties will be carefully considered in the following section.

A RHETORICAL ACCOUNT
OF THE AUDIENCE

The various modern perspectives on the audience—whether they appear independently or in a mélange—all operate under two basic assumptions: (1) the audience is simply "out there," waiting to be addressed; and (2) if rhetors wish to take account of the audience, they must somehow discover, with certainty and finality, what makes this audience "tick." For all four approaches (intentionalist, empiricist, pluralist, idealist), as for David Tracy, the audience is external to the speaker; the speaker's task is to learn about the members of the audience in order to address them.

This externalization of the audience seems natural enough, for we have become accustomed to think of speaker and listener as separate entities. In a technologically dominated age, the communicative relationship is often treated by analogy to the process of transmission and reception: the audience is considered a receptacle into which the rhetor can measure out eternal verities. Both audience and speaker are reified, and the argument itself becomes no more specifiable than a radio wave.

This view of human communication effectively neutralizes the diverse assumptions, opinions, and ideological commitments with which human beings approach the rhetorical task.[66] People are not merely channels through which communication flows; they are the source and destiny of language, and they actively shape both the message that is "sent" and the message that is "received." As we observed earlier in this chapter, the speaker's objective is to persuade the audience to *identify* with a particular position. The rhetor seeks to move, even to *impel*, the audience toward a particular point of view—and thence to action. The audience is not simply "out there," waiting to be persuaded; rather, it is much more integrally related to the rhetor who addresses it.

THE AUDIENCE AS
A RHETORICAL CONSTRUCT

Lurking among the various definitions of the audience in *The New Rhetoric*, we find the following comment:

The audience, as visualized by one undertaking to argue, is always a more or less systematized construction. Efforts have been made to establish its psychological or sociological origins. The essential consideration for the speaker who has set himself the task of persuading concrete individuals is that his construction of the audience should be adequate to the occasion.[67]

From this observation we can derive a working definition of the relationship between the rhetor and the audience: *The speaker or writer constructs an audience that is adequate to the occasion.* From a rhetorical perspective, speakers determine their audiences just as surely as they determine the content of their speeches.

More precisely: Speakers and writers construct their audiences *through the very way in which they select and deploy their arguments.* By choosing certain arguments over others, rhetors include and exclude certain people from the audience. Of course, if they hope to be persuasive, they cannot construct the audience *ex nihilo*; they must try "to form a concept of the anticipated audience as close as possible to reality."[68] But as we discovered in the previous section, this reality can never be perfectly known. Even with the spoken word, when the audience is often physically present, the speaker will be unable to predict the eventual scope and range of the speech. In writing, *a fortiori*, the author has no choice but to construct the audience in an imaginative way: readers must be made up, "fictionalized."[69] Either way, the audience is created in the process of discovering the available means of persuasion—the process that the Roman orators called *inventio*, and that Aristotle called simply *rhētorikē*.

Clearly, this relationship between the choice of arguments and the constructed audience will not always be brought to consciousness by the speaker or writer. Rhetors may claim that their audience comprises only one or two groups of people and yet choose arguments that invite the attention of those whom they had planned to exclude (or that fail to attract the attention of those whom they believed they were including). Similarly, the claim to address a wide audience may be betrayed by an argumentative structure that makes the text accessible only to a few specialists.

The construction of an audience would include, on the most obvious level, the use of a natural language in which to phrase the argument. Often the rhetor will have little choice in the matter; for instance, I would be well advised not to attempt to write this book in a language other than English. I would not have that many choices; and even in the languages I know well, writing a book of this length and complexity would be a formidable project indeed. Nevertheless, by choosing to write in English, I construct my audience: I exclude those who cannot read English. Similarly, the most eloquent and impassioned speech, when offered in French, will rarely persuade a room full of people who can understand only Russian. Poems and prose written in gibberish are effective only to the extent that they are understood in a quasi-musical way—or as a kind of code into which a recognizable language has been transmogrified.

But the choice of a natural language is only the first step; the features of the constructed audience are also determined through a wide range of argumentative choices. For example, when I write a technical treatise with hundreds of footnotes and a jargon-ridden vocabulary, I am constructing my audience. Nothing prevents me from claiming that my work is meant as a candidate for the *New York Times* best-seller list; but if I were to make such a claim, most critics would judge my effort a dismal failure. Or, I may claim that I do not intend anyone to read this work, other than a few carefully selected academic specialists; this claim, however, will not prevent one of my students from foolishly taking it off my office shelf and flipping through the pages as a means of passing the time. From a rhetorical perspective, my audience is determined not by a declaration of intent but by the arguments I have selected.

> It is not just that a writer "needs an audience": the language he uses already implies one range of possible audiences rather than another, and this is not a matter in which he necessarily has much choice. A writer may not have in mind a particular kind of reader at all, he may be superbly indifferent to who reads his work, but a certain kind of reader is already included within the very act of writing itself, as an internal structure of the text.[70]

The audience is actively constructed by the rhetor, whether consciously or otherwise. "No one writes simply for oneself. There is always an Other; and this Other willy-nilly turns interpretation into a social activity, albeit with unforeseen consequences, audiences, [and] constituencies."[71]

In fact, the notion of a constructed audience seems strange to modern ears precisely because we tend to construct our audiences unconsciously. This is why Kenneth Burke devoted so much of his work to the study of human motives: motives help us describe why people do what they do, regardless of how they may describe their own acts. A rhetor's motives for deploying a particular argument may be very different from the motives that she or he overtly declares. But once we recognize the possibility (likelihood?) of this divergence, we can begin to seek other avenues for discovering the rhetor's motives—of which, more anon.

The notion of a constructed audience bears some similarities to what literary theorists call *the implied reader*. In Wolfgang Iser's theory, the implied reader "embodies all those predispositions necessary for a literary work to exercise its effect—predispositions laid down, not by an empirical outside reality, but by the text itself."[72] But too often, this theoretical implied reader is made a product of the autonomous text, without reference to the flesh-and-blood person who wrote that text.[73] This differs from the notion of a constructed audience, which pushes the analysis back to the moment of production of texts and speeches. Specifically, it designates the speaker or writer as the actual agent of construction. Thus, the constructed audience is closer to Wayne Booth's notion of readers who are made by the writer:

> The author makes his readers. If he makes them badly—that is, if he simply waits, in all purity, for the occasional reader whose perceptions and norms happen to match his own, then his conception must be lofty indeed if we are to forgive him for his bad craftsmanship. But if he makes them well—that is, makes them see what they have never seen before, moves them into a new order of perception and experience altogether—he finds his reward in the peers he has created.[74]

Here, Booth supports the thesis that the audience is constructed by the writer or speaker; but he also suggests that these constructions can be evaluated. He claims that the audience may be "created badly" or "created well." On what basis can such evaluations be made?

The answer to this question has already been introduced: the quality of a particular construction depends on the degree to which it is "adequate to the occasion." Of course, the rhetor both identifies the situation and sets the criteria for adequacy; thus, from the rhetor's point of view, the constructed audience is almost always "adequate to the occasion." (*Almost* always, because speakers may deliberately argue in ways that they judge to be formally *in*adequate, as in the use of irony.) If the constructed audience does indeed turn out to be "adequate for the occasion"—that is, if those who read the text or hear the speech are persuaded—then the rhetorical event is judged a success. If only some are persuaded, then it may be a partial success; if no one is persuaded, then the effort fails. In other words, the success or failure of an argument is often determined by whether the speaker managed to construct an audience that, when judged with the advantages of hindsight, seems to have been "adequate to the occasion."

Consider, for example, the discussion of Karl Barth in the previous section. Barth seems to have constructed an audience composed of two major groups of people: those firmly committed to his own Evangelical confession, who would probably agree with him; and those firmly committed to other confessions (such as Roman Catholicism), who would respect his position but would undoubtedly oppose him. As we noted, Barth quite accurately predicted these results, and with these groups his argument was at least partially successful. Yet his constructed audience did not include those pluralists and ecumenists who believed that "no Church should take itself or other Churches with final seriousness."[75] (We can discover this by analyzing his texts; he offers few arguments against such a position and thus apparently did not expect its advocates to read his work.) Yet a number of these pluralists did encounter Barth's arguments, and—needless to say—did not find his position terribly persuasive. In this case, at least, Barth's construction of his audience was only partially "adequate to the occasion."

This analysis might seem to suggest that rhetors need an uncanny degree of insight in order to persuade their audiences. But speakers and writers do not construct audiences in the abstract; they analyze successful constructions by other rhetors in other situations and then apply this analysis to their own situation. Indeed, hundreds of such rhetorical examples were compiled into those textbooks which, from the Roman period through the nineteenth century, reduced the faculty of rhetoric to mere memorization and duplication. But even without recourse to textbook rhetoric, speakers and writers can make use of the persuasive successes of others. The successful writer or speaker is one whose constructed audience is learned "not from daily life but from earlier writers who were fictionalizing in their imagination audiences they had learned to know in still earlier writers, and so on back to the dawn of the written narrative."[76] Thus, although speakers and writers may think they work alone, they never work without examples of successful persuasive discourse.

Moreover, the constructed audience can be revised, based on various forms of feedback that the rhetor may receive. In a weekly lecture series, the speaker might rework each lecture in light of the discussion that followed the preceding one. Some speakers alter their construction of the audience during a speech, attending to feedback observed during the delivery itself. At the other end of the scale, a speaker who sits alone at a radio microphone may have no information on which to base any reconstruction of the audience. In the case of writing, of course, any comprehensive feedback *in media res* is almost impossible, because the entire audience is rarely physically present at the time of composition. Yet writers do occasionally revise their work for a second edition, and successive drafts of a manuscript often depend upon advice received from interested readers.

Whether the medium of communication is oral or written, rhetors can create an opportunity to reconstruct their audiences each time they pause long enough to receive some form of response. Reconstruction can thus occur whenever the rhetor ceases, temporarily, to be the rhetor, and instead becomes the auditor of someone else's speech—in other words, whenever there is a change of speaking subjects. Here we may employ Mikhail Bakhtin's notion of the *utterance*:

> The boundaries of each concrete utterance as a unit of speech communication are determined by a *change of speaking subjects*, that is, a change of speakers. Any utterance—from a short (single-word) rejoinder in everyday dialogue to the large novel or scientific treatise—has, so to speak, an absolute beginning and an absolute end: its beginning is preceded by the utterances of others, and its end is followed by the responsive utterances of others (or, although it may be silent, others' active responsive understanding, or, finally, a responsive action based on this understanding).[77]

With each new utterance, then, the speaker can reassess and thereby reconstruct the audience. This reconstruction provides a way of increasing the likelihood that the audience will be persuaded.

This suggests that, as the number of people in the actual audience decreases, the opportunities for explicit feedback during the process of an argument will often increase, enabling the speaker to reconstruct the audience over and over again. Thus, the smaller the number of people whom the speaker is addressing, the greater the opportunity for successful persuasion. And at the limit case, in which the audience consists of only one person, the result is dialogue—in which the rhetor can very quickly come to know a great deal about the addressee. Nevertheless, dialogue is but a special case of persuasion in general; we may choose to give it the kinder name of *conversation*, but it is not thereby vacated of agonistic structures. A conversation is simply two rhetorical events moving in opposite directions simultaneously. The conversational model was favored by Plato, and with good reason: for the skilled orator, dialogue allows for frequent reconstructions of the audience and thus provides one of the most effective methods of persuasion.

Regardless of its size, though, the audience is never entirely static and external to the rhetor, but is actively constructed in the very way in which arguments are selected and deployed. This constructivist view of the audience actually subsumes the four perspectives outlined in the previous section while avoiding most of their inadequacies. Like the intentionalist view, it recognizes that the rhetor defines the audience; but it does not assume that the final destiny of the argument can be controlled. Like the empiricist perspective, it tries to attend to the audience that will actually encounter the argument, by making the speech "adequate to the occasion"; but it recognizes that even the "thickest" description of an audience will be incomplete. Like the pluralist view, it admits the diversity of the audience; yet it still attempts to address the audience as a whole. It even subsumes the universal audience (though not its tendency toward idealism) by recognizing that even this universality is constructed by the rhetor. This, I believe, is precisely the role of the universal audience in *The New Rhetoric*, even though it was rarely read in this way. Many years later, Perelman made another attempt to define the universal audience: "The thesis defended in *The New Rhetoric* is that every philosopher addresses himself to the universal audience *as he conceives it*, even in *the absence of an objectivity* which imposes itself upon everyone. The philosopher develops an argumentation thanks to which he aspires to convince any competent interlocutor whatsoever."[78] On this reading, even the universal audience is a conscious construction; it is simply a more optimistic one, aspiring to include as many people as possible.

All arguers construct their audiences; however, some acknowledge this fact, while others deny it. This denial may take the form of an idealistic appeal to a universal audience, the empirical specification of an actual audience, or a psychologizing appeal to an intended or pluralistic audience. All of these appeals tend to obscure the speaker's implied assumptions, thereby masking the speaker's social location, material conditions, political sentiments, and ethical commitments. But when the audience is recognized to be a construction of the speaker, sociopolitical matters become much more important—and much easier to identify. These commitments now deserve our attention.

CHOOSING SIDES

The readers and auditors to whom arguments are addressed
are not abstract thinking minds. They are human beings, and
they bring to the rhetorical situation particular commitments.
They think in certain ways; they have specific likes and dis-
likes; and they live under particular social, economic, and
political conditions. Yet these commitments have typically been
ignored in modern theological discourse (and, for that matter,
in much modern discourse generally). They are ignored
because audiences are treated not as constructions of the
speaker, but as abstract externalities to which the speaker may
transmit a message.

Viewed from a rhetorical perspective, however, discourse
does not simply transmit information; it persuades others to
action. Moreover, as we have discovered, the relationship
between speaker and audience is much more complex than the
transmitter–receiver model would suggest. Thus, even purely
academic discourse—and perhaps *especially* such discourse—
must be examined with respect to the concrete commitments of
rhetor and audience.

This goal is well served by rhetoric, which assumes polemic
and partisanship to be the norm. Traditionally, as Walter Ong
has noted, "rhetoric fixed knowledge in agonistic structures."
Indeed, he claims, "until the age of romanticism reconstituted
psychological structures, academic teaching of all subjects had
been more or less polemic, dominated by the ubiquitous
rhetorical culture, and proceeding typically by proposing and
attacking theses in highly partisan fashion."[79] The polemical
nature of persuasive discourse does not mean that speakers
and writers need to be unpleasant to one another. In fact,
among academics, the "programed fighting spirit" which
rhetoric encourages is often "let loose on the social order more
than on their subject matter or colleagues."[80] Regardless of the
target of the argument, however, persuasion always involves
some degree of commitment to a particular point of view.

Persuasive discourse, then, is partisan; moreover, it urges audiences not just to *think* in particular ways, but also to *act* in particular ways. And because action takes place within a particular
polis, the partisanship of persuasive discourse cannot be divorced

from political life. Thus, a rehabilitation of rhetoric calls for attention to the social and political implications of persuasive language. A speaker may insist that a particular argument is presented merely for an audience's disinterested enjoyment; but ideological commitments are never far away. As Kenneth Burke suggests, "In accordance with the rhetorical principle of identification, whenever you find a doctrine of 'nonpolitical' esthetics affirmed with fervor, look for its politics."[81]

Indeed, this political emphasis is a hallmark of Burke's extension of the classical rhetorical tradition. "Burke's work may be read as an attempt to explode the myth of disinterest. His definition as a political thinker may be located precisely in his effort to place our 'autonomous' activities as intellectuals within the larger capitalist project whose purpose is always to prepare the sheep for market."[82] Burke insisted that, if rhetors were unwilling or unable to express their political intent, then the task of rhetorical criticism should be to seek out this intent and display it to them. The political emphasis of rhetoric has also been recognized in recent literary criticism; for example, Steven Mailloux defines rhetoric as "the political effectivity of trope and argument in culture."[83]

The thinkers of the Enlightenment had hoped to undermine vested political interests by resorting to a discourse of liberalism or pluralism. They believed that, if every point of view were given a voice, no single ideological structure would be able to take absolute control. This "public" attitude has gained widespread currency in the modern age; we tend to assume that, if all options were discussed openly and rationally, then special interests would vanish and all the participants would be made better persons. Unfortunately, however, such an assumption

> usually grossly overestimates this transformative power, considers it in isolation from any determining social context, and can formulate what it means by a "better person" only in the most narrow and abstract of terms. . . . Liberal humanism is a suburban moral ideology, limited in practice to largely interpersonal matters. It is stronger on adultery than armaments, and its valuable concern with freedom, democracy and individual rights are simply not concrete enough.[84]

On this account, the discourse of humanism is simply a different way of masking concrete political interests, which will still be carried out by other means.

Any speech or writing that seeks to persuade will operate with particular commitments and interests. These interests will often be masked, either because the rhetor prefers that they remain hidden, or because the rhetor has not become aware of them. Whenever ideological interests are thus enshrouded, they can be effectively exposed through the process of rhetorical criticism.

Specifically, rhetoric can help identify political interests by examining the concrete relationship between speaker and audience. To learn about a speaker's audience, we need not hypothesize the speaker's intentions, nor poll the actual listeners and readers, nor even listen to the speaker's own description of the audience. The audience is implicit in the rhetor's choice of arguments, because those arguments are chosen with a particular audience in mind. Thus, by examining the structure of a rhetor's argumentative choices, we can learn much about the commitments that the speaker holds, as well as the commitments with which the speaker has endowed the audience. In the process of attempting to move the audience from one set of commitments to another, rhetors reveal their own commitments as well.

IMPLICATIONS FOR
CHRISTIAN THEOLOGY

The conclusions reached thus far in this chapter have significant implications for the practice of the Christian faith. These implications will be developed at length, below. Meanwhile, I want to make a few observations about how this perspective might affect Christian theology's self-understanding and its methodological standards.

The constructed nature of the audience implies that Christian theology is a polemical and partisan activity, and cannot be reduced to a discourse of neutral observation. Every theology operates with certain commitments, and it constructs a committed audience as well. Even a theology that claims to champion pluralism has made a commitment—specifically, a commitment to pluralism.[85] Theology is thus necessarily polemical and partisan, even when disavowing these labels. All theology is controversial theology, for all theology seeks to persuade. A theologian does not ask, "Shall I make a commitment?" but rather, "What commitment shall I make?"

When a theology's commitments are ignored or deliberately subverted, its persuasion becomes a hegemonic discourse that binds itself to structures of power and influence. In this case, Christian theology would become one more discourse of power, competing with other such discourses in a world of commodities. Unfortunately, the history of Christian theology is filled with such masking of interests and complex struggles for dominance. Christian theology has become, at various times in its history, a mouthpiece for any number of glorifications of human power: nationalism and fascism, capitalism and socialism, racism and sexism, warfare and environmental destruction.

But although a theology may explicitly deny or disregard its own commitments, it does not thereby insulate itself from critique. Its motives can always be assessed with the tools of rhetoric. A rhetoric of Christian theology will ask: What does this theologian think will move the audience? To what authorities does the theologian appeal? What specifically Christian commitments would members of the audience need to bring to the rhetorical situation, in order to become interested in listening to the argument (and thus be open to the possibility of persuasion)?

Even those theologians who are most reticent about their partisan commitments often reveal a great deal about themselves by how they construct their audiences. By examining the deployment of a theologian's arguments and the standards of judgment to which these arguments appeal, a critical observer can begin to discern the complex relationship that has been constructed between rhetor and audience. In this manner, the rhetorical critic can offer a new perspective on the ideological commitments of the speaker or writer.

This approach produces a sociopolitical analysis of the rhetor's constructed audience, of which the description of

Tracy's audience at the end of the previous section was a very brief example. I suggested that Tracy's audience was an audience with specific assumptions about rights, responsibilities, the University of Chicago, the citation of academic authorities, and so forth. These observations were made not by psychoanalyzing Professor Tracy, nor by asking him whom he thought he was addressing. Rather, they were made by examining the arguments he offers.

This is not the place for a full-scale rhetorical commentary on *The Analogical Imagination*. Nevertheless, as an example of the sorts of commitments that can be discerned in Tracy's work, I offer a few observations about his constructed audience. Among those who are included: readers who appreciate the citation of a wide variety of academic intellectuals; readers who can be persuaded that the metaphor of *conversation* accurately describes the theological task; and readers who are willing to accept, as "Christian theology," a volume that makes only passing reference to traditional theological *loci* such as the Trinity, sin and atonement, and the liturgy. Among those who are excluded: the particularist (for no explicit argument is made in favor of pluralism); the fundamentalist and the authoritarian (as both are denounced without argument);[86] and the politically committed activist, for whom all appeals to the model of conversation are simply strategies for maintaining hegemony.

The notion of a constructed audience thus implies that theology is an inherently political activity. All writers and speakers approach the theological task with particular political commitments, even though these are rarely made salient (and are sometimes even intentionally hidden). These commitments, too, can often be critically reconstructed from the arguments that are deployed.[87] Such political criticism is often strengthened when the critic has access to biographical information about the author as well; this matter will concern us in chapter 3.

A theology's political interests can also be ascertained by considering its concrete political effects. For example: How does a particular theological position affect the poor and the outcast? To what degree does it move its audience toward a *praxis* that Matthew Lamb has called "solidarity with victims"?[88]

Does it offer hope for the future to those who are oppressed? In order to make salient a theology's political presuppositions, rhetorical criticism asks about the specific practices it produces. We cannot evaluate theologies simply through theoretical inquiry; we must also "ask what sort of social agenda they would serve."[89]

In other words, a theological position cannot be evaluated merely on the basis of its theoretical plausibility. A theology may appeal to a myriad of speculative theories, and yet not yield a practice in which Christians can participate. Even the most theoretically sound theology "may very well have the role of justifying a morally indefensible social situation—or perhaps simply of masking this situation by a discourse that is doubtless 'true,' but that is irrelevant or inopportune, because it distracts the mind and 'detours' the attention of the faith vis-à-vis the urgent tasks of a given conjuncture."[90] This is not to say that only practical results can justify a theological argument; it is simply a reminder that a tree is known by its fruits (Matt. 7:16–20).

Because Christian theology often takes highly theoretical forms, it can tend to isolate itself from the concrete political world. For example, the field of biblical studies has recently been indicted for its frequent pretension "to 'scientific' modes of inquiry that deny their hermeneutical and theoretical character and mask their historical-social location."[91] Similarly, when theologians resort to discourses of pluralism and universalism, the astute observer will suspect that political implications are being trod underfoot. If theologians claim to be disinterested observers, we should follow Burke's advice: "Look for their politics."

If the audience of Christian theology is not simply "out there," but is instead a construction of the theologian, then Christianity can no longer understand itself as a neutral, objective discourse on the Christian faith. Rather, it is itself an act of faith—or, at any rate, a faithful act. Theologians are not neutral observers, abstracted from the real world of Christianity. Rather, they are rhetors, attempting to persuade an audience that *their* vision of the Christian faith is a vision *worthy* of that faith. For

this reason, the doing of Christian theology is best characterized as an act of faithful persuasion.

CONSTRUCTING THE AUDIENCE
OF CHRISTIAN THEOLOGY

Given this revised understanding of the discipline of Christian theology, how might it affect the concrete ways in which
theologians go about their task? I want to suggest that, in order
to construct an audience that is "adequate to the occasion," theologians may need to take into account a number of factors that,
during the modern age, have rarely appeared on the theological
agenda. Because these concerns will frequently affect how the
audience evaluates a theological argument, their articulation
will be a central feature of a rhetoric of Christian theology.

In a sense, this section points toward the development of
rhetorical commonplaces (*topoi*) for Christian theology. In
Aristotle, the *topoi* were lines of argument; assembled in systematic form, they formed an incomplete catalogue from which
the speaker could select arguments that would be appropriate
in a particular context. In order to develop a list of *topoi*, the
speaker would need to examine the various factors affecting an
audience's judgment. Thus, the project here is to offer a very
preliminary sketch of some of these factors: discerning the
way, setting the scene, and practicing the faith.

DISCERNING THE WAY

Arguments can be evaluated through a wide variety of
means. In an age dominated by logic and other analytic methods, *evaluation* usually calls to mind rules of logical inference
and advice on the detection of fallacies. In practice, however,
these techniques may have little value; auditors will often base
their judgments on matters that the logician would consider
irrelevant. (I return to the inadequacies of logic in chapter 4.)

A rhetorical perspective is not limited to logic and thus allows for the possibility of distinctively Christian approaches to the evaluation of arguments. Christian theology concerns some matters that are not capable of purely empirical or logical demonstration: God, grace, revelation, atonement. A specifically Christian perspective on these matters may lead the audience to discern some very different "ways of evaluating" than those to which we may be accustomed.

First, as Aristotle knew, the emotions often have a significant effect on how an audience comes to a decision. While the modern age characterizes the emotions as irrational, Aristotle understood them as rational. This was not a mere leap of speculative psychology but a *rhetorical* insight: because passions can be shaped by argument, they must be related to human reason. As Larry Arnhart suggests, people "are continually talked into or out of their passions, either by themselves or by others. Passions do respond to arguments."[92]

The modern prejudice against the passions has come under close scrutiny in a number of quarters, including moral philosophy, feminist theology, and literary criticism.[93] These critiques dovetail with the rehabilitation of the emotions in argumentation theory. For example, in Wayne Booth's view, any argument can become a "good reason," even if its appeal is primarily emotional.[94] Of course, not all persuasion is purely emotional; however, emotion can—and frequently does—play a legitimate role in persuasion.

The role of the emotions in judgment was recognized by John Henry Newman, who applied them more specifically to Christian belief. "Newman's language and method are clearly appropriate to just those kinds of indeterminate questions he is at pains to have us recognize, those that are relative to the emotional, moral, spiritual, as well as cognitive capacities of people."[95] This approach is not a mere emotionalism, nor a privileging of the emotions over some other mode of judgment. It is, rather, a recognition that in Christian theology, as in many activities, people make judgments in cumulative, associative, and practical ways, rather than through abstract logical demonstration. "If we insist on proofs for everything, we shall never come to action: to act you must assume, and that assumption is faith."[96]

Second: Audiences will not necessarily respect the rationalistic distinction between *facts* and *values*. This distinction, employed primarily by noncognitivist moral philosophers, claims that value judgments have no cognitive status.[97] By removing such status from all statements of value, noncognitivism effectively elevates the significance of statements of fact. But from a rhetorical perspective, so-called statements of fact have no greater *a priori* epistemological status than any other statement.

> Statements of fact are after all *statements*, which presumes a number of questionable judgements: that those statements are worth making, perhaps more worth making than certain others, that I am the sort of person entitled to make them and perhaps able to guarantee their truth, that you are the kind of person worth making them to, that something useful is accomplished by making them, and so on.[98]

What we have been taught to name *facts* and *values* are both, from a rhetorical perspective, simply two perspectives on *judgment*. As the authors of *The New Rhetoric* remind us, we cannot ultimately distinguish so-called judgments of fact from judgments of value.[99]

A theological example: In arguments concerning the Resurrection, modern theologians have often emphasized a difference between the story (as it is described, from various perspectives, in the Bible), and the historical event which one might have witnessed, had one been present at the time. This approach claims that the biblical witness is merely a story; as *Geschichte*, it is permeated with the values of those who wrote about it. The event as observed by an eyewitness, on the other hand, would be a fact; it would be *Historie*. From the noncognitivist viewpoint, only the fact could have any cognitive value; the only relevant question would be: Did the Resurrection actually occur or not?

But such sharp distinctions are intentionally blurred by a rhetorical perspective, which recognizes that this dualism of perspectives misconstrues the basis on which many members of the audience will judge the theological argument. Indeed, upon closer inspection, the attempt to distill the Resurrection into these component parts seems quite ill conceived.

> It is possible to be so preoccupied with the chronology of Easter Sunday and the subsequent weeks or months (or years), or with the endlessly intriguing literary history of the resurrection stories that the question of why the resurrection should be good news *now* almost disappears. And this can produce the [opposite] reaction whereby 'resurrection' becomes simply a metaphor for grace, or triumph over adversity, or hope, or any other general human phenomenon, without its being related very clearly to the actual execution of a supposed rebel and/or blasphemer by the Roman colonial administration.[100]

The audiences that evaluate arguments about the Resurrection will not always seek to reduce this complex element of the faith to "a fact" and "a value."

Third: Audiences will often be persuaded by the effective use of figurative language. While figures of speech are often regarded as mere stylistic ornamentation, they affect the audience's judgment in subtle and sometimes mysterious ways. Naturally, not all figures will always have this persuasive effect; but when they do, they are no less "argumentative" than the most tightly constructed syllogism, as many communication theorists have observed.[101] Indeed, the classification of language under the headings of *figurative* and *literal* is a very questionable endeavor and makes sense only within a concrete rhetorical situation. "It is impossible to decide in advance if a given structure is or is not to be regarded as a figure, or if it will be an argumentative or a stylistic figure."[102]

The use of figurative language—and especially metaphor, allegory, and analogy—plays a particularly important role in Christian theology. If theology takes seriously the notion that human beings cannot achieve complete knowledge of God through their own endeavors, then the discipline should also recognize that the language of empirical description will be incapable of providing a complete vocabulary for talking about

God. Metaphor is thus central to Christian theology because it helps bridge the gap between the familiarity of empirical language and the relative strangeness of talk about God. "The interesting thing about metaphor, or at least about some metaphors, is that they are used not to redescribe, but to disclose for the first time. The metaphor has to be used because something new is being talked about."[103] Theology must rely upon metaphor to disclose the "wholly other" reality which is taken as the subject of its inquiry.

When the scope of metaphorical language extends beyond the particular tropic instance and encompasses a larger segment of prose, the result is typically called *allegory*. Allegorical discourse and allegorical interpretation can provide a particularly appropriate channel for theological discourse. Far from the irrational or dishonest use of language (as it is often labeled), allegory helps remind us of the depth of a text—a depth from which a wide variety of meanings are often plumbed.[104]

Metaphor and allegory are closely related to *analogy*—yet another way of speaking that does not depend completely on the assumptions of empiricism and scientific rationalism. Analogy is similar to metaphor in that it attempts to stretch language to operate beyond its (so-called) literal limits. It tends to be less jarring than metaphor, simply because it consciously affirms its status as "unusual" language. In the Thomistic tradition, analogy was often considered a path toward a knowledge of God that could be held with great certainty. However, some recent commentators have suggested that analogy can also remind us of the great difficulty with which human beings can speak of God at all.[105]

Finally: Audiences may make their decisions based upon common wisdom, or the *sensus communis*. As Vico described it, the *sensus communis* is the collective wisdom that guides action and discourse in a particular situation.[106] Instead of attempting to label certain actions or statements as eternally true or false, the *sensus communis* takes into account the concrete situation in which an action is performed or a word is spoken. It suggests an ability to act and think and speak rightly, according to the standards of the community and the concrete location of the agent. It is related to the notion of practical reason (*phronēsis; prudentia*), but it also includes the notion of speaking well (*eulogia; eloquentia*). As noted in chapter 1, the *sensus communis* is, not simply common sense, but the sense that nurtures community.

Community develops through common responses and common judgments that are not always well understood but that can be counted on to occur under particular circumstances. These responses and judgments are neither absolutely required nor inevitable; nevertheless, they are highly predictable. For example, members of a community will typically have a highly stylized way of responding when another member of the community has just experienced a death in the family. In the time and place in which I live, I can anticipate my own response: a certain form of words ("I'm so sorry, I know you were very close"); a certain immediate action (an embrace); a certain set of actions over the next few days (trying to assist the bereaved in everyday tasks such as cooking and housekeeping). Of course, these activities are culturally formed, and members of other communities might respond very differently. But in a particular time and place, the *sensus communis* would prescribe the responses that are appropriate toward those in grief—as well as what sorts are not (insulting them, telling them jokes, making immediate demands on their time and energy). These social conventions help constitute the community as a community.

A rhetorical appropriation of the *sensus communis* can be especially appropriate in theology. As Rebecca Chopp has noted, the theologian cannot even begin to understand Christian *praxis* without recognizing the importance of appeals to the spirit that holds the community together. Only thus can we hope to understand the Church's "conversations and actions, its sermons and worship, its fellowship and practices *as a community*."[107] The questions with which a community is typically preoccupied can often be answered only through an appeal to the *sensus communis*.

In sum, a rhetorical approach to the audience opens up a wide range of possible modes of evaluation. Through an act of discernment, the audience finds its own way to the most appropriate mode for a particular case. These alternative modes should be taken into account by theologians; in constructing their audiences, they should not assume that arguments will be evaluated according to some generally accepted criterion of rational assessment. Instead, the theologian must seek to discover those means of persuasion that can move the audience; and these can include appeals to modes of evaluation that may not have received the blessing of modern rationalism.

PREPARING THE SCENE

Audiences may be formed by a wide variety of stories, histories, linguistic assumptions, and cultural self-identifications; and these factors shape the context within which an argument is evaluated. To use Kenneth Burke's dramatistic terms: the *scene* of the argument helps to determine the *act* of judgment that the audience performs. "There is implicit in the quality of a scene the quality of the action that is to take place within it."[108] This is not to say that context absolutely determines an audience's judgment; nevertheless, it may restrict the range of possible judgments. "One could not deduce the *details* of the action from the *details* of the setting, but one could deduce the *quality* of the action from the *quality* of the setting."[109]

The context in which the audience evaluates an argument is described well by Hans-Georg Gadamer's apt metaphor of the *horizon*. A horizon is a boundary, but not a fixed boundary; a horizon is public, yet perspectival and mobile. According to Gadamer, the historical human life "is never utterly bound to any one standpoint, and hence can never have a truly closed horizon. The horizon is, rather, something into which we move and that moves with us. Horizons change for a person who is moving."[110] Without attempting to justify Gadamer's "two-horizon" model and his discussion of their "fusion," we can nevertheless respect this metaphor for its ability to emphasize simultaneously both human finitude and human capacity for change.

An audience's horizon situates the audience in a context. The horizon depicts the set of symbols, definitions, assumptions, motives, and beliefs according to which the members of an audience live their lives. The scene changes over time; but without it, the act of communication would be impossible. We may like to think that we are free to believe and argue about anything we like; but we are limited by the horizons that bound the scene within which we try to communicate.

> The inherited complex of symbols fixes the framework for communication within the group. Having had the courage to make use of my own understanding, I may decide that the way in which those around me perceive and describe the world is radically mistaken. I propound an alternative, bend old words to new use, concoct new words and construct new metaphors. If my readers are benign, they will shake their heads in amused bewilderment. If they are less tolerant, they will exclude me from their society (be it academic, ecclesiastical or political) as heretical, subversive or insane.[111]

We may move our audiences little by little; giant leaps will be either politely ignored or rather less politely suppressed.

Essentially the same point is made by Gadamer in his effort to rehabilitate the notion of tradition. Although some readers of *Truth and Method*—including both proponents and detractors—have seen in it an uncritical submission to authority, Gadamer's other writings do not support this view. He simply argues that we cannot avoid the tradition in which we stand.[112] The tradition is an authority for particular auditors of an argument, not because they *submit* to the tradition, but because it has made them who they are and because it pervades the scene within which they communicate. They have no pure platform of perception from which to view the argument disinterestedly.[113]

Indeed, audiences are formed by a wide variety of traditions; and this variety can provide rhetors with a way of setting the scene. The very opposite of a facile surrender to the tradition, this process recognizes that even the most stable traditions are constantly being reappropriated and reinterpreted. In this way, even the most "traditional" text can become the basis for political commitment and for the critique of ideology.[114] Indeed, the recovery of tradition is always a politically committed activity, like all persuasive acts. Without idealizing tradition or expecting that its appropriation will be utterly nonproblematic, we can recognize the significant role it plays in how audiences evaluate an argument.

In Christian theology, the audience's horizon will frequently be constituted by Scripture and by its effective-history, as well as by the tradition of the Church. Obviously, these sources will be variously interpreted, and the importance of their relative roles will differ, depending upon the formation of the audience and its judgment of the relevance of such materials to the argument at hand. I will return to discuss some of the ways in which these materials are appropriated in chapter 4.

PRACTICING THE FAITH

Christian theology takes as one of its essential presuppositions that the Christian faith continues to be believed and practiced by a community of the faithful. Even those commentators most intent on regarding theology as a secular enterprise are forced to admit that "theology as such would not even be possible except for the prior existence of the Christian witness of faith."[115] This faith can be identified by a number of distinctive practices; and participation in these practices will contribute significantly to the audience's evaluation of theological arguments. In order to describe this role, I want first to comment on the nature of practices in general; I shall then turn to some of the distinctive practices of the Christian faith.

The nature of practices

Many recent theological accounts of practices[116] take as their starting point the work of Alasdair MacIntyre, who defines a *practice* as

> any coherent and complex form of socially established cooperative human activity through which goods internal to that form of activity are realized in the course of trying to achieve those standards of excellence which are appropriate to, and partially definitive of, that form of activity, with the result that human powers to achieve excellence, and human conceptions of the ends and goods involved, are systematically extended.[117]

This definition, while adequate, says little about the scope of a practice, and this leads to serious ambiguities. While MacIntyre insists that "the precise range of practices is not at this stage of first importance,"[118] he makes some rather arbitrary judgments as to what activities might be labeled practices.

For example, MacIntyre argues that the game of chess is a practice, but that tic-tac-toe is not. The internal goods of chess, he says, include analytical skill, strategic imagination, and competitive intensity.[119] But *pace* MacIntyre, tic-tac-toe may be played for these same ends; the scale may be smaller, but the difference is clearly of degree, not kind. Admittedly, between two masters of the game, tic-tac-toe always ends in a draw. But the same would be true for two perfect masters of chess; anyone able to foresee all possible future permutations of the moves of the game can prevent the opponent from winning. In chess, the number of such permutations is greater; but for both games, exhaustive calculation is theoretically possible. (This is why computers can be programmed to play either game: tic-tac-toe, perfectly; chess, very well but imperfectly, since exhaustive calculation would be time consuming.)

MacIntyre's apparently arbitrary distinction between these two activities stems from the vagueness of certain terms in his definition of a practice. For example, he would probably argue that chess is complex, whereas tic-tac-toe is not. But complexity is a matter of judgment, and therefore a *rhetorical* matter— a matter that depends on the response of a specific audience. MacIntyre offers no guidance concerning *how* complex an activity needs to be in order to be a practice—nor concerning *who* might make that judgment. Consider, for example, other activities involving the placement of playing pieces on a grid, with little or no involvement of chance: activities such as the games of checkers or pente.[120] In complexity, these activities rank somewhere between the extremes of tic-tac-toe and chess; but which would be complex enough to be considered practices?

Issues of scale and scope may seem minor, but they describe a very basic failure of MacIntyre's definition: it is insufficiently attentive to context. For people who have engaged in practices such as chess, tic-tac-toe may seem fruitless. But children love the game; they seem to be able to play it endlessly without the slightest notion that they are failing to engage in a practice. Whether or not a particular game could count as a practice depends entirely on the context in which it is played.

A similar judgment could be rendered on other activities that MacIntyre excludes from the realm of practices, apparently because they are insufficiently complex. For example, MacIntyre argues that bricklaying is not a practice. But for all his emphasis on the contextuality of our judgments, he ignores the context in which bricklaying occurs. If bricklaying is one's trade, then it is undoubtedly a practice. But if I slap mortar on a few bricks to repair my patio, I certainly do not engage in bricklaying as a practice. (If done only as a household chore, it does not fit the rest of MacIntyre's definition.)

The contextualization of practices helps to explain why certain arguments are sometimes persuasive and sometimes not. Those who are engaged in a practice develop certain notions about standards of excellence, about the goods internal to that practice, and about its effect on more general notions of excellence. Consequently, those who participate in a particular practice will be more readily persuaded if the rhetor appeals to the standards of excellence that they have developed through their participation. Yet the very same appeal might be lost on someone who does not engage in the practice. No matter how mundane a particular practice may seem, it will still affect a person's judgment.

The practices of Christianity

How members of an audience participate in Christian practices will frequently shape their judgments. When evaluating a theological argument, members of an audience "must and do decide by the principles of thought and conduct which are habitual to them."[121] Christians are typically engaged in a wide variety of practices, some or all of which may impinge significantly on their evaluation of theological arguments.

Christians engage in a variety of activities, which may be personal, communal, or both. For some people, these activities may play a very small role in their lives; for example, some may participate in Christian worship only occasionally or in a very distracted manner. Such persons are not really participants in a *practice*, under a contextualized definition of practices. But other Christians may participate in the same activity in such a way as to strive for excellence in that activity, and thereby realize its internal goods. In such cases, they are participating in a Christian *practice*, and such practices will affect their standards of judgment when evaluating arguments.

For example: among the most celebrated "arguments" in theology are the so-called proofs for the existence of God. Too often, these arguments are described and discussed with no reference whatsoever to the persons to whom they are addressed. In their original context, the arguments often relied on particular practices of the audience in order to achieve the status of persuasive argument. For example, St. Anselm's ontological argument, as well as the five ways of St. Thomas Aquinas, were directed at those engaged in particular practices: Anselm's argument is set in the context of a prayer to God; Thomas addresses the *Summa theologiae* to novices in the study of theology. When evaluated by audiences engaged in Christian practices, these arguments clearly *are* proofs—and successful ones, because they appeal to the practices of prayer and theological study as contexts for evaluation. On the other hand, when torn from their rhetorical context, the arguments lead only to endless quarreling and confusion among students of the philosophy of religion.

Christian practices may also include study, meditation, and prophecy. Study seeks knowledge about God, humanity, and creation, which can come through a variety of activities: reading Scripture, studying the history of the tradition, and even criticizing the institutional structures of the Church. Meditation is a path to discernment—an openness to guidance from others concerning one's thoughts and actions. Prophecy includes both testifying to God's will and receiving this testimony from others. These practices need not take place within an institutional context; some have discerned a prophetic statement in a classroom lecture, an act of civil disobedience, or a popular essay on social justice.

Christians also engage in community-oriented practices. These may include regular gatherings for prayer and worship, and for the acknowledgement of community life. They may also include practices that address the wider human community—that is, action on behalf of others. Communal practices may be even more important for the formation of an audience's processes of judgment; for in the context of such communal practices, people learn about transformation and action— which operate at the very center of rhetorical activity. In its most vital incarnations, the Christian community

> is not static and staid, it does not exist merely as a building where individuals may be gathered or bureaucracy may be housed. First and foremost this community acts in its life together: worship, service, care, mission, ethics. And all these practices are corporate ways and means of transformation, the ongoing practice of life together in community.[122]

In community, people learn what motivates action and how change occurs. Thus, not surprisingly, the practices of a community may play a major role in the evaluation of an argument.

Theological arguments often fail to consider community practices; instead, the audience is assumed to be composed of autonomous individuals who evaluate arguments without reference to community standards. For example, arguments about the use of inclusive language in the Christian liturgy are often presented without a realization that an audience's judgment has already been partially formed by its participation in specific linguistic practices, both liturgical and otherwise. Thus, if the members of an audience participate in practices marked by the use of inclusive language (perhaps in the academy or the workplace, if not in the Church), they may be more sensitive to the exclusivity of the grammatically masculine language that has dominated Christian worship. On the other hand, for an audience formed primarily by the practice of traditional (often masculine) linguistic forms of the Christian liturgy, the problems inherent in such language may not be as patently obvious as its detractors often assume. Each side may fail to see the other's perspective: "the anguish that led many women to call for an inclusive language lectionary is countered by the anguish of the Orthodox and the distress of many traditionally oriented women over its use."[123] This is not to suggest that audiences can never alter their participation in a practice; indeed, precisely the opposite assumption motivates the entire rhetorical enterprise. But only by taking account of these varying practices can a rhetor hope to build a persuasive argument.

The audience is actively constructed by the theologian; it is not radically external to the rhetorical process. Therefore, how the audience evaluates an argument becomes much more nuanced. No longer can notions of logical validity and self-evidence be expected to enforce a "correct" judgment. Those who read and hear theological arguments make judgments based on "what seems to them to be the case" (the *doxa*), not on timeless standards of accuracy and rationality. Thus, theologians need to expand their notion of what counts as a basis for judgment. When coming to a decision, audiences may rely on a diverse range of practices, particularized horizons of judgment, and widely varying modes of evaluation.

CATECHESIS AS
A RHETORICAL ACTIVITY

In taking a rhetorical approach to Christian theology, the theologian self-consciously constructs the audience. Rather than assuming that an audience is simply "out there," ready and waiting to be persuaded, theologians actually construct their audiences by the very way in which they select their arguments. They appeal to the biblical text because they have constructed an audience that finds such appeals persuasive; or they avoid such appeals because they have constructed an audience which will *not* find them persuasive. As a result, their audiences are always already embedded in their theology.

Through the deployment of certain arguments, theologians are, in effect, saying: "this is what I want my audience to be; these are the kinds of people that I want them to become." The traditional name for this activity is *catechesis*—a theological activity, but also a thoroughly rhetorical activity. Catechesis is often derided as mere indoctrination; but its traditional role has been the instruction of inquirers in the ways of the faith. When theologians present their arguments, they are addressing an audience that they hope will find their appeals persuasive. As such, they are building up the faith of the members of their audiences; but the faith they seek to build is a particular faith. It is the Christian faith *as the particular theologian understands it.*

Theologians, then, are catechists; and whether they realize it or not, their theological arguments construct an audience. The theologian operates from a commitment to certain points of view and hopes to persuade the audience to hold those points of view. Some speakers and writers become truly adept at making an audience; that is, they learn how to shape an audience that is "adequate to the occasion." By learning from the persuasive success of other rhetors, and by paying close attention to the feedback they receive from their own audiences, they discover what makes an argument effective. By learning to persuade successfully, they learn not only how to *project* an audience, but also how to *transform* an audience.[124]

This implies that the theologian bears a considerably heavier burden than is commonly assumed. Christian theology cannot consist of mere intellectual gymnastics, because those who judge its arguments are inescapably influenced by its claims. Theologians cannot simply declare that a particular work is addressed to the academy, without reference to the effect that the work may have on those to whom it is not consciously addressed. A rhetorical approach to theology demands that theologians "own" their theology—not in the sense of private ownership, but in the sense of taking responsibility for the audiences that they create. They become responsible for insuring that all their acts of persuasion will be acts of *faithful* persuasion.

Consequently, a rhetoric of Christian theology cannot be limited to an examination of persuasion by means of the audience. It must also take into account the character of the person who presents the argument. The speaker may have constructed a perfectly appropriate audience; but if that speaker does not seem worthy of belief, the argument may still fail to persuade.

For example, in the closing arguments of the trial of Oliver North, both attorneys read from the Bible. Because all twelve members of the jury were black, the attorneys felt justified in constructing an audience for whom an appeal to the Bible would be highly persuasive. Yet after the verdict was rendered, one of the jurors remarked,

> I didn't like that [when they read the Bible]. Especially when Mr. Sullivan said, "I've never done this before but I'm going to do it now." I wanted to say, "If you've never done it before, leave it alone." I didn't like Mr. Keker doing it. They figured, you know, "Black people go to church."[125]

The jurors were, in fact, Christians. They did, in fact, read the Bible. They prayed together in the jury room. For such an audience, surely, an appeal to the Bible would be "adequate to the occasion"—would it not?

Yet the argument failed to persuade; an appeal to the audience is not always successful on its own. That appeal must be credible; it must be *authorized* by the person who presents the argument. In this case, the appeal to the Bible was presented by someone who was not authorized to make such an appeal—at least from one juror's point of view. The attorney was not authorized to read from the Bible because he had "never done this before." An argument that would seem persuasive under some circumstances may come from a source whose authority is in question—as St. Paul suggested when he told the Galatians that "such persuasion does not come from the one who calls you" (Gal. 5:8).

The authority of the rhetor, then, is often as important to the appeal of an argument as is the "state, condition, or experience" of the audience. In order to understand more fully the speaker's role in the process of persuasion, we must move out of the realm of the world to which theology speaks, and into the realm of the character with which theology speaks. Thus we turn now to persuasion by means of *ēthos*.

3

Ēthos

The Character
with Which
Theology Speaks

According to Aristotle, one of the three means of persuasion is the moral character (*ēthos*) of the speaker. The speaker's character will affect the degree of confidence with which a speech is received.

> The orator persuades by moral character when his speech is delivered in such a manner as to render him worthy of confidence; for we trust such persons to a greater degree, and more readily. This is generally true for all types of argument, and absolutely true when there is uncertainty [*amphidoxein*] and room for doubt. But this confidence ought to be due to the speech itself, and not left up to some preconceived idea of the speaker's character. It is not the case, as some writers of rhetorical treatises hold, that the worth of the orator in no way contributes to his power of persuasion; on the contrary, moral character may almost be called the most potent [*kuriōtatēn*] means of persuasion.[1]

Here Aristotle sides with Isocrates and against the Sophists. Persuasion is not simply a matter of employing clever arguments—nor even a matter of correctly constructing the audience. The rhetor must also give the members of the audience some reason to believe that the person to whom they are listening is worthy of their attention.

The audience's confidence can be influenced a number of different ways. The listeners may form an opinion of the speaker's character before they hear the speech; or, some future event or action may influence their evaluation retrospectively. Alternatively, their opinion about the rhetor's character may be shaped primarily by the speech or text itself. According to Aristotle, this last option should be favored by the rhetor, since it provides for the greatest exercise of control.

But this seems a troublesome notion: Should the moral character of the speaker really be allowed to qualify the outcome of an argument? Does this not represent a step backwards—a retreat from the modern goals of neutrality and objectivity? Does it imply, once again, that rhetoric functions primarily as a means of deceit? And how can an audience ever expect to know the speaker's true character? Does Aristotle's description not leave the door open wide for every variety of coercion and manipulation?

The relationship between moral character and persuasion is complex—and will become more so when applied to arguments within Christian theology, where disputes about character often play a central role. Moreover, the term *ēthos* demands some clarification. Just as *pathos* suggests more than simply the audience's emotions, so *ēthos* suggests more than simply a list of the speaker's virtues and vices. The term also refers to the entire range of characteristics that describe how people live their lives—as suggested by the Greek *hexis* or the Latin *habitus*. This is the sense of the term stressed by Martin Heidegger in the "Letter on Humanism":

> *Ethos* means abode, dwelling place. The word names the open region in which man dwells. The open region of his abode allows what pertains to man's essence, and what in thus arriving resides in nearness to him, to appear. The abode of man contains and preserves the advent of what belongs to man in his essence.[2]

This passage requires two judgments. First, a negative one: words such as *essence* and *appearance*, because of their abstractness, can be used to justify the most horrific political consequences—as Heidegger himself should certainly have known by 1947. But second, and more positively: Heidegger seems to recognize a broader territory for *ēthos* than the highly restricted sphere typically signified by *ethics*. One's *ēthos* is one's dwelling place; and this signifies a particular approach to living, an entire range of actions and passions—not simply a list of misdemeanors and foibles. We are thus challenged to develop this expanded understanding of *ēthos*, and yet to find ways of describing this *habitus* in terms far more concrete than Heidegger's.

In the first section of this chapter, I consider the traditional role of *ēthos* in rhetoric and theology and how its role has been eclipsed in the modern age. In the second section, I provide a description of how persuasion occurs by means of character; this will entail questions about who judges character, and how these judgments are formed. I then turn, in the third section, to a brief inventory of the theological elements of character—i.e., an analysis of how audiences evaluate the character of Christian theology. I conclude by examining some of the larger theological implications of this discussion.

CHARACTER IN RHETORIC
AND THEOLOGY

Many accounts of the nature of argument pay no attention whatsoever to the character of the person making the argument. Standard textbooks on argumentation or reasoning typically offer examples for analysis that have been abstracted from their rhetorical context; the question of who offered the argument does not even arise.[3] In fact, any attempt to draw connections between the argument and the arguer is usually labeled a fallacy: the *argumentum ad hominem*. But as we will discover, this modern inattention to character results primarily from the rationalistic attempt to render illegitimate any personal involvement in the process of persuasion. This variety of reductionism has had disastrous results for Christian theology, which had traditionally given a very large role to matters of character.

THE ROLE OF CHARACTER
IN PERSUASION

Both rhetoric and ethics concern themselves not with analytically necessary facts, but with matters that could be otherwise. Thus, when a particular rhetor puts forward an argument, the audience may often react with the question: "Why should I believe this particular person?" Most audiences will come into contact with an enormous range of apparently coherent arguments, which will support widely varying (and often mutually exclusive) positions. The members of the audience will not always be able to adjudicate among conflicting arguments. They will ask: "Why should I believe this argument instead of that one?" In other words, they will seek ways to authorize some positions and cast doubt on competing positions. Authorization depends on the varying degrees of confidence that an audience places in those who advocate competing positions.

Consequently, the authority of a particular argument is closely connected to how the audience evaluates the person who offers that argument. As the audience judges the speaker's character to be more or less worthy of confidence, the speaker's arguments are accordingly considered more or less authoritative. The connection may be clarified by following the sojourn of Aristotle's notion of an appeal to *ēthos*. In the writings of Quintilian, this notion becomes an appeal to *auctoritas*: not so much "character" as "warrant," "authorization," or "authority."[4] Perhaps Quintilian's language helps explain why Aristotle says that judgments about the character of the speaker may provide the most powerful means of persuasion.

The significance of judgments about character in determining authority results from the close relationship that exists between language and language-users. When we hear a speaker or read a book, we naturally make connections between the words employed and the person who employs them. Whether consciously or not, we make judgments about the speaker's language traditions, personal experiences, limitations, and historical and social circumstances.[5] Moreover, these judgments will be made differently in different circumstances. We cannot simply compile a list of persuasive characteristics that will be effective in every case. Of course, we could enumerate the virtues, as does Aristotle in the *Nicomachean Ethics*; but as Aristotle himself admits, the content of those categories will vary according to time, place, and circumstance.

The degree to which character affects the persuasive quality of a speech depends very much on the degree to which the question is in dispute. When an issue is especially difficult to resolve, audiences must rely on other kinds of judgments—e.g., judgments about character—in order to discriminate among options. Thus, character rarely plays a role in arguments within conventional systems; most audiences do not need an additional authorization for accepting an argument about which there is widespread agreement, such as "two and two make four." Indeed, conventional systems (such as those employed in some branches of mathematics) are meant to eliminate contingency altogether. Of course, one may need to be persuaded to adopt the convention in the first place (I shall return .to this problem in chapter 4). Once the convention is established, however, judgments about a particular rhetor's character become irrelevant, as does the entire enterprise of persuasion. On the other hand, most arguments are not purely conventional; in fact, people can only be said to have an argument over matters that could be otherwise. As the authors of *The New Rhetoric* observed, "Euclid's morality in no way influences the validity of his geometrical proofs; but if the person who recommends a candidate hopes to draw a considerable personal advantage from his nomination or election, the weight of his recommendation will inevitably be greatly affected by it."[6] Audiences naturally consider the character of the speaker or writer when rendering judgments in contingent matters. In Aristotle's terms: whenever persuasion is possible, it will be influenced by judgments about character—especially in those matters which are most open to dispute.

This openness to dispute characterizes most arguments about concrete and practical matters. While abstract generalizations may lend themselves to widespread agreement, such agreement retains a merely formal quality. Any attempt to specify more particular, practical implications will very likely lead to dispute. In such cases, says Newman, we are in great measure thrown back into that condition, from which logic proposed to rescue us. We judge for ourselves, by our own lights, and on our own principles; and our criterion of truth is not so much the manipulation of propositions, as the intellectual and moral character of the person maintaining them, and the ultimate silent effect of his arguments or conclusions upon our minds.[7]

In matters which involve concrete practice and action, audiences cannot rely upon the canons of logic alone (if at all). They must rely on their judgments about a particular speaker's authority to speak; for they have no other way of adjudicating among a number of differing options (all of which may seem warranted). Uncertainty leads directly to judgments about character.

As I have argued throughout this book, such uncertainty is part and parcel of the enterprise of Christian theology. In the great tradition of the *via negativa*, theologians must admit that no argument will be finally definitive, no human words will be ultimately determinative. Their audiences will be faced with a number of uncertain, insufficient, and admittedly incomplete arguments about the Christian faith. Varying accounts will gain authority only through the character of the theologian who employs them. Thus, character has traditionally played a central role in Christian theology.

THE ROLE OF CHARACTER
IN THEOLOGY

In the Christian tradition, the ultimate "character reference" is provided by God. One argument is authorized over another because it is claimed to be God's argument, rather than a human being's. This authorizing character of God's speech is a central feature of the witness of both the Old and New Testaments. As George Kennedy has suggested,[8] the Old Testament frequently offers examples in which a human claim is disputed, and in which the dispute is resolved by appealing to the authority of God.

But Moses said to the Lord, "O my Lord, I have never been eloquent, neither in the past nor even now that you have spoken to your servant; but I am slow of speech and slow of tongue." Then the Lord said to him, "Who gives speech to mortals? Who makes them mute or deaf, seeing or blind? Is it not I, the Lord? Now go, and I will be with your mouth and teach you what you are to speak. (Exod. 4:10–12)

The techniques of persuasion that Moses claims to lack are more than amply recompensed by the (divine) authority with which he speaks.[9]

The appeal to the character of God is made more personal and more concrete in the New Testament; for here, a particular human being is perfectly identified with God. The character of Jesus Christ thus takes on immense significance; to Christians, the arguments advanced by Jesus are the ultimately authoritative arguments. But Jesus' authority will be variously assessed:

Now when Jesus came into the district of Caesarea Philippi, he asked his disciples, "Who do people say that the Son of Man is?" And they said, "Some say John the Baptist, but others Elijah, and still others Jeremiah or one of the prophets." He said to them, "But who do you say that I am?" Simon Peter answered, "You are the Messiah, the Son of the living God." (Matt. 16:13–16; cf. Mark 8:27–29; Luke 9:18–20)

Needless to say, the identity that various audiences assigned to Jesus affected their assessment of his character, and thereby affected the authority with which he spoke. For the disciples, he was the Christ; for others, a prophet. For others still, he was the very opposite of an authority; in fact, Peter could have added, "Others say you are a devil" (cf. Matt. 12:24 par.). Jesus' character is of great significance to the writers of the gospels, who tell us that "he taught them as one having authority, and not as the scribes" (Mark 1:22).

Similarly, character plays an important role for St. Paul, who knows that his words will be variously received depending on how much confidence they can inspire. So in his epistle to the Galatians, where he is apparently addressing a hostile audience, he begins with a bold declaration: "Paul an apostle— sent neither by human commission nor from human authorities, but through Jesus Christ and God the Father, who raised him from the dead" (Gal. 1:1). Clearly, Paul wants to remind the

Galatians that, among the various "gospels" they have heard, the one that comes from him is the authorized one—because it also comes from Christ.

Paul's self-description as an "apostle" already asserts a claim to authority—a claim to a direct relationship with Christ, and therefore a claim which is meant to inspire confidence.[10] It gives Paul's audience a reason to consider him a person of good character. (Again, *good character* is used here not in the sense of "moral righteousness," but in the sense of a life lived according to the will of God.) Of course, anyone could make such a claim; simply to maintain that one's authority is of divine origin does not make it so. Nevertheless, such claims are more likely to be accepted if they are supported and validated by the life of the claimant. This is precisely how Paul seeks to substantiate his appeal to his own authority:

> For I want you to know, brothers and sisters, that the gospel that was proclaimed by me is not of human origin; for I did not receive it from a human source, nor was I taught it, but I received it through a revelation of Jesus Christ. You have heard, no doubt, of my earlier life in Judaism. I was violently persecuting the church of God and was trying to destroy it. I advanced in Judaism beyond many among my people of the same age, for I was far more zealous for the traditions of my ancestors. (Gal. 1:11–14)

Paul's story describes his character: one who had been zealous in persecuting the Church received a direct mandate from God to preach the Gospel. Paul's lived-through experiences thus help authenticate his self-description, which in turn gives authority to his teaching.

Theological interest in character has continued throughout the history of the Church; appeals to character occur and assume great importance in the works of Tertullian, Origen, the Cappadocians, and Augustine, as well as in Anselm, Thomas, Luther, and Calvin. I would like to offer one example of how theologians have sought to persuade by means of *ēthos*—an example provided by the writings of St. Gregory of Nazianzus.

St. Gregory's orations emphasize the importance of the theologian's character. For example, he cautions his listeners against accepting the arguments of "just anyone" who might claim to be engaging in Christian theology: "Not to everyone, my friends, does it belong to philosophize about God; . . . because it is permitted only to those who have been examined, and are past masters in meditation, and who have been previously purified in soul and body, or at the very least are being purified."[11] Gregory's strong emphasis on purification might be seen by some as mere moralizing; and yet, he does not appear to argue for radical ascesis as the only way to prove one's character. Rather, he emphasizes that the theological task requires a significant level of spiritual and intellectual preparation, and should not be done merely for one's own amusement. Only because we are "being molded and molding others by Holy Scripture," he argues, can we "enter upon theological questions."[12]

Gregory believes that theologians must live the sort of lives that will, on the one hand, allow them to recognize the truth of revelation, and, on the other hand, lend credibility to their arguments. Gregory reminds his listeners that only a Moses will be able to go up to the mount and take away the veil from his face. An Aaron would have to stand outside the cloud; a Nadab or an Abihu would stand yet further away; and those of the multitude would need to stay below.[13]

As Gregory's use of the appeal to *ēthos* should indicate, a discussion of character need not advocate the invasion of every theologian's closet in search of skeletons. Theologians are not exempt from the paradoxical condition of humanity: created in the image of God, and yet constrained by so many limitations. "All have sinned and fall short of the glory of God" (Rom 3:23); theologians are certainly no exception. On the one hand, this means that they are capable of choosing badly and, indeed, of doing evil; and their actions may play a significant role in the evaluation of character. Moreover, specific incidents may indicate larger character flaws, and these need to be discussed openly and critically.[14] I shall return to this issue at the end of the chapter.

On the other hand, to focus only on specific wrongdoings is to operate with too limited an understanding of *ēthos*. I want to suggest that character affects theology in much broader ways— i.e., that the entire life of the theologian can provide a warrant whereby the audience evaluates a theological argument.

Judgment may be affected, for example, by the audience's perception of the theologian's faith; for faith is also a virtue, a _habitus._[15] How Christian theologians live their lives will affect, and should affect, how their message is received.

THE MODERN DISTASTE
FOR CHARACTER

The persuasive role of character was seriously devalued during the Enlightenment. The rise of experimental science emphasized the goal of neutrality, which was thought to be guaranteed only through radical detachment: subject and object were thus torn asunder. On this view, an experiment needed only to take place under properly controlled conditions; the character of the experimenter was considered irrelevant. Empirical experimentation tended to focus attention away from how things appear in nature, and toward exceptions to the rule.[16] This narrow focus contributed to the reduction of the meaning of _ēthos_ from a complex, holistic _habitus_ to a mere series of rules and regulations. The significance of character has been obscured by other modern assumptions as well: fact/value distinctions, restrictions on the concept of proof, and noncognitive approaches to moral philosophy.[17] Finally, as Wayne Booth has suggested, the best-known ethical criticism—such as that of Plato, Johnson, and Marx—displays a "vigorous tone of condemnation" that has sometimes been interpreted as an attempt at censorship.[18]

But perhaps the most important reason for the modern distaste for _ēthos_ is the problematic status of _personhood_ in recent philosophy. Certain strands of Enlightenment thought tended to idealize an autonomous subject, completely severed from community and world: a subject who acted in perfect freedom, unencumbered by the traditional constraints of heaven above and hell below. The notion of a purely autonomous subject has fallen under such heavy attack that it has become little more than a parody of itself. But if the transcendental subject is no longer the central focus of thought and action, what role remains for the speaker in the rhetorical situation? Do all arguments simply take place inside the minds of their auditors? Is the rhetor nothing more than an instantiation of the wide variety of social, political, and economic forces that impinge upon and constitute the so-called self? Or are arguments really made by *persons?*

In the field of literary criticism, these questions have often been discussed under the heading of *authorial intent.* In the days when the autonomous subject was taken for granted, critics quite logically assumed that a text provided some sort of access to the mind of the author. The text meant whatever its author intended it to mean. This view was rejected by the devotees of New Criticism, who called it *the intentional fallacy.*[19] The New Critics claimed the author's intended meaning is of no value in interpreting a text.[20] Instead, they argued, meaning is to be found in the text itself.

On the one hand, the New Critical attempt to locate all meaning in a text is clearly called into question by the rhetorical tradition, which highlights the central role of the writer or speaker. Nevertheless, the negative conclusion of New Criticism was an important one: we do not rely solely on a rhetor's intentions in order to give meaning to a text or speech. Even when authors and speakers state their intentions clearly, we have no way of judging the accuracy of their claims—nor of deciding whether their purpose is to deceive. More often, the rhetor's intentions are not plainly stated; and members of the audience rarely have an opportunity to ask for a clarification of intent. Thus, any reliance on authorial intention seems to imply a degree of psychoanalytic insight which few critics could claim to possess.[21] But the problems associated with an appeal to authorial intention go well beyond the mere difficulty of crawling into another person's mind.

The attempt to rely on an author's intention ignores the complexity of the process of communication. Arguments are evaluated on the basis of hundreds of disparate factors (some of these have been explored in chapter 2). Many of these factors are altogether unrelated to the speaker—let alone to the speaker's mental state. Moreover, as Terry Eagleton has noted, the claim that authorial intention should adjudicate interpretive disputes implies that discursive acts are nothing more than commodities to be exchanged.[22] Like the *sender-receiver* model criticized in chapter 2, this *commodity* model of communication tends to characterize the self as a merely passive receiver of data. Both models seem to imply a hidden ideology—a "collapsing of conceptions of motives, powers, and action into the subject-agent," which Kenneth Burke labeled a "capitalist psychosis."[23]

But if this critique of hermeneutical intentionalism is pressed to its limits, it would seem to imply that any appeal to the character of a rhetor would be misguided at best. It would turn our attention away from persons and toward texts, toward *écriture*—not toward the character of the writer or speaker. According to Michel Foucault, for example, the new questions that we should be asking about texts manifest "little more than the murmur of indifference: 'What matter who's speaking?'"[24]

Yet despite the significance of these critiques, rumors of the "death of the author" have been somewhat exaggerated. To be sure, the self, as speaker or writer, is not the transcendent, self-sufficient entity that the devotees of nineteenth-century romantic hermeneutics had hypothesized. To this extent, the decentering of the self offers an important correction. However, this does not justify the assumption that audiences do not care who is speaking, nor that all arguments are simply manifestations of societal and structural power. While admitting the force of the postmodern critique of the autonomous self, we can still attempt to construct a notion of personhood that can account for the personal and directed nature of discourse. The speaker is certainly not the purely autonomous entity that many Enlightenment thinkers (both rationalists and romantics) imagined. Nevertheless, the speaker still remains a concrete locus to whom character is attributed.

This important caveat to the postmodern understanding of personhood has been affirmed by a number of commentators in rhetoric, philosophy, and literary criticism. These critics recognize that, after all, writing and speaking imply human activity. For example, Calvin Schrag argues that "the tracking of meaning within the sociohistorical interstices of the conversation and practices of mankind does no more than resituate, relativize, and decentralize the role of the author. It does not entail his

displacement."[25] Similarly, the authors of *The New Rhetoric* insist that "the person is the best context for evaluating the meaning and significance of an assertion, especially when the
statements are not integrated in a more or less rigid system."[26]
And even Foucault recognized that the question is not *whether*
to investigate the speaking or writing subject, but rather *what
kind* of investigations to undertake.

> We should suspend the typical questions: how does a free subject
> penetrate the density of things and endow them with meaning;
> how does it accomplish its design by animating the rules of dis-
> course from within? Rather, we should ask: under what conditions
> and through what forms can an entity like the subject appear in the
> order of discourse; what position does it occupy; what functions
> does it exhibit; and what rules does it follow in each type of
> discourse?[27]

These are precisely the questions that rhetorical analysis
should ask; and they are particularly important questions for
the task of Christian theology.

Christianity has always given significant weight to the notion
of *personhood*—an emphasis that has played itself out in biblical studies, doctrine, ethics, and worship. In early Christian
thought, the person is understood as existing in relationship to
others; personhood thus necessarily implies community. Christianity had developed this highly nuanced approach long before
the advent of the autonomous self of the Enlightenment. And
although sometimes swept along in autonomy's tide, Christianity can still reflect a notion of personhood very different
from the atomized, individualistic model so prevalent in the
modern age. Christianity's more communal and relational model
of personhood is now being recovered by a wide variety of
theologians.[28]

Theological and philosophical concerns about personhood
are addressed well by a rhetorical method, for rhetoric provides
us with ways to speak of the subject as an actor, without the
metaphysical baggage that the Western philosophical tradition
has attached to the act of authorship. We can allow for multiplicity and equivocity, and yet continue to speak meaningfully

of the subject. Drawing on the very different views of Nietzsche and of G. H. Mead, Calvin Schrag suggests that the "decentered subject" that we have inherited from the postmodern critique is admittedly an ensemble of multiplicity, "whose identity is an acquisition rather than a given, achieved within the play of difference."[29] Nevertheless, this multiplicity need not prevent us from specifying a subject—especially when we turn our attention to the rhetorical sphere.

> Discourse and action, as we have seen, assume different forms of language and life against the background of multiple social memories, variegated customs, habits, and institutional practices. The presence of the subject within this network of communicative praxis is that of a postured response to the ongoing conversation and to the prior action upon the subject. In this response there is a "responding center" in terms of an existential sphere of interest and concern, a base of operations "from where" something is said and something is done, a stance of critique and assent; but this is neither a metaphysical nor an epistemological center.[30]

That is, personhood does not denote that self-authorizing, autonomous center that the Enlightenment idealized but, rather, the locus where a variety of concrete interests and assumptions intersect. A rhetorical analysis of the speaker does not seek a turn to the subject, but only a critical analysis of how a speaker's interests and purposes are constructed and judged by a particular audience.

We are now in a better position to consider the relationship of rhetoric to debates about the intentional fallacy. Admittedly, we cannot appeal to the author's intentions in order to determine a text's meaning; but this should not prevent us from considering the role of character in determining a text's persuasive appeal. To understand why a text may persuade a particular audience is a far cry from pronouncing a sentence on the text's meaning—or even on its range of possible meanings. In fact, a rhetorical approach tends to minimize questions of meaning, turning instead to the question of whether an audience is persuaded.[31] Thus, we need to stop asking *whether* character will play a role in persuasion and turn instead to the question of *how* it persuades.

HOW DOES CHARACTER
PERSUADE?

I want to examine the relationships between an argumentative claim and the character of the claimant. After discussing the
nature of the audience's evaluation of character, I explore the
mediations of character—that is, the variety of ways in which
the audience obtains information affecting its evaluation of
character. A few concluding remarks explore the wider implications of this analysis.

CHARACTER ACCORDING TO WHOM?

Many of our day-to-day decisions would be less complicated
if we knew how to separate those persons whom we should respect from those whom we should ignore. Our lives would be
easier if speakers wore a badge carrying a rating that allowed us
to evaluate their character intersubjectively. With such information, the relative reliability of all communication would be clear;
we would know which candidate's speech to believe, which
witness's testimony to accept, even which religious leader's
exhortation to obey.

But—fortunately!—no such evaluations are available. Even if
they were, they would generate more disagreement than con-
vergence, for the evaluation of character is a highly perspectival notion. The character of the speaker or writer will be
evaluated differently by different audiences, and these evaluations will be influenced by a wide range of factors. Character,
then, is always character as perceived by someone. The rhetor's
character is not in itself persuasive; however, an audience's
judgments about character can dramatically affect how an argument is received.

Even in the relatively homogeneous world of the Greeks,
judgments of character were not considered univocal. As
Aristotle noted, an action considered a virtue in one city-state
might be treated as a vice in another. We can give names to the
virtues—*justice, courage, temperance, magnanimity*— but
their content will always remain in dispute. We may agree that

whatever is noble is productive of virtue; but various accounts of *nobility* are still possible.

> The special characteristics proper to a people are noble; also any distinctive marks or habits that are admired among a particular people. Thus in Lacedaemon it is noble to wear the hair long, as that indicates the free man; for with the hair worn long it is not easy to do any servile work.[32]

Aristotle's approach to character in the *Rhetoric* accords with his discussion of virtue in the *Nicomachean Ethics*. There, the table of the virtues is abstract and generalized, whereas the specific examples are appropriate to restricted cultural assumptions about what is praiseworthy or blameworthy. His examples of the virtues may have seemed obvious to many Greeks, yet ludicrous to contemporaries in Egypt or Persia. Sometimes, they seem strange to modern readers in the West, even though we live in a world strongly influenced by the norms of ancient Greek culture. We are unlikely to dispute that justice, courage, and temperance are virtues; but we will probably define them differently from Aristotle.[33]

Even with this caveat, however, Aristotle's emphasis on the virtues has certainly not won universal acceptance. For example, the virtues have played a relatively minor role in modern accounts of moral philosophy. After the Enlightenment, ethics tended to become

> an investigation of character-properties which attach to a moral subject. These character-properties, defined as "values," were viewed as having their origin in a valuing subject. This valuing subject, posited as the center in a moral theory of the self, had conferred upon it a position and function similar to the knowing subject of modern epistemological theory. . . . Value and knowledge became viewed as properties possessed by a subject.[34]

We have already admitted the force of postmodern critiques of the knowing subject. But the notion of a *moral* subject is even more pernicious, in that it can support a radical individualism that depicts selves as autonomous moral agents—acting purely on the basis of the will, and making decisions independently of societal, psychological, and economic influences.

This notion of moral autonomy was brought under radical questioning by the materialist critiques of the nineteenth century; but it lingers, to the present day, in some forms of *laissez-faire* economics, individualistic religious belief, and existentialist philosophy. In practical terms, the illusion of moral autonomy manifests itself in an ethical decisionism that emphasizes the ability of the free-acting individual to determine a plan of action by performing the required level of casuistry. But such stark assertions of autonomous decision-making are extremely difficult to maintain.

The response to decisionism

Our decisions, after all, are *not* autonomous; they are shaped by our education, our friendships, our commitments—that is, by the way we live our lives. Moreover, given the expanded understanding of *ēthos* that I am advocating here, any investigation into the nature of ethics must go beyond mere decision making and instead attempt to understand why people live their lives as they do.

These concerns have led a number of commentators to suggest that we should examine our place in the narratives that structure our world. A narrative approach to *ēthos* would argue that, within a given community, the distribution of praise and blame (and therefore how character is understood and evaluated) can best be understood by examining the stories that the community tells. As Stanley Hauerwas has observed,

> the field of a story is actions (either deeds or dreams) or their opposite, sufferings. In either case, what action or passion is seen to unfold is something we call "character." *Character*, of course, is not a theoretical notion, but merely the name we give to the cumulative source of human actions. Stories themselves attempt to probe that source and discover its inner structure by trying to display how human actions and passions connect with one another to develop a character.[35]

Some narrative theorists make a further claim: these stories not only describe, but actively contribute to the *formation* of, the community's judgment and its hierarchy of values. The recovery of narrative as a source for ethical reflection has become increasingly prominent in moral philosophy, literary criticism, and argumentation theory.[36] Narrative has also played a key role in theology, and especially in theological ethics.[37]

Although many critics agree that narrative provides a much-needed corrective to the emphasis on the autonomy of the agent, the use of narrative as an analytical tool has stirred considerable controversy. Here, I can make no attempt to adjudicate the question of whether narrative provides an appropriate paradigm for any or all of the fields in which it has been employed. I simply want to investigate the role it might play in our attempt to understand the ethical appeal of an argument.

At the outset, narrative interpretation seems a promising place to begin, if we want to understand the relationship between the audience and the *ēthos* of the speaker. Narrative was certainly a central category for Aristotle, who drew many of his examples of the virtues from the Greeks' archetypal stories—the Homeric epics. Stories do tend to reveal judgments about character; they probably help to form character (and judgments about character) as well, as our use of stories in the nurture of children would suggest. Finally, narratives can help build identity between speaker and audience, because they implicate the narrator in the story that is being told.[38] In all these ways, narratives help to provide or to develop common ground between speaker and audience.

Moreover, narrative interpretation has the important methodological advantage of making salient the tension, in all readings, between immanence and transcendence. It offers the critic a way of attending to social conditions and practices, but it also helps account for certain continuities in the evaluation of character that seem to transcend restrictions of time and space. The tension between these two aspects helps to explain why Aristotle's table of the virtues can seem both culturally specific and strangely contemporary. These immanent and transcendent functions of narrative interpretation need further unpacking.

On the one hand, the appeal to a common narrative presents us with concrete, material descriptions of how people live their lives. In the process of relating a narrative, the storyteller may describe (and, at least implicitly, evaluate) material conditions, political hegemony, and cultural assumptions. This specificity of stories helps to explain why they are not always literally translatable into other languages: for their effectiveness, they rely on a complex network of values and relationships that will not always remain firmly in place when a story is retold in a different time and place.

On the other hand, this very specificity of context makes room for the possibility that a story might be similarly heard across wide temporal and spatial gulfs. A story can allow listeners to construct what we might call an *analogy of context*. Knowledge about the symbols and symbolic relationships of another period or another place can enable the listener to recognize similar circumstances in the present. For example, by examining the relationship between two characters in a story, readers can draw inferences about their own relationships to others. These inferences will likely not be identical to those drawn by people who heard the story hundreds of years ago; nevertheless, the construction of an analogy of context can give us a means of applying old narratives to new situations.

Narrative thus situates itself in two contexts simultaneously—in the milieu where the story takes place, and in the situation in which the story is told. This produces both an immanent and a transcendent quality, both a concrete and an abstract function. This dual contextuality—precisely what has given narrative its celebrated success in clarifying moral discourse—can help narrative play a similarly positive role in evaluating the ethical appeal of an argument. Nevertheless, dual contextuality also poses certain problems that prevent narrative from offering a complete description of how *ēthos* persuades.

The insufficiency of narrative

When analyzing the virtues, Aristotle made significant use of the Homeric narratives. Thus, he had an advantage we do not:

coherent, well-accepted stories on which he could rely. He could expect his readers to have been familiar with them, and many of his references to the claims of these stories would have been utterly unproblematic. Other cultures and ages have had other such normative stories: for example, particularized interpretations of the Torah, the Qur'an, or the Bible. Similarly, Descartes and Hegel provided their own stories as a foundation on which to construct a systematic edifice.

Today, such universally familiar stories are extremely difficult to locate. Even if the search were to be restricted to a single culture (which might itself be difficult to define), we would not discover the degree of commonality that Aristotle was able to expect from his readers. "Where once agents could be presumed to share a common social knowledge from which moral action might emanate, that presumption has become all but untenable in an age of increased specialization and the concomitant proliferation of technical knowledge."[39]

The fragmentation of our moral and cultural discourse has naturally led to a call for some means of restoring order. Thus, for example, Alasdair MacIntyre argues that a reappropriation of the ancient Greek narratives could help to repair our moral fragmentation. By framing the choice as "Aristotle or Nietzsche," MacIntyre depicts narrative as an alternative to chaos and madness. But in seeking to avoid fragmentation, he unwittingly advocates the very sort of moral universalism which his book had set out to critique. While he clearly does not want to duplicate the abstract and individualistic tendencies of a work such as Moore's _Principia Ethica_, MacIntyre nevertheless seems confident that the traditions of the Greeks can serve as a new universal story for a considerable portion of Western culture. This difficulty has been described by Thomas Frentz:

> If the question were asked, which moral ends, which practices, or which virtues are best, the ultimate grounds for responding, I fear, would be the very grounds MacIntyre strives so diligently to avoid—the collective wills of the group or community in which moral action takes place. As long as the ultimate good _for humanity_ is something which can be exclusively defined, changed, and acted upon _by humanity_, the moral philosophy which results will turn out to be another form of an emotivist moral system.[40]

MacIntyre sometimes seems as convinced of the Greek understanding of virtue as G. E. Moore was of the Victorian understanding. Certainly we may praise MacIntyre's preference for Greek
communitarianism over Victorian individualism; yet both
approaches are pervaded by attitudes toward race, gender,
nation, and class that a great many contemporary readers would
prefer to shun.

Of course, this quandary is not MacIntyre's alone. Any attempt
to make significant use of narrative analysis must grapple with
the major problem of the greatly varying *scope* of the communities that are formed by narratives.[41] At one extreme, a nearly
universal scope is suggested—as in MacIntyre's appreciation
for the tradition of the Greeks, or the perennial call for a return
to the Great Books.[42] In each of these cases, a particular narrative or group of narratives is assumed to be of value in shaping
the understanding of the good—in Western society generally,
and among "educated" persons in particular.[43]

But at the opposite extreme, the community formed by a particular narrative may be very small—such as a local congregation, the citizens of a small town, or even the members of a
single family. Most people belong to a number of such communities. Each group may be formed by a different set of stories;
many people will thus find themselves living in a number of very
different moral worlds. They use one form of language at work,
and a different form at home. They adhere to one set of ethical
standards while playing with their children, and a very different
set when negotiating with their supervisors.

Within these constantly shifting scenes, our various sets of
moral presuppositions offer precious little stability. We are all
moral transients, constantly on the move from one ethical
arrondissement to another. Thus, in attempting to describe the
moral life of humanity in the modern age, we can say practically nothing of significance. It will be even more difficult to
make the claim that *all* people have been formed, even in a
very weak sense, by some one great tradition.

Variations in the scope of a community are highly significant
for rhetorical analysis, because they direct us back to our central question: Who evaluates character? The simple answer—

the audience—leaves unexamined the larger question of how the audience's standards of judgment are formed. According to narrative analysis, an audience's judgment will depend on the stories that it tells. But this answer will not suffice, for the members of an audience are formed by an infinite variety of stories: not only classic stories of Western civilization, but also local stories too numerous and too diverse to specify. The moral formation of people today is far more diverse than was that of the typical Athenian citizen; we belong not simply to a particular city-state, but to a wide range of overlapping communities.

Hence, the audience will evaluate the character of the speaker differently in every rhetorical situation. In one instance, the listeners' judgment will be controlled by the values of just one of their constituent communities, say, the community formed by their coworkers. But in a different rhetorical situation, the same listeners might pay no attention to their coworkers, instead harkening to the call of another community to which they belong, such as their neighbors or their families. Because the members of the audience participate in a variety of communities, and because their various appropriations of the virtues are derived from so many different (and even conflicting) narratives, their standards of judgment will vary from one instance to another.

While narrative analysis rightly reminds us that audiences are not autonomous entities, rhetorical analysis reminds us that the communities by which audiences are formed are often multiple in quantity and uneven in quality. Consequently, in each rhetorical situation, the audience draws on varying values and commitments in order to *construct the character of the speaker*—much as the speaker constructs an audience to which the speech will be addressed. The personhood of the speaker is not a triumph of the autonomous self but precisely the opposite. In the particular rhetorical situation, the speaker's personhood and character are determined by those who are addressed.

Therefore, in order to understand how the persuasiveness of a speech is affected by the character of the speaker, we cannot rely simply on a single narrative by which all members of the audience are assumed to have been formed. Their stories will vary enormously. Moreover, they will have a number of different perspectives on the speaker, because they will have been exposed to the speaker through a wide variety of channels. This brings us to a further complicating factor in the analysis of character.

HOW IS CHARACTER MEDIATED?

In order to construct the speaker's character, audiences rely on information gleaned from two primary sources: the speech or text itself (along with any nondiscursive practices that might accompany it); and whatever knowledge about the rhetor they may gather, either before or after the event. But regardless of its source, all information about the character of the speaker is mediated to the audience through a great variety of channels; the effect that this information will have on the audience's judgment will depend largely on the nature of the mediations that it has undergone.

The rhetorical event

We may have no information about the speaker other than the speech or text itself. Interpreted very narrowly, this might mean that we hear only a voice. The scenario is unusual, but possible: an individual whose name we have never heard, and whose associations and opinions we do not know, sits in front of a microphone; we are in another room and hear only a voice. Our impression of the speaker's character is formed only by what we hear.

While this circumstance is rare, it does occur. Radio personalities—from disk-jockeys to talk-show hosts to comedians—are sometimes judged on voice alone. (Of course, the radio itself is a medium; we will return to this point below.) Even less information about the author is conveyed by a written text; nevertheless, the reading of a pure text is as rare as the hearing of a pure speech. Almost always, a text is connected to a name; the name is connected to a profession, an institution, a publishing company, and a brief biography (and sometimes to a picture of the author as well). The only exceptions would be anonymous or pseudonymous texts; but even these remain "pure" texts only until the first review is published.

On these rare occasions when the audience forms an opinion of the speaker's character *purely* on the basis of the speech or text itself, the rhetor has a great deal of power in creating an impression. By embracing or avoiding certain subjects, by allying one's own positions with those of the audience, even by the manner of style and arrangement, the speaker can have a tremendous influence on the context wherein the audience evaluates character. Depending on the format of the rhetorical event, a number of other elements may also have an effect: if the speech will be heard but not seen, the speaker may use tone of voice, volume, and pitch to increase the audience's confidence. If the speech will be seen as well as heard, one may employ gesture, facial expression, and visual background (which may include location, setting, and entourage). Even if the rhetorical medium is a written text rather than a speech, the writer can rely upon a number of tools for increasing the audience's confidence—from particular figures of speech to the overall level of diction employed by the writing (discretion or bombast, brevity or prolixity, kindness or contempt).

Collateral information

Only rarely does an audience rely solely on a speech or text to evaluate a speaker's character. More often, the audience has at its disposal a considerable body of preestablished information. In fact, the very existence of a rhetorical situation suggests that the members of the audience will know something about the speaker; otherwise, they would not be giving the speech or text any special attention. Some evaluation of the character of the rhetor is implied by the event itself, by the very fact that a lecture is scheduled, that a speech is covered by the media, or that a book is selected for publication.

In most cases, the speaker's name will be known; it may have been mentioned in the broadcast or print media, observed on dustcovers of books, and cited by other writers and speakers. The rhetor's previous speeches or writings may have been discussed with friends and colleagues, or may have been praised (or ridiculed) by others—others whose reputations, in turn, will be variously evaluated by the audience. In short, most audiences are surrounded by information about the speaker before they hear or read a single word. As the authors of *The New Rhetoric* have pointed out, "in most cases the speaker is known, either because he is speaking to a familiar audience or because he is known through the press and all the modern methods of publicity. The speaker's life, insofar as it is public, forms a long prelude to his speech."[44] This prelude may reach the audience by way of a number of different channels.

First, an audience may gain an impression of a speaker's character by listening to the evaluations of others. These judgments can range from informal appraisals ("I've heard he's very generous") to comments on professional reputation ("she's very prominent in her field"). Such evaluative statements are themselves thoroughly mediated; while they may have originated through personal contact, they are more often gleaned from newspaper accounts, television reports, or hearsay. Thus, these evaluations are subject to the same additional mediations as the original rhetorical event. Moreover, after the original impression was made, the evaluation has probably been passed down through any number of channels and subjected to the revisions that naturally occur in such circumstances.[45]

One's evaluation of the character of a foreign head of state, or of a corporate executive, for example, will almost always be based on this sort of information. It may have come to us through an exasperatingly large number of intermediaries: the head of state is known through an associate, who in turn is known only through a bureaucrat, and so on down the line: spokesperson, reporter, wire service, print media, broadcast media, television viewer. The viewer might form an opinion and convey it to a colleague, who might then pass it along to a friend; such mediations can continue almost indefinitely.

Second, an audience may know some of the basic details of the speaker's life: when and where born, educational background, previous occupations, current occupation. Such information seems more concrete than general reputation; nevertheless, it is still thoroughly mediated. Information such as date of birth and occupation does not bring with it a preformed evaluation of character in the way that the speaker's reputation does (though it may be used by its recipient in order to make such evaluations); however, biographical data plays varying roles, depending upon its context. For instance: occupational status conveys character in one way if it appears on the flap of a book's dustcover, and in quite a different way if it appears on a criminal record. Moreover, as all critical readers of biographies know, very few of the details of an individual's life are unaffected by how the biographer tells the story.

Third, some members of an audience may have had previous encounters with the speaker's rhetorical skills: one may have read a book or an article written by the speaker, or one may have heard or seen a recording of a speech. Again, this is certainly not a pure exposure to the speaker's character; it simply indicates the possibility of evaluating a speaker based on that person's own work rather than by relying only on the opinion of others.

Fourth, one may have had personal contact with the speaker. This might have amounted only to a handshake; but it might also range from a short conversation to an ongoing correspondence. Such experiences, even when very brief, can often play a major role in the way we construct a person's character; and again, this information has probably not been mediated by as many other factors as for the other scenarios already described.

Fifth, one may have had enough contact with the speaker to be able to say, "I know what kind of life that person lives." Typically, this sort of contact is rare—restricted, in most cases, to family members and very close friends. However, it is also experienced by the members of a religious order, or by coworkers in certain highly collegial professions. Of course, even this level of insight to a person's character does not mean that the judgment is an accurate one. However, we tend to have more confidence in information that is less thoroughly mediated.

These five levels of mediation certainly do not provide an exhaustive or definitive typology of the information about a speaker that may be available to an audience. Nevertheless, they remind us of the qualitative differences among the pieces of information that we use in order to construct the character of the rhetor. They also suggests that the audience's evaluation of a speaker's character may differ vastly from one rhetorical situation to the next. Thus, the sort of life that the rhetor actually leads may or may not be adequately reflected by the character that the audience will construct.

Additional mediations

At least three other factors influence our reception of information about the speaker's character. The first is that of quantity: any of the above mediations may be modified by duration, frequency, repetition, or intensity. A frequent reader of Plato evaluates the character of Socrates differently from the reader who has quickly glanced at the *Apology* only once; the journalist who has conducted repeated interviews of a person has more information than someone whose contact has been more casual. Of course, the categories of mediations differ and cannot always be compared quantitatively; an ounce of personal contact is worth a pound of hearsay.

A second additional factor is the disposition of the evaluator when the information was received. This harks back to our consideration of the audience in chapter 2. We know that the audience's assumptions and practices will shape how it receives the speech. But information about the speaker's character may be gathered over a long period, during which time the audience's disposition may change. The reception and evaluation of data that bears on the speaker's character is relative to the state of the audience, just as is the reception of the speech itself. (Those who read Dickens for fun probably have a higher opinion of him than those who are forced to read him under penalty of repeating eleventh-grade English.)

Our evaluations of character are rarely based exclusively on one type of information but instead rely on a combination of variously mediated sources. Audiences construct the speaker's character from information that has reached them through circuitous paths; the adequacy of such information can never be guaranteed. But this does not stop audiences from using it, for it provides their only means of determining whether a particular argument is authorized by the character of the person who puts it forward.

IMPLICATIONS

This analysis suggests that the audience's construction of a speaker's character is a highly complex matter, and that the members of an audience will construct character in a wide variety of ways. More radically, these considerations remind us of some of the more troubling implications of the integral connection between the speaker and the speech. In a sense, the character of the speaker is grafted onto the argument and becomes a part of its persuasive force. Thus, to attack a person's character is to attack the arguments that the person deploys; and, conversely, an assault on a person's argument is also an assault on that person's character.

This gives a new meaning to a way of arguing that has traditionally been regarded as fallacious—the *argumentum ad hominem*, or argument directed toward the person. If we think rhetorically, instead of adhering only to the canons of scientific rationalism, we are forced to admit that *all* arguments are in fact directed toward persons. Even if the argument is ostensibly directed against only the opponent's position or tactics, it still strikes a blow against the opponent's person—because an argumentative position is authorized by the character of the rhetor. The position will succeed only if its argumentation is recognized as legitimate; and this requires a personal authorization by the speaker.

This claim has been frequently underscored by communication theorist Henry W. Johnstone. Commenting primarily on the field of philosophical argumentation, he notes that all appeals to "alleged facts or evidence" rest on a decision as to what counts as facts or evidence; all such appeals must therefore be authorized by the character of the speaker who makes the claim.[46] But given our account of the relevance of character in assessing an argument, it seems that, not just for philosophical arguments, but for any act of persuasion whatsoever, we may justifiably claim that all arguments are *ad hominem*—directed toward the person.

Johnstone asserts that the *ad hominem* nature of argumentation can have surprisingly positive implications. If we recognize that our arguments are *ad hominem* attacks, we are urged to address our opponents more directly and thereby evoke a more personal response. Arguments can function as a call "to a life of reason, a life in which consistency matters and one can't duck one's responsibilities by making trivial decisions."[47] When we argue a point, and when we truly mean what we say, our arguments *should* affect people personally. We argue with people, not simply to hear ourselves talk, but to show other people why they should think and act in certain ways. As we discovered at the end of the previous chapter, our arguments may often have a transformative effect upon our audiences. Thus, any analysis of the communicative process cannot avoid matters of *ēthos*, in the fullest sense of that word.

But in addition, the recognition that all arguments are *ad hominem* arguments suggests a need to exercise caution. When a particular argument comes under attack, so do the life and character of the person who deploys it. Thus, according to Johnstone, argument should never be undertaken in the spirit of revenge. Anyone who offers a word of criticism

> is implicitly appealing to his interlocutor to do better, to produce a better argument. He criticizes *con amore.* . . . Whether a critic is criticizing *con amore* or not cannot be determined from his criticisms as such. . . . It is revealed only in the way he goes about his work—lovingly or viciously.[48]

"To criticize with love"—a remarkable phrase to appear in the work of a communication theorist, and one who otherwise shows little obvious interest in ethics or theology. The same motto could easily be the stated goal of a rhetorically sophisticated understanding of Christian theology. Let us keep Johnstone's phrase in mind as we develop a more concrete analysis of the character with which theology speaks.

THE ELEMENTS
OF CHARACTER

Consistent with his point of view in the *Ethics*, Aristotle argues that the evaluation of character is not based on any absolute standard, but on the norms of a particular community or group. In book 2 of the *Rhetoric*, he describes three elements that influence an audience's confidence in the speaker: practical reason, excellence, and good will (*phronēsis kai aretē kai eunoia*).[49] Although the names of the three elements remain constant, the characteristics that they describe will vary according to the standards of the communities in which the members of an audience participate.

The three elements structure the present section, which offers a theological and rhetorical analysis of the elements with which character is constructed. Using a slightly different terminology and in a different order from Aristotle, I want to suggest that an audience develops its perception of a speaker's character through three different kinds of information: excellence or virtue is assessed on the basis of the speaker's associations; good will is assessed by evaluating the speaker's attitudes; and practical reason is assessed on the basis of the speaker's actions. The analysis in this section will suggest that some perennial theological disputes can be clarified by attending to certain aspects of the character with which they are spoken.

ASSOCIATIONS

The individuals or groups with whom a speaker is identified are the speaker's *associations*; by means of these associations, audiences judge the virtue or excellence (*aretē*) of a particular arguer's position. The importance of associations is underscored by Perelman and Olbrechts-Tyteca, who note that rhetors are always members of a group.

> Membership in a given group can, in fact, raise the presumption that certain qualities will be found in its members and this presumption will gain in strength as the feeling of class or of caste is more pronounced. . . . Certain ways of behaving conform to the idea a person has of the members of a group. The behavior of aristocrats is aristocratic; that of serfs is servile; that of Christians is Christian; that of men is human. The behavior is often described by the name of the group, and it reacts on the image that is formed of the group.[50]

This definition, while thought provoking, evokes two criticisms. First, by its very abstractness, it leaps over some very difficult questions (e.g., What specific behaviors are aristocratic or servile or Christian?). Second, the definition is static: the terminology of *members in a group* suggests too fixed a view of the relationship between the rhetor and other individuals. Rather, this membership shifts from one group to another, and such shifts may even be engendered by the speech itself.[51] The dynamism of these constantly shifting alliances is highlighted by the use of the term *associations*.

In Christian theology, a speaker's associations will often affect the persuasiveness of an argument. Audiences will be more confident in a speaker whose associations are most like their own (whether actual or hoped for). Thus, for example, non-Christians may very well question the clarity of a Christian's theological vision; and, conversely, Christians may consider non-Christians to lack insight. Moreover, to the extent that the listener has loyalties to a particular denomination, arguments presented in the name of that denomination may be given more authority. This, as Aristotle reminds us, explains why it is easy to praise Athens among Athenians.

But unlike differentiations among Greek city-states, theological questions are more ambiguous: Who is a Christian? Who is not? Both questions will not always turn simply on whether or not the speaker claims to be a Christian. For instance, the evaluation may be made on the basis of denominational alignment alone: some auditors might consider Lutherans and Methodists to be Christians but might exclude Mormons and Unitarians; others might be more or less restrictive in drawing the boundaries.

This casts a new light on a perennial theological question: Must one be a Christian in order to do Christian theology? As traditionally posed, the question would seem to seek an answer about the essence of the theologian, as though the attribute *Christian* were univocal. This has led to two typical responses: an exclusivist view, suggesting that only those formed by the story of the Gospel can adequately speak about the faith; and a universalist view, arguing that theology can be done by Christians and non-Christians alike. The exclusivist position is criticized as a way of insulating Christian theology from all external argument; conversely, the universalist position is criticized for ignoring very real differences between Christians and non-Christians, especially in their structures of knowledge and belief. And so it goes: the conflict seems intractable.

This question might be more productively investigated by inquiring more broadly into the character of the theologian, rather than attending only to some preconceived essence of the speaking or writing subject. Instead of discussing whether the theologian need "be" a Christian, we might ask whether a particular audience (of Christians, for example) can construct a character for the non-Christian speaker that authorizes that person to say something about the Christian faith. Clearly, these constructions will vary. They will depend on how Christianity is defined by the audience, on the audience's knowledge about the speaker, and on the speaker's other associations.

Yet despite its variations and ambiguities, this approach better describes how a theological argument can persuade. Clearly, a Christian audience might be persuaded to belief and action by listening to a Jewish Holocaust survivor such as Elie Wiesel, even though the faith perspectives of speaker and audience are labeled differently. Similarly, the same audience might not be moved by listening to British theologian Don Cupitt propound arguments for "taking leave of God," even though they might respond similarly when asked their own religious preference. Audiences do not make judgments based on the essence of the speaker, nor even necessarily on the labels that have been assigned to the speaker. Audiences judge on the basis of their construction of the speaker's character—a construction that may not follow traditional categories. By turning our attention to the highly contextualized and concrete rhetorical situation, we need not attempt to answer the perennial, abstract, noncontextual question of who can do theology.

Character may also be constructed on the basis of institutional associations. We associate teachers with an academy, government officials with a specific branch of government, journalists with a newspaper. Some institutional associations may be purposely hidden, in an attempt to dissuade the audience from passing an unfavorable judgment. In Christian theology, the mention of institutional commitments calls to mind the significance of denominations—not as a set of beliefs but as an official group of which the speaker is considered a member.

Membership in a denomination may play an important role in arguments about polity, organization, worship, and life in the community.

Similarly, a rhetor may have a certain relationship to a secular, church-related, or church-operated academic institution. The institution's purpose may be to train ministers (for a variety of denominations, or for one denomination only); or it may be engaged primarily in the production of graduates who will generate wealth. Or, the theologian may be employed by a think-tank, primarily for the purpose of offering an *apologia* for a particular political platform.

Thus, to speak of a theologian's institutional commitments is not simply a means of closing off discussion about certain uncomfortable matters. These commitments provide the structural material with which the audience constructs the speaker's character. Thus, the effectiveness of an argument will depend, in part, on the degree of authority that its audience invests in the institution with which the speaker is associated. For example, theologians who are recognized as speaking for the Church will be more persuasive among those who endow the Church with greater authority.

Sometimes an institutional relationship is magnified by a degree of official participation: the person who presents an argument may hold a particular office, chair a committee, or represent another person (or a group) in some official capacity. A person who holds an office claims to represent the interests of a larger group, thus reminding the audience of the additional weight of those interests. "The office of a speaker, no less than his person, forms a context which has an undeniable influence. The members of a jury will judge the same remarks quite differently according as they are pronounced by the judge, the counsel for the defense, or the prosecutor."[52] The jury should recognize that the judge speaks for the interests of justice, whereas the defense attorney speaks for the defendant's interests and the prosecutor speaks for the plaintiff's interests. The *office* is not itself a separate category of associations, but it can strengthen an institutional association.

Turning to Christian theology: an institutional association may be strengthened by ordination. While the authority of ordination typically rests in a particular office, this authority must be (at least in part) embodied in a person in order to be actualized. Moreover, those who are ordained usually declare a certain degree of allegiance to the authority of their Church, and consequently they are often judged to be speaking for the Church in a way that differentiates clergy from laity. Similarly, a particular denomination's acceptance of the teaching authority of the episcopate will affect how arguments are authorized. This authority is not simply a matter of hierarchical authoritarianism, but also a matter of the character that the audience constructs for the source of the argument. Episcopal authority can provide an _ēthos_ that affects the persuasiveness of arguments about faith and morals.

Finally, a speaker may be associated with other individuals. These personal associations may be professional ("That sociologist is a student of B.F. Skinner"); they may have to do with authorities on whom the speaker relies ("Our minister seems to mention Paul Tillich in every sermon"); or, conversely, they may depend on the reputation of those who cite the speaker as an authority ("Her work is respected by a number of well-known anthropologists"). Associations such as these invite the audience to pass similar judgments on the persons being associated with each other.

For Christianity, one of the most widely recognized authorities is the person of Jesus. The speaker who is associated with Jesus is authorized to speak, for Jesus is the person to whom "all authority in heaven and on earth has been given" (Matt. 28:18). Allegiance to Jesus therefore indicates good character: "No one speaking by the Spirit of God ever says 'Let Jesus be cursed!' and no one can say 'Jesus is Lord' except by the Holy Spirit" (1 Cor. 12:3). But the appeal to Jesus' character can remain abstract, and thus may not help settle an argument. Two communities whose members continue to proclaim that "Jesus is Lord" may find themselves at war with one another, because their understanding of Jesus varies so greatly as to preclude any agreement. Nevertheless, an allegiance to Jesus can sometimes provide the common ground where productive disagreement can occur. After all, to proclaim someone as Lord (_kurios_) is precisely to claim that the character of that person provides, as

Aristotle calls it, the "most powerful" (*kuriōtatēn*) means of persuasion.

ATTITUDES

A second element that audiences use to construct the rhetor's character is *attitude*. The speaker's attitudes, as exemplified by his or her demeanor and moral purpose, can provide information about what Aristotle calls good will (*eunoia*). After considering how these attitudes can be specified, we will investigate their significance for the assessment of theological texts.

Specifying the rhetor's attitudes

First, speakers may be judged on their general demeanor, which is often determined by the tone with which an argument is pursued. We can imagine a number of spectra within which we might try to place the tone of an argument. For example:

conciliatory—absolute
ruthless—mild
clear—obscure
questioning—answering
simple—complex
novel—ordinary
univocal—ambiguous

These spectra do not assume that a tendency in one direction is always better than a tendency in another. As Aristotle argues throughout book 3 of the *Rhetoric*, sometimes one stylistic extreme is called for; at other times, the opposite extreme is needed.

In speaking (as opposed to writing), the role of gesture, facial expression, and general comportment should not be neglected. These factors were recognized by Aristotle, and were endlessly classified and systematized in the Roman handbooks and their successors. While we can offer no universal account of persuasion by personal appearance, we can admit its importance—especially in the age of the decentered self, in which embodiment plays a larger role than does the abstract idea.[53] Theologically, the nondiscursive aspects of communicative practice serve to underscore the persuasive aspects of various liturgical forms. While the full implications of this matter cannot be pursued here, we can emphasize that theology persuades by the nondiscursive practices that accompany its language, as well as by the language itself.[54]

When a speaker makes predominant use of one stylistic tendency at the expense of another, this information may be assimilated into the evaluation of her or his character. If a writer's work seems obscure in every instance, apparently disregarding the audience's abilities and interests, then we will begin to attribute obscurity, not just to the work itself, but to the writer as well. These judgments are not always the result of reading a text or listening to a speech; they may also be judgments of personal observation, whether intermittent or continuous.

Any consideration of style causes some anxiety,[55] because it calls up the specters of aesthetic subjectivity, individualistic judgment, and the greatly devalued notion of taste: *de gustibus non disputandum.* But perhaps style is not just a matter of individual preference. If it were, we would be powerless to explain why, in certain contexts, some styles are predictably more persuasive than others. We are not trying to identify good styles and bad styles but, rather, styles that are more or less persuasive under particular conditions.

> *One thing is needful.*—To "give style" to one's character—a great and rare art! It is practiced by those who survey all the strengths and weaknesses of their nature and then fit them into an artistic plan until every one of them appears as art and reason and even weaknesses delight the eye. . . .Whether this taste was good or bad is less important than one might suppose, if only it was a single taste![56]

Style remains a basis for the audience's judgment, no matter how often such judgments are labeled irrational or deceptive.

In addition to general assessments of the speaker's style, we can also speak of the rhetor's *moral purpose.* This is Aristotle's term; today, we might prefer the word *interests.* What motivates the speaker to speak? What is the goal behind it all?

Again, the audience will make this evaluation as much on the basis of nondiscursive elements as on discursive ones. Does the speaker have a vested interest in the outcome of the argument? What does the writer stand to gain (money, power, fame) if the argument succeeds? Who else would benefit from the success of the argument? How are these individuals related to the speaker?

Rhetors are frequently judged on the degree to which their arguments seem to reflect particular ethical and political commitments. These matters are a natural part of any persuasion by means of *ethos* and should not be jettisoned as irrelevant to the argument. As Terry Eagleton has noted,

> It must be a question of political and not only of "moral" argument: that is to say, it must be *genuine* moral argument, which sees the relations between individual qualities and values and our whole material conditions of existence. Political argument is not an alternative to moral preoccupations; it is those preoccupations taken seriously in their full implications.[57]

Such an evaluation is often based on the speaker's associations, as we have already discussed: university, think-tank, denomination—all may be in a position to convey a reward to the speaker who puts forward a persuasive argument. But those who stand to gain and lose from the argument's success may not be so closely connected to the speaker. What impact will the argument's outcome have on people in varying social classes? Or on people living under a wide range of political climates?

Matters of demeanor and moral purpose (or interest) can be difficult to identify. However, we can make some sense of these elements by attending to a rhetor's deployment of *ultimate terms*. This method was suggested by rhetorical theorist Richard Weaver, who points out that a single word can have rhetorical force far beyond its denotation, especially when it is coupled with an opposing word. This suggests that persuasion depends very much on how things are named.[58] Weaver characterizes some of the common ultimate terms at the time he wrote his essay—including "god-terms" such as *progress* and *fact*, and "devil-terms" such as *communism* and *prejudice*. While Weaver's substantive analysis will eventually become dated (as he no doubt realized), his method of inquiry can reveal much about the demeanor and the moral purpose embodied in a speech.

Assessing theological attitudes

In order to suggest how this analysis might clarify arguments in Christian theology, I want to examine some of the ultimate terms in four texts concerning the issue of infant baptism. The first passage appears in the writings of Karl Barth:

> It is the perverted ecclesiastical practice of administering a baptism in which the baptised supposedly becomes a Christian unwittingly and unwillingly that has obscured the consciousness of the once-for-allness of this beginning, replacing it by the comfortable notion that there is not needed any such beginning of Christian existence, but rather that we can become and be Christians in our sleep, as though we had no longer to awaken out of sleep. We must not allow infant baptism to induce in us this comfortable notion.[59]

In this passage, two elements deserve attention. First, certain forms of infant baptism are called "perverted"—thus signaling a strong tone of condemnation and at least a degree of outrage on the part of the writer. On the other hand, outrage is balanced by a certain level of self-critique. By turning from the third person ("the practice") to the first person ("we"), Barth includes himself among those who are tempted to indulge in the comfort of effortless repentance.

For most readers, however, the self-critique in this passage will seem mild compared to the stories that they may have heard about Barth's strident tone and his absolutism. As Stephen Sykes has noted, the English reader of Barth cannot but have been influenced by the (frequently anecdotal) comments of his detractors, many of whom have themselves read little of Barth's work.[60] Such widespread and often ill-informed assumptions about a theologian's attitudes can irreparably damage the reception of her or his thought, for these assumptions provide the context for the reception of the written product. Those who have been influenced primarily by stories and jokes about Barth are more likely to give special weight to the occasional shocking term (e.g., *perversion*); those who evaluate Barth's attitudes more positively might be more inclined to focus on Barth's frequent self-criticism and even self-effacement. In either case, we fool ourselves if we claim to base our judgment on "the arguments alone."

A second text on the subject of infant baptism comes from John Macquarrie:

> The question of whether baptism is to be administered in infancy or delayed until adolescence cannot be treated as one of indifference, and well-intentioned persons who think that opposing views on the matter could be accommodated by making infant baptism optional are deeply in error and have not understood the nature of a sacrament, and above all, have not understood the meaning of "incorporation."[61]

To claim that another person is "deeply in error" about a particular theological position is quite mild, compared to some attacks. Nevertheless, making such a claim affirms the certainty of one's own position very adamantly indeed. Macquarrie's tone in the volume from which this passage is taken is generally mild and conciliatory; in fact, if his famous one-volume systematic theology is to be faulted, it might be for its tendency to collapse toward the center.[62] But when the discussion turns to infant baptism, it becomes white hot.

The reasons for Macquarrie's absolutism regarding infant baptism are unknown to me as a reader; those readers with more information will doubtless evaluate this section differently. But the significant shift in tone that occurs in this section of Macquarrie's book indicates that he attaches some special significance to this matter. One can imagine a range of personal and institutional commitments that would make this issue quite important.

Our third example dates from 1530; it is taken from *The Ordinance of God* by Melchior Hofmann:

> [Baptism] is the sign of the covenant of God, instituted solely for the old, the mature, and the rational, who can receive, assimilate, and understand the teaching and the preaching of the Lord, and not for the immature, uncomprehending, and unreasonable, who

cannot receive, learn, or understand the teaching of the apostolic emissaries: such are immature children; such also are bells which toll for the dead, and churches, and altars and all other such abominations. For nowhere is there even a letter in the Old or the New Testament in reference to children.[63]

The argument of the passage is built on two major assumptions: that the covenant of God is meant for those who can actively understand it; and that the biblical witness is sufficient to authorize the argument. The second point is important for our purposes, for it reminds us that Hofmann shared with the magisterial Reformers a willingness to embrace the notion of *sola scriptura*. It was this very emphasis on the biblical witness that made the radical Reformers such thorns in the flesh to Luther, and most especially to Zwingli, who otherwise shared so many of their assumptions. The radical Reformers were able to turn Zwingli's own views against him. "They accepted *sola scriptura*, the theme of the Great Minster sermons since 1519, and insisted that they were simply carrying his own teaching to its logical conclusions."[64]

But despite the overwhelming degree to which matters of the covenant and the interpretation of Scripture control this passage, they are almost outweighed by the single word *abominations*. This word alone suffices to remind most readers of some of the more sensational aspects of the radical Reformation— whether characterized as an ill-conceived excess of iconoclastic enthusiasm, or as a fully justified assault on idolatry. Moreover, the radical Reformation had extremely subversive political implications that may often play a role in theological argument. For most audiences, the character of the radical Reformation precedes the texts that it has handed down to us.

Even the choice of a word to name the baptismal practices of the radical Reformers carried a strong evaluation of their attitudes, as our final passage (from Zwingli) illustrates:

You would not speak here of the church's baptism, but of heretical baptism, that is your sect's, and this, as it is born outside the church, is justly called pseudo- or catabaptism (some prefer "anabaptism"). . . . [B]y your baptism you crucify Christ again (for as he was once dead and once was raised from the dead, so it is his wish that one who loves him should be baptized once only); you do not dare to call your baptism catabaptism, but you call "baptism" that which is rebaptism.[65]

Rather than referring to the radicals as "baptists," Zwingli makes certain that the process of naming is also a process of condemning. The prefixes that he uses (*pseudo, ana, cata*) all cast doubt on the validity and legitimacy of the baptisms that his opponents perform. A similar process is still at work today.[66]

Zwingli's passage employs perhaps the most strident tone of all. To accuse another Christian of having "crucified Christ again" is one of the most vitriolic condemnations imaginable. (The words allude to Hebrews 6:6, where "crucifying the Son of God again" [*anastaurountas*] describes the act of apostasy.) The attitude reflected by the passage might be described as absolutist, condemnatory, and accusatory.

However, as in the other three examples, the degree to which the tone of this passage will influence the reader's evaluation of Zwingli depends on the weight accorded to any other relevant information to which the reader might have access— whether discursive or not. Moreover, this evaluation will necessarily be influenced by one's prior judgments about (and level of commitment to) the matter under discussion. The strong advocate of infant baptism will be prone to regard the passages by Barth and Hofmann as unjustifiably virulent, whereas the quotations from Macquarrie and Zwingli might be labeled "appropriate righteous indignation." Conversely, the opponent of infant baptism will evaluate the character of the four passages in a very different way.

We have repeatedly observed that the evaluation of character varies according to the perspective of the audience. And among judgments about character, those concerning the demeanor and moral purpose of the speaker are most likely to vary from one rhetorical situation to another. Thus, when a member of the audience judges the speaker to be ruthless or mild, absolutist or conciliatory, ambiguous or univocal, no objective evaluation of the speech or text is being offered. Nevertheless, by examining a text's ultimate terms, we can come to some provisional conclusions about its general tone.

Another conclusion seems warranted as well: the use of a particularly strident tone may not always have its intended effect. Those who construct theological arguments frequently seek to convey an attitude of indignation, accusation, or anger as a way of increasing the argument's persuasive appeal. But these stylistic features may only reinforce an audience's negative image of the speaker's demeanor, or general moral character, or both. Moreover, given the integral connection between speaker and speech, an inflammatory attack on a particular position becomes an attack on a person as well. In this context, Johnstone's request that argument be carried out *con amore* takes on some very suggestive theological ramifications.

ACTIONS

The final category of clues by means of which an audience constructs the speaker's character is *actions*. What are the speaker's special talents and skills? How does the speaker spend his or her time? In what other activities is he or she involved, aside from the construction of persuasive arguments? Recalling Aristotle's list of the elements that inspire confidence, this category corresponds most closely (though certainly not precisely) to *phronēsis*. Aristotle places this first on his list; we come to it last because many of these evaluations develop directly from the elements I have labeled *associations* and *attitudes*.

Audiences are affected by a speaker's actions, especially when they are connected to the matter at hand. Part of the persuasiveness of the civil rights movement, for example, was its emphasis on relating action to argument. Anyone can stand up in a college cafeteria and speak of the virtues of peace, justice, and equality. But such arguments are more persuasive when accompanied by actions that demonstrate the speaker's commitment to the ideals that the speech seems to advocate. Those who rode the buses, sat at the lunch counters, and subjected themselves to physical attacks acted in ways that authenticated their words.

This is a point worth emphasizing, for we tend to assume that rhetoric can refer only to discursive practices and actions that are integrally related to discourse, i.e., gestures and facial expressions. But rhetoric is concerned with all forms of persuasion; and activity can be *as* persuasive—sometimes *more* persuasive—than discourse.

> The activities of individuals and groups are performances of social and historical meaning. . . . A protest march, as a pattern of institutional action, is a rhetorical display or making manifest of social ideals and goals. A political rally is an endorsement of a candidate through the sheer presence of the gathered bodies. The performance of a religious ritual announces the inscription of sentiments or valuation that preserve a tradition. In all this there is a rhetorical expression of variegated forms of meaning within the body politic of communicative practices. This expressivity can at times be more consequential and more revelatory than the rhetoric of the spoken or written word.[67]

In general, actions and potential actions are integrally connected to how we evaluate character. This does not mean that, whenever we think of the action, we necessarily think of the speaker as well; nevertheless, any "dissociation of the act and the person is never more than partial and precarious."[68] We characterize people not merely by what they say; we also pay attention to what they do.

And we also characterize people by what they do *not* say and do. Not only action and speech but also stillness and silence may affect the evaluation of character. Theologians will be judged not only according to that whereof they speak, but also that whereupon they remain silent. Silence can also speak, as the Orthodox theologian Vladimir Lossky knew well:

> The words of Revelation have then a margin of silence which cannot be picked up by the ears of those who are outside. . . . This silence which accompanies words implies no kind of insufficiency or lack of fulness of Revelation, nor the necessity of adding to it anything whatever. It signifies that the revealed mystery, to be truly received as fulness, demands a conversion toward the vertical plane, in order that one may be able to "comprehend with all saints" not only what is the "breadth and length" of Revelation, but also its "depth" and its "height" (Eph. 3:18).[69]

Lossky's comments suggest that those who would seek to persuade through the language of Christian theology can do so only from within a greater and more profound silence—a silence that provides the context for an event of faithful persuasion. Theology must begin by heeding the divine admonition: "Be still, and know that I am God" (Ps. 46:10).

What sorts of action (and inactions) affect the audience's construction of theological character? As we noted when we spoke of the theologian's associations, the speaker may have ties to a particular Church. But the significance of this association can vary considerably; it may be little more than an affiliation required by the profession, or it may be the theologian's primary commitment. Thus, audiences may evaluate character on the basis of questions such as these: In what other activities is the speaker involved? For example, is the speaker committed to public worship within a local congregation? Involved with a congregation in other ways (committee work, teaching, leadership)? Interested in the general welfare of the neighborhood, the city, the world? The answers (or even the presumed answers) to these questions will have an impact on the audience. They will certainly not be suspended in order to consider the argument "objectively."

To take another example: The theologian may teach in a secular setting, say, a non–church-related college or university. Yet such settings still provide opportunities for a number of different levels of involvement. How does the individual use her or his free time? Involved with campus ministry groups? Willing to spend time working for the community? How are questions about faith treated in the classroom? What attitude is expressed toward the traditions of the Church? How is time balanced between discussions of conservative orthodoxy and radical interpretations? Again, one particular set of answers will not be persuasive in every situation.

The theologian's actions necessarily have social and political ramifications as well. Of course, not all theologians align themselves with particular political parties or causes; they may even claim complete apoliticism. Nevertheless, if we "look for their politics," we will always discover a certain relationship to sociopolitical structures.

It is a truism that theologians are social agents—that they "do theology" in and from some determinate social locus, make use of the
means society offers them, and formulate cognition and meaning
endowed with a determinate social existence and finality. . . . This
being the case, any theology, in its quality as a determinate social
practice, and as a "signifying" product—just as any theologian, as
someone working in a specific area of knowledge and significa-
tion, and as a social agent—is socially situated, inserted, indeed
"engaged" . . . in the articulation of a social conjunct, regardless
of whether this theology or this theologian be "traditionalist" or
"progressive."[70]

Political and social structures cannot be avoided; thus, they will
always affect the evaluation of theological character. For
example, the audience may consider the risks that speakers
have taken, under oppressive political regimes, in order to present their arguments. If the argument was so important that the
speaker risked his or her life to present it, then it will usually be
judged worthy of attention.

This very appeal was frequently employed by St. Paul: "If we
are being afflicted, it is for your consolation and salvation" (2
Cor. 1:6). Theology may be done in extremely comfortable situations or in battle zones. Some speak and write where it is relatively easy to carry out their work; others can do theology only
by risking their lives. Those who suffer for the sake of others
are often judged to be persons of good character—primarily
because they are less likely to be working out of pure self-inter-
est. Thus, a particular theology can be authorized by the suffer-
ings its practitioners endure. "For theology to have authority, in
the present situation, it must, rhetorically and pragmatically
speaking, not merely talk about suffering but have the authority of suffering."[71]

At the extreme, persuasion is affected by one's willingness to
die for one's cause. Martyrs offer a witness (*marturia*) precisely
in this sense: by their self-sacrifice, they bear witness to the
authority in whose name they speak and act.

The martyr bears witness to the living God and the coming of
his Kingdom. By his death he contests all attitudes which would

absolutize the present state of affairs, and he affirms his faith in eternal life. Yet Christian hope does not demobilize us with regard to engagement in history. On the contrary, it supplies reasons for such involvement and the courage to undertake it.[72]

To bear witness to the Gospel at the risk of death is to endow one's arguments with an ultimate appeal to *ēthos*: in this sense, one's whole life becomes an argument for a particular theological position.

Any ethical evaluation of a rhetor's actions will be a delicate matter indeed. We have already mentioned the difficulties encountered by the ethical criticism of literature; but the path will become even more perilous when we turn to the realm of Christian theology. This point is recognized by Donald MacKinnon who, commenting on the troublesome politics implied in Plato's *Republic*, raises the question with caution: "Granted that unmistakable human goodness can make no man or woman a genius, can we suppose that its total absence leaves unaffected any man's claim to be numbered among the master-spirits of our age?"[73] MacKinnon offers some specific examples: Bertrand Russell, who displayed a "detached arrogance in sexual behavior"; Gottlob Frege, "a racialist of the most bigoted sort, narrowly nationalist, obsessively anti-Catholic as well as anti-Semitic"; and Gerhard Kittel, who used his skills as a New Testament scholar to defend the Nuremberg Racial Laws.[74] As MacKinnon points out, we are often quite willing to allow matters of personal and social morality to pass by unnoticed. We rationalize, we point to extenuating circumstances, we ask ourselves whether we would have reacted any differently had we been placed in that person's position. But we also recognize, as this chapter has repeatedly argued, an integral connection between the speaker and the speech—just as between the tree and its fruit.

MacKinnon's essay provides us with the first of two theological examples of the persuasive force of a theologian's actions. He focuses primarily on two books about the life of Paul Tillich—one by Tillich's wife and the other by his close friend, Rollo May.[75] MacKinnon finds in both books a very unflattering portrait of a man otherwise regarded as a theological giant.

Tillich emerges as ready to use his unquestioned powers as a teacher, as an intellectual prophet, to attract women into his orbit, whom it would seem that he often seduced. He emerges as wilfully promiscuous, and in his promiscuity coldly cruel towards his wife. As evidence of the reality of this cruelty, the appearance of Hannah Tillich's record is unquestionable evidence.[76]

MacKinnon then notes that May's book, though more apologetic, takes little away from the serious charges that Hannah Tillich makes. In fact, May seems to confirm much of her testimony.[77]

Whatever one's evaluation of Paul Tillich's *ēthos*, one cannot help but take such matters into account when evaluating his theology. Not everyone will judge it harshly; in a review of the same two books, Harvey Cox declared himself more, not less, proud to claim Paul Tillich as his teacher.[78] MacKinnon, on the other hand, sees the revelations primarily in a negative light. "The flaws of which Hannah Tillich writes inevitably infect the texture of her husband's *oeuvre*. We are aware of an element of fraud, of hypocrisy here as so often 'the tribute vice pays to virtue.'"[79] Whether evaluated positively or negatively, Tillich's actions can have a direct bearing on how his theological project is assessed.

MacKinnon's essay shows a willingness to "grasp the nettle" in a way which few other theologians have. He has recognized that judgments about the life and work of those who speak persuasively about Christian doctrine cannot be separated from the arguments they make. Additionally, we may note that such judgments are not made once-for-all at the time of the rhetorical event. MacKinnon clearly sees a need to reevaluate Tillich's theology in light of the reconstruction of Tillich's character.

We now turn to consider, more briefly, a very different example. Dietrich Bonhoeffer was born twenty years after Paul Tillich, and certain elements of his moral formation would be comparable. Yet Bonhoeffer's martyrdom shows a willingness to put words into action in a way that many audiences will identify as virtuous. Especially against the background of Nazi horror, Bonhoeffer's decisive actions against Hitler's regime will bring to mind the names of the virtues: courage, magnanimity, justice, and—in the Christian tradition—faith, hope, and love as well. The persuasiveness of Bonhoeffer's theology cannot be disconnected from his life and his death.

Eberhard Bethge's biography of Bonhoeffer opens with the sentence, "Dietrich Bonhoeffer was a powerful man."[80] Bethge follows this with a description of Bonhoeffer's stature, dress, abilities, and attitudes; but we might just as easily read the sentence as a statement about Bonhoeffer's authority as a theologian. He is powerful for some audiences precisely because many audiences have constructed for him a character that authorizes his theological insights. Those who read his writings do so with the knowledge that this man seemed willing to die for the life of the Church—and not only to die, but to risk, in his own estimation, the very salvation of his soul.

The examples of Tillich and Bonhoeffer may at first seem a facile juxtaposition of evil and good; but this is not the primary lesson to be learned from the two theologians. Indeed, one finds no dearth of theological literature which praises Paul Tillich, not only as a scholar but as a human being—and which makes no mention of any sexual misconduct.[81] Conversely, it should be remembered that, just after the war, some saw Bonhoeffer's activity in the German underground, and especially his involvement in plots to assassinate Hitler, as improper interference in the divine orders of creation. Bethge observes that "Lutheran church representatives refused to accept [Bonhoeffer] as a Christian martyr when they made the unpleasant discovery that this biblical scholar was a political plotter."[82] The evaluation of *ēthos* is determined by specific audiences—not by a universal account of good and evil.

Of course, a person's actions are not usually revealed with the level of drama present in these two examples. But audiences often do have access to such information, and they will be influenced by whatever information they have. As we have noted, the speaker's character is constructed with the help of information that is mediated to the audience in a great variety of ways. This information may come from a biography, an autobiography, a book's dust jacket, or the comments of a friend; but it will always have an effect on the persuasiveness of the argument.

CONVERSION AS A
RHETORICAL ACTIVITY

This chapter has emphasized that the character of the speaker is a constructed reality. It is not an essence, waiting to be truthfully revealed; rather, it is actively constructed by a particular audience in a specific rhetorical context. Audiences make concrete (and varying) evaluations of the character with which theology speaks—and thereby decide whether a particular theology speaks with authority, or merely as one of the scribes.

A theology that does speak with an authoritative character can become more than an act of intellectual gymnastics: it can also become a way of winning converts to the faith. In this sense, conversion is not simply an interiorized dialectical moment, but a rhetorical activity. "Dialectic seeks an act of the intellect, judgment, and secures its religious end in contemplation. Rhetoric seeks an act of the will, assent, and secures its religious end in conversion."[83] A properly authorized argument persuades others not simply to *think* about Christianity but to adopt the Christian life as their own.

How can theology speak with a character that will bring about true conversion? It can do so only when theologians are clear about their own interests and purposes. Audiences will tend to attribute certain motives to theologians in any case, so they may as well try to state their interests clearly. This will be difficult; like all scholars, theologians have become accustomed to ignoring or suppressing their commitments in the name of imagined objectivity. But as I suggested in chapter 2, we need to rehabilitate the role of commitment in the evaluation of arguments. This means getting our motives on the table— good motives, bad motives, ulterior motives. By admitting this admixture of motives, theologians can make significant and effective statements, despite the tentative and inherently unfinished nature of Christian theology. Though our motives are never completely pure, we must still "put in our oar"; only thus can we speak the word which theology must speak.

Theological speech becomes possible only under the recognition that all decisions are human decisions—and that, consequently, all decisions are produced by mixed motives. In

Christian theology, as in the closely related enterprise of jurisprudence, the "decision is made by people, not handed down by God, but the system does all it can to strengthen the decision by arriving at it in a certain way. It is a proceeding of radically impure motives."[84] Jurisprudence "works" because it recognizes that people do not typically act on the basis of pure altruism. Thus, safeguards are constructed to ensure that decisions will be made and people will be changed—even though our knowledge remains incomplete. The theological equivalent is the doctrine of original sin, according to which none of us acts from pure motives or speaks with complete knowledge. The theologian's goal should be to speak and act in ways that acknowledge this incompleteness and impurity, and that do not seek to hide behind a cloak of objectivity or neutrality.

As suggested in chapter 1, the difference between persuasion and sophistry is based, not on a particular form of argument, but on the moral purpose of the discourse. Even the modern usage of the term *sophistry* is a moral usage; audiences use it to describe speakers whose language is unauthorized (that is, not worthy of sustained attention). But if the audience can construct for the speaker an authoritative character, then the speech is not sophistry, but persuasion. In the context of Christian theology, this means not persuasion simply, but *faithful* persuasion; for only when theological discourse is believed to be authorized by its faithful character will its audience pay attention to the *word* it speaks. This word—and indeed, the *Word*—will occupy our attention in the next chapter.

4

Logos

The Word Which Theology Speaks

Having examined the roles of the audience and speaker in some detail, we turn now to the most obvious aspect of the rhetorical situation: the argument itself, which is the third of Aristotle's three means of persuasion:

> Persuasion is produced by the arguments [*dia tōn logōn*] themselves, when we establish the true [*alēthes*] or the apparently true [*phainomenon*] by the means of persuasion applicable to each individual case.[1]

Thus, according to Aristotle, rhetoric is concerned not only with speakers and audiences but also with the arguments themselves—that is, to the *logoi* (words, or language) in which the arguments are cast.

At first glance, Aristotle's third means appears to make a radical departure from his typical approach, for here he seems to suggest that the contextual elements of persuasion—speaker and audience—can temporarily be shelved, leaving only what he will call, simply, the *argument*. This would imply that arguments can be identified and examined in isolation from their concrete and particular rhetorical context. But given the significant roles that Aristotle has already assigned to speakers and audiences, can the arguments themselves really be identified in the abstract? Can they even *exist* apart from their specific rhetorical contexts? Does *logos*, as one of the three means of persuasion, have any real content?

Although *logos* is one of the three means of persuasion, Aristotle never treats it as an isolated category. He always interweaves his discussions of arguments with considerations of the specific times, places, and circumstances in which the arguments are employed. Thus—an initial impression to the contrary notwithstanding—they are not detached from analyses of the speaker, the audience, and the overall rhetorical dynamic.

Following Aristotle's approach in the *Rhetoric*, I turn to persuasion by means of *logos* only after having discussed *pathos* and *ethos*—an arrangement that underscores the highly contextual nature of argumentation. Arguments are not absolute structures; they do not somehow mirror the natural order of things.[2] Rather, arguments function differently in different rhetorical situations, and their appeals are not necessarily transferable from one context to another. We can only speak of "the arguments themselves" if we keep in mind their situatedness within the larger rhetorical context.

In this chapter, I want to deconstruct the commonly received notion of *argument* and display the inadequacies—both rhetorical and theological—of the account offered by formal logic. A description of various alternative notions of argumentation that are offered by rhetoric will suggest certain theological advantages of these other approaches. These advantages, in turn, can be concretized by investigating their impact on a perennial methodological argument in Christian thought: the problem of *theological sources*. The approach of this chapter will help us recognize the argumentative character of Christian theology in general.

A CRITIQUE OF PURE LOGIC

We begin with an inquiry into the typical modern understanding of the word *argument*. While the word is sometimes used to describe any adversarial conversation ("They were having an argument"), its technical use in modern philosophy and theology has focused on the category of formal (deductive) logic. Modern thinkers have assumed that, in order to be admitted to the public arena, an argument must be valid; and validity is only possible for deductive arguments.

Occasionally, induction—argument by example—is also permitted. However, induction is often treated as suspect; for as Hume demonstrated, the arguer cannot exhaustively enumerate all examples and thus may omit the one exception that disproves the rule. And if the argumentative status of induction is in doubt, then so much the worse for any other form of argumentation. The notion that an entire range of argumentation might exist that is neither inductive nor deductive has rarely been given serious consideration.

When current assumptions about the methodological priority of deductive logic are brought under scrutiny, deductive logic will begin to appear relatively useless for most of the arguments which we encounter in our day-to-day lives. So, too, for the use of logic in theological method: a "logic of theology" cannot provide an adequate vehicle for understanding "the word which theology speaks."

A RHETORICAL CRITIQUE OF LOGIC

Formal logic seeks to guarantee its argumentative authority through the category of *validity*—thus suggesting that the strength of an argument is unaffected by its ability to persuade. A valid argument is always valid, regardless of whether the person by whom it is employed is virtuous or vicious. Even the most saintly individual cannot argue that "temporal order necessarily implies cause and effect" without committing the fallacy of *post hoc ergo propter hoc*; and all arguments that rely on such a deduction are invalid. Moreover, a fallacy remains fallacious, even if the audience is completely convinced by an argument that relies on it. According to formal logic, then, arguments are unaffected by their persuasive appeal.

In making the criterion of validity the supreme arbiter of judgment, formal logic attempts to give argument some degree of intersubjectivity. It should not matter, the logician argues, who promulgates the argument, or to what audience; we judge its validity independently of such "subjective" factors. But this appeal depends on awarding an epistemological priority to objectivity—an assumption that has been subjected to increasing scrutiny in recent years, even in the natural sciences.[3] We need to take time to unpack the notion of validity; for as long as we remain under its domination, we will be unable to recognize the persuasive nature of most forms of argumentation.

The logical standard of validity is widely accepted as a universal law of reason. For example, an argument can be called *valid* when it can be expressed as a well-formed categorical syllogism:

> All human beings are mortal;
> You and I are human beings;
> Therefore, you and I are mortal.

Yet the validity of this syllogism is guaranteed *only* for those who have accepted various logical conventions (e.g., the law of excluded middle) as part of their way of living. But within a different language game, I can violate the categorical syllogism and still make my point—as George Orwell did in *Animal Farm*:

> All animals are equal;
> Pigs are animals;
> But some animals are more equal than others.

This "syllogism" makes its tragicomic point by denying the exclusion of the middle term.

Similarly, the *post hoc* fallacy is called a fallacy by those who accept a notion of causation that relies not strictly on temporal order but on a considerably more complex analysis of actions and events. Within a different cultural milieu, precedence and causation might be considered completely commensurate. Thus, the rules for formal validity are not eternal truths, but conventions that have been adopted as part of a particular way of life. They might be called a particular aspect of one's *habitus.*

Of course, some conventions are so widely accepted that they take on an aura of absolute authority. Indeed, conventional standards of validity provide the means by which communication can occur; they create a system of agreement within which disagreement can become possible. This need not imply a conventionalist view of all language; but if all conventions were to disappear, communicative practices that we so often take for granted would become extraordinarily difficult. Nevertheless, to label these conventions *arguments* is to give rise to confusion; for arguments often depend on persuasion, and persuasion plays no role once the linguistic convention has been adopted.

Consider, again, those conventions embodied in the categorical syllogism, or in the *post hoc* fallacy. Anyone in a position to be persuaded by such conventions—that is, anyone who does not already accept them—will not be persuaded by their mere invocation. Those who refuse to accept these conventions are simply not playing the game; they are not accepting the rules that one is required to accept if one wants to indulge in the game of formal logic.

Rejecting the categorical syllogism is something like rejecting the number system. Imagine the following argument between two college students.

A: "7 plus 9 equals 10, of course."
B: "What? Don't be obtuse. Any first-grader knows that 7 plus 9 equals 16."
A: "There you go, transforming conventions into reality."
B: "Convention or not, who's going to believe you when you claim that 7 plus 9 equals 10?"
A: "Most any computer programmer."

And most any computer programmer would believe this statement, because computer programmers often work with hexadecimal (base sixteen) numbers. Seven plus nine equals 16_{10} or 10_{16}. Numerical conventions can always be rejected, but only by trading one set of conventions for another. Arguments about color are similarly conventional. Remember Wittgenstein's remark: "How do I know that this colour is red?—It would be an answer to say: 'I have learnt English.'"[4]

Formal logic, the number system, color—all depend on linguistic conventions in order to maintain coherence. They may seem to have fallen from the sky as timeless truths, but only because we rarely bring to consciousness their conventional status. Anyone who questions the convention is thought to be a poorly formed member of that particular community of discourse. So, for example, outside the hallowed halls of philosophy departments, the law of noncontradiction almost never causes a stir. Anyone who demands a demonstration of this law does so, in Aristotle's terms, only out of *apaideusia*—a lack of proper habituation.[5] To ask for a demonstration of the law of noncontradiction is to go back one step too far—much like the person who asks how we know this color is red, or someone who refuses to accept that 7 plus 9 equals 16. "Explanations come to an end somewhere."[6]

But in a larger sense, even these highly conventional structures depend on persuasion and are therefore related to rhetoric. We may not need to persuade people that 7 and 9 make 16. But what shall we do with the obstinate computer programmer who insists on transforming all numbers into hexadecimal, even when at the grocery store? If we hope to convince such a person to stop such nonsense and operate according to a decimal system like everyone else, we will need to rely on persuasion. One need not be persuaded of the truth of a convention (whatever that would mean); but one may need to be persuaded to adopt a particular convention in the first place. Aristotle tells us that no one uses fine words to teach mathematics;[7] but this assumes that the student has agreed to abide by the conventions. The teacher may still need fine words in order to persuade a student to study mathematics in the first place.[8]

And similarly for the law of noncontradiction. We typically assume that we must accept this law simply because it is a law— as though it had been ordained from the beginning of the age. But the contrary is actually the case: we call it a *law* precisely because it is so widely accepted. We normally speak and act in ways that make the law of noncontradiction utterly unproblematic. But a philosopher may introduce an alternative system of logical conventions that need not heed a law of noncontradiction. Indeed, Michael Dummett has shown that an intuitionistic logic, which depends on "warranted assertability," has no difficulty reconciling mutually contradictory propositions.[9]

The conventions we have mentioned rely on the acceptance of a larger system within which their validity can be judged: a system of cardinal numbers, a system of logic, a system of descriptive words for color. These matters do not call for persuasion, except insofar as we argue for one set of conventions over another. Indeed, their status as convention depends on a certain agreement about the meaning and usage of their terms. But how often can we expect a near-universal acceptance of univocal conventions? How often are our arguments decided on the basis of logical validity? Indeed, if a particular dispute hinged upon logical validity alone, why would people even bother to argue about it?

Most of our arguments take place precisely because we have no general agreement about the rules of the game; and the absence of such universally accepted conventions makes persuasion essential. Arguments do not usually rest on whether or not the syllogism is a valid form of reasoning; that is, nothing is really at stake in the validity of the categorical syllogism. Even when the argument can be encapsulated in a syllogism (which is rare), the dispute will not hinge on the syllogism's validity; rather, it will hinge on issues such as the truth of the premises, or perhaps the univocity (or equivocity) of terms used in the premises and the conclusion. The syllogism's logical validity—or the validity of any other argument, for that matter—can be decisive only if the rules of the game are unambiguous and widely accepted.

When assessing the role of validity in evaluating an argument, everything depends on context. We want to say that anyone who questions the law of noncontradiction, just like anyone who tries to convert all numbers to base sixteen, shows signs of *apaideusia*. But what of someone who speaks of a Jesus Christ as "powerless, yet all-powerful"? Similarly, a poet may claim that

> Time present and time past
> Are both perhaps present in time future
> And time future contained in time past.[10]

It would be useless to claim that such statements are invalid, since within their particular contexts (theology, poetry), the laws of formal validity cannot be decisive. Why not? Because in such contexts, we have no set of generally accepted conventions on which to rely. Instead, we have to attempt to *persuade* others to accept one set of standards over another.

An interlocutor's position can show signs of *apaideusia* only in those contexts in which the rules of the game are universally known and accepted. The scope of such contexts will vary greatly, depending on a particular group's coherence. For example, in a relatively well-defined social system such as that of the ancient Greeks, *apaideusia* may help to define the limits of moral discourse. But can it do so for us, today? To know what *apaideusia* is, we must generally agree about the content of *paideia*; and this, as every curriculum committee knows, is precisely what is in dispute.

Hence, as useful as this notion may have been for Aristotle, we simply cannot transfer it out of its place in the Greek *polis* and attempt to make it constitutive of all discourse. And in fact, defining *apaideusia* may have been considerably more difficult, even for the Greeks, than we would often like to believe. (After all, if the Athenians had been so univocal as to what constituted *paideia*, they would have been less divided on the question of whether or not to execute Socrates.) *A fortiori*, attempts to define *apaideusia* will be more divisive for us today, living as we do in a considerably more fragmented world.

Indeed, Aristotle himself seemed aware that different circumstances called for different categories of argument. In the *Rhetoric*, he pays close attention to speaker, audience, and other contextual factors. But in the *Prior Analytics*, he suggests that the circumstances and context of an argument are irrelevant. There, arguments proceed by syllogism, which is defined as "discourse in which, certain things being stated, something other than what is stated follows of necessity from their being so."[11] However, as Aristotle clearly indicates, such context-free argumentation is possible only for terms which are univocal. Thus, the discussion in *Prior Analytics* applies only to instances of "scientific demonstration" (*apodeixis*); it does not apply to arguments within the more equivocal provinces of dialectic and rhetoric.

These comments recall our explorations of Aristotle's method in chapter 1. We could now say: enterprises which rely on generally accepted conventions can make use of analytic methods, whereas those fields without such conventions must rely on dialectical and rhetorical methods. Dialectic and rhetoric deal with matters that could be otherwise; they call for persuasive argumentation rather than depending on logical validity. In fact, an analytic method is only serviceable for applications that are relatively empty—those lacking material content. This Aristotelian insight has been admirably retrieved in the work of Stephen Toulmin, who argues that "for substantial arguments, whose cogency cannot be displayed in a purely formal way, even *validity* is something entirely out of reach and unobtainable."[12] While an analytic method can prove that 7 and 9 make 16 (in base ten!), it cannot prove that decimal notation is superior to hexadecimal notation. To make that substantive argument, persuasion becomes essential—and the notion of validity becomes fairly useless.

Unfortunately, however, many modern Aristotle scholars fail to restrict the formal notion of validity to the apodictic arguments that Aristotle investigated in some of his treatises. Instead, modern commentators have often attempted to stretch logic to cover arguments about any matter whatsoever. Thus, Aristotle's simple division of methodological labor into analytic and dialectic modes has, in the modern age, been turned into a hierarchy. For example, Richard McKeon claims that the dialectical and rhetorical approaches are, for Aristotle, "a second-best method distinct from the method of science."[13] Similarly, Wayne Booth expressly disavows an Aristotelian approach to his "rhetoric of assent" on the grounds that "Aristotle is much too interested in being scientific."[14] Thus, Booth and McKeon—like all too many ostensible defenders of rhetoric—have subordinated Aristotle's rhetorical insights to his comments on scientific demonstration.

This interpretation of Aristotle has come under increasing attack.[15] A more defensible view is that the choice of rhetoric over logic (or *vice versa*) is based on the field of application, rather than on a preconceived hierarchy of method. As communication theorist Olivier Reboul has emphasized, the rhetorical mode of argumentation is not the poor man's logic! Its uncertainty, its lack of rigor, are a matter of its very object, or, if you will, of its field of application. When it is a question of judicial, economic, political, or pedagogical matters, perhaps also ethical and philosophical, we are concerned not with the true in itself, but with what is more or less probable [*vraisemblable*]. Inversely, in a world of certitudes, there would no longer be either action or argumentation.[16]

Because persuasive arguments are, by definition, open to dispute, they cannot be reduced to logical validity alone.

Once we have rid ourselves of the false assumption that the worth of an argument is based on its formal validity, we can begin to see how great a role persuasion must play in the evaluation of an argument. This suggests that we will need to develop a new understanding of what counts for argument. Before turning to that task, however, we need to examine how the tendency to privilege the category of deductive logic has affected Christian theology.

A THEOLOGICAL CRITIQUE OF LOGIC

From a theological perspective, the foregoing critique of formal logic may seem to be deployed against a straw figure. After all, no theologians are suggesting that the subtleties of Christian theology can be reduced to categorical syllogisms. Nevertheless, the categories drawn from logical analysis have often dominated theological arguments, especially when theology has come into contact with analytic philosophy. For example, the essays collected by Flew and MacIntyre in *New Essays in Philosophical Theology*[17] are strewn with references to formal logic—complete with p's and q's and plenty of symbol-pushing. While the *New Essays* are no longer very new, they represent a strong current in theological method that still surfaces from time to time—for example, in Wolfhart Pannenberg's discussion of theology as a science.[18]

Even more recently, Dietrich Ritschl produced a book entitled *The Logic of Theology*.[19] Ritschl believes that logic can investigate theology's assertions, because, he claims, "there are 'implicit axioms', 'regulative statements' which make a difference to the thought and action of believers, which have a particular logic."[20] Thus, he suggests, logic can improve our understanding of what supports theology's claims and what validates its arguments. Specifically, he is convinced that analytic philosophy will be of great use in theological reflection. Ritschl's book will provide us with a few examples of the kinds of theological difficulties faced by an appeal to the analytic category of *logic.*

At the outset, Ritschl seems to guard against the potential excesses of an analytic method. For example, he is not afraid to debunk the commonly assumed hegemony of the natural sciences, arguing that not only scientists but also poets can tell the truth. "Not only the poet but also the forester sees the forest in a particular perspective. In recent decades very helpful ideas have been developed about 'perspectivistic truth'."[21] And Ritschl even seems interested in rehabilitating the theological tools that the Enlightenment had sought to discredit. For instance, rationalistic approaches might be expected to dismiss an appeal to the theologians of the early Church—perhaps on the grounds of their "unscientific" worldview and their location in the distant past. Ritschl, on the other hand, makes a strong argument for what he calls "the special significance of Patristics."[22] In sum, Ritschl hardly seems an analytic extremist; he acknowledges quite frankly the need for theology to broaden its notion of what counts for argument.

Yet surprisingly, he adamantly maintains that *logic* should serve as a fundamental category for Christian theology. Indeed, he holds to this position so absolutely that he is frequently blinded to the incompatibilities among his various claims. The book illustrates well how the modern attachment to logic can have damaging theological consequences. In this instance, an otherwise astute commentator is prevented from developing an adequate perspective on theological method.

Ritschl's book exemplifies four significant problems with the use of logic in theological method. First, logic fails to account for what I have called the tentative and fragile nature of theological reflection. Second, logic encourages us to stop asking critical questions too soon, leaving in relative obscurity the origins of many theological claims. Third, logic tends to divorce theology from ethical commitment. Finally, logic imposes unacceptable restrictions on theological language.

The absolutism of logic

Logic suggests solidity and finality, as opposed to the contingency of dialectic and rhetoric. Ritschl emphasizes this definitiveness, and his choice of philosophical conversation-partners confirms this choice. "What Kant's criticisms meant for the theology of the nineteenth and early twentieth century, analytic philosophy will be able to achieve for the theology of the end of the twentieth century and the century to come."[23] Although Ritschl explicitly disclaims his project to be a positivism or a nominalism, he nevertheless embraces a mode of philosophical thinking that seems incompatible with the provisional nature of all talk about God.

A concrete example: Ritschl dispatches too easily complex theological arguments by labeling them "pseudo-problems." Without actually clarifying why a particular problem should be given the label *pseudo*, he lists a number of "mistakes" from which such problems can arise. These include: "mistakes in translating the biblical texts"; "wrong assessments of historical data"; and "wrong biblical interpretation."[24] But Ritschl's use of the adjectives *wrong* and *mistaken* in these contexts implicate him in some very serious category errors. His analysis operates under the influence of a notion of logical validity, in which such terms would be relevant. But Ritschl does not consider that, in these instances, such univocity might be quite difficult to achieve. Terms like *wrong* and *mistaken* cannot be applied so easily to contingent matters such as translation, historiography, and interpretation.

Of course, an error in translation can arise from mistaken orthography or syntax; but Ritschl seems to have more substantive matters in mind, since he associates mistakes in translation with "wrong assessments" and "wrong interpretations." These phrases call for an investigation into the grammar of the word *wrong*: Wrong according to whom? Wrong on what basis? Wrong according to what standards? Unfortunately, Ritschl does not investigate such questions; he simply assumes that the standards are already in place. He pays little heed to the complex ethical and political issues raised by the production and reproduction of translations, of historical discourses, and of interpretations of texts.[25] Moreover, Ritschl seems to have an unwarranted degree of optimism about the resolution of hermeneutical conundrums. He believes that pseudo-problems can be "recognized easily"; that their wrongness is "easily demonstrable"; and that they "could originally have been avoided."[26]

Logic's failure to question

One of the primary purposes of logic is to guarantee the certainty of a result, without having to investigate how it was achieved. Theologically, this procedure results in a failure to ask penetrating questions that would otherwise reveal the origins and sources of theological claims, for logic tends to focus on products rather than processes, on results rather than causes. In Ritschl's book, this problem manifests itself most clearly in the invocation of psychoanalytic categories.

Ritschl is convinced that psychopathology can provide a sort of testing ground for theological concepts. How adequately he appropriates and applies psychoanalytic categories is beyond my competence to judge; in fact, his approach may have important implications for practical theology. Nevertheless, his undifferentiated use of terminology that contrasts "the psychologically sick person" to the "normal person" suggests a positivistic reliance on the canons of psychology without reference to the degree to which these social constructions undoubtedly mask unjust power relationships.[27]

Consider, for example, Ritschl's analysis of the "sick soul," which recurs at various places in his book. The reader will scarcely disagree with Ritschl's general observation that Christian pastoral theology has never really come to terms with its need to minister to the mentally disturbed. But his argument is not simply a pastoral one. Instead, he uses psychoanalysis as a way of identifying and classifying theological disagreements. For example, disagreements in biblical interpretation and in ecclesiology are reduced to their "psychological symptoms."

Anyone with experience in pastoral work knows that psychologically disturbed individuals can differ very widely from those with a
balanced psychology in what they derive from biblical texts, sermons, and prayers. . . . Psychologically abnormal people are recognized by the privatization of their language; it is here that help
or therapy must begin. This observation applies not only to individuals but to groups. Sects also express themselves in "privatized"
language.[28]

The imposition of psychoanalytical categories provides a
frighteningly effective way of dismissing some theological
positions on the basis of their "imbalance" or "abnormality."
Such discourse is too easily produced within Ritschl's analytical
paradigm; within the assumptions of logic, minds—like everything else—can be classified and "scientifically" evaluated. This
approach is dangerous because it masks its own commitments
and sociohistorical location by employing the objectifying label
of *science*.

Logic as an uncommitted enterprise

Logic claims to achieve unbiased results, regardless of the
attitudes of its practitioners. Hence, an undue emphasis on
logic is unable to recognize the decisive role of *ēthos* in
theological arguments. As might be expected from a work that
so emphasizes logic, Ritschl's book tends to label any stance of
ethical commitment *ideological*.

Ideological positions, too, for example in favour of the poor as
over against the rich or the victims over against the victors, the suf-
ferers over against the strong, offer caricatures—even though at
first sight they might appear to be biblical—which in fact constantly do injustice to the new man and can open up gulfs.[29]

In this passage, Ritschl uses the word *ideological* as an antonym
to the word *biblical*, a rather strange usage that the author does
not attempt to justify. If *ideological* is simply a euphemism for
"that with which I disagree," then it becomes a way of (quietly)
denying the importance of commitment. And indeed, Ritschl
frequently seems to imply that his own position is free of any
stain of ideology. He believes that the theologian can somehow

obtain an objective, undistorted standpoint: "Much depends on the uncompromising separation of faith from ideology."[30]

Later in the book, Ritschl frames the entire political/ethical problematic as a question of whether the Church should be "partisan or neutral." While he admits that "a 'neutral' attitude is also a political position,"[31] he does not recognize that a neutral position is also a partisan and committed position (i.e., committed to neutrality, with all the urgent ramifications of such a commitment). Ritschl believes that Christians should free themselves of ideological positions so they can see the "truth" about the world. But his claim involves substantial difficulties, some of which begin to surface in his division of partisanship into committed and uncommitted forms:

> There is no possible doubt over the correctness of the statement that the church must take the part of the sick, the weak, the poor, those without rights, those discriminated against, the imprisoned and the persecuted. In this sense the church must be partisan. But it goes against its task and is ethically intolerable if through its spokesmen it holds fast to this or that political ideology and gives a partisan description of the historical truth, as it often does in East and West, North and South. In this connection the church must have the courage for objectivity and real neutrality.[32]

This is, in many ways, a most amazing paragraph. While it affirms the notion of political commitment, this commitment is required to be somehow transperspectival. The text seems to imply that we can ascend to the heights and see the world as it really is ("the historical truth"), rather than offering our own partisan descriptions. But as we discovered in chapter 2, all theological descriptions are partisan descriptions and thus imply commitment. The invocation of logic too quickly removes such commitments from consideration.

Logic as linguistically inflexible

Logic assumes that words and things must correspond on a one-to-one ratio. Univocity is essential; without it, logical conventions could not claim certainty for their results. Consequently, Ritschl's use of logical categories unduly restricts the theological significance of language. For example, he attempts to undermine any notion of a "heightening of language" about Jesus by describing Jesus as "the minimal man."[33] But why, one might ask, must these two alternatives be set so strongly against one another? Ritschl's logical framing of this question almost seems to suggest that a believer cannot simultaneously affirm both the divinity (heightened language) and the humanity (minimalized language) of Jesus Christ. Need this be labeled a logical contradiction? In this instance, the category of *logic* becomes the basis for methodological reductionism.

A similar reduction of theological language is found in Ritschl's treatment of the category of *narrative*. Clearly Ritschl has followed recent discussions about narrative theology, but some elements of his language betray a logician's pessimism about the potential of narratives to be revelatory. For example, he uses the word *fiction* to dismiss the whole enterprise of biblical theology.[34] The label itself is ill-conceived, for we have come to realize that a fiction can never be "dismissed as a fiction"; a fiction can posit truth-claims and can be evaluated as such. Nevertheless, Ritschl almost always uses the word *fiction* dismissively;[35] his comments reveal little reflection on the complex evolution of this word in literary theory and rhetoric.

Similarly, Ritschl obscures the enterprise of narrative theology and limits its scope by demanding that it meet the standard of logical rigor. He finds the category of *story* insufficiently analytical:

> A deliberate reduction of language to story language would be a renunciation of differentiated concepts. But without concepts there is no theorizing, and without that no control of the world and no ethical putting to the proof. Here too is the basis and justification for the main objection to the present proponents of a narrative theology. Theology itself is regulative and not narrative.[36]

This very desire for "control of the world"—for regulation and for justification—is, in my view, precisely what Christian theology must call into question.

Ritschl cannot be faulted for his earnest search for a category that could help to resolve some perennial theological quandaries. He is understandably tempted by the lures of logic. After all, logic is definitive; its attraction is due to a quite natural human anxiety about irresolvable problems and internal contradictions. If we could just find a bit of bedrock on which all our theologizing could be based, we could eliminate pseudo-problems, heal sick souls, adjudicate political strife, and speak with unmistakable precision. Such efforts might even help us move toward the realization of the unity of the Church.

Yet the elusive search for bedrock tends to produce more anxiety than solidity. Life cannot always be divided into logical categories—though of course, we do not therefore stop seeking solid ground. As Donald MacKinnon notes, we never seem to tire of attempting "to seek escape from the authority of the tragic, to avoid reckoning with the burden of inescapable fact," and—in general—to posit wholeness and unity where we find none.[37] Indeed, we make matters worse by trying to rationalize and objectify both the fragility of human existence and the painful inadequacy of our knowledge about God. Very little is gained by positing theological problems (and then seeking solutions). More fruitful for theological discourse would be a recognition that the world in which human beings dwell does not function problemlessly. Life is fragile, oblique, sometimes opaque. Thus understood, life calls for ways of thinking and acting that are neither definitive nor final. "The opacity of living is what bids forth rhetoric."[38]

EXPANDING THE RANGE
OF ARGUMENTATION

The inadequacies of formal logic lead us quite naturally toward a rehabilitation of rhetorical modes of argumentation in general and to three "expansions" of the range of argumentation in particular. First, I return to Aristotle for a consideration of enthymemes and examples, and I investigate the expansion of these argumentative structures in the work of Chaïm Perelman. Second, I examine the more organic notion of informal inference—an approach advocated by John Henry Newman in the nineteenth century, and by Wayne Booth and others in the twentieth. Third, I turn to the work of Kenneth

Burke and explore his investigations into the linguisticality of argument. A variety of examples will suggest how these expansions of the range of argumentation might enrich and enliven theological disputes.

ARGUMENTATIVE STRUCTURES: ARISTOTLE AND NEO-ARISTOTELIANS

Given his highly specific analysis of speakers and audiences, Aristotle is surprisingly vague about *logos* as the third means of persuasion. The lack of specificity has led some commentators to reduce all discussion of *logos* to Aristotle's two primary modes of argumentation: enthymeme and example. As we will discover, recent scholars of Aristotle believe that his use of the word *logos* covers a considerably wider territory; nevertheless, enthymemes and examples constitute his two central argumentative structures, and we need to begin by examining their role.

The enthymeme

Outside the field of argumentation theory, the *enthymeme* is typically defined as "two-thirds of a syllogism"—i.e., a syllogism in which the major premise has been omitted. So, for example, the standard categorical syllogism is structured thus:

> All human beings must eventually die;
> You and I are human beings; therefore
> You and I must eventually die.

According to the common definition, the enthymeme is less formal; it takes for granted the knowledge of the major premise (here, that people are mortal) and thus has only two stages of argument:

> You and I are human beings; therefore
> You and I must eventually die.

This argument will work only if the audience agrees with the major premise. (For this example, of course, that likelihood is relatively high.)

Yet this definition of the enthymeme, while very widespread, is fundamentally inaccurate; it has been explicitly rejected by several recent commentators on Aristotle.[39] What Aristotle seems to say is only that the enthymeme is "some sort of syllogism,"[40] rather specifying it as partial syllogism or a defective one. In his commentary on Aristotle's *Rhetoric*, Larry Arnhart has helped to clarify the issue:

> Aristotle does not confirm the common assumptions that the enthymeme is by definition an incomplete syllogism. Although he lays it down as a practical maxim that speakers need not verbally express elements of an enthymeme that would be familiar to or easily inferred by the listeners, he does not take this to be a necessary characteristic of the enthymeme. It is a practical rule of procedure that forms no part of the definition of the enthymeme.[41]

Arnhart (following Grimaldi) then suggests an alternative to the common interpretation. An enthymeme differs from a syllogism in the same way that rhetoric differs from analytic modes of inquiry. Whereas a syllogism concerns matters that are conventional or that can be determined only within a closed system, the enthymeme concerns matters that deal with the apparent and the probable—that is, with contingent matters. In this sense, the "enthymeme" offered above is really no enthymeme at all; it is simply another *syllogism*, for it deals with logical deduction of an analytic truth. Although abbreviated, it retains its syllogistic character.

According to this revised definition, an enthymeme concerns matters that might be otherwise. Thus, the following argumentative structure would be an enthymeme:

> All human beings are born in sin;
> You and I are human beings; therefore,
> You and I are born in sin.

And of course, the enthymeme can also be abbreviated, in which case the major premise is once again taken for granted:

> You and I are human beings; therefore,
> You and I are born in sin.

The enthymeme differs from the syllogism, then, not in form, but in content. Let us examine this difference in detail.

Our first example had a major premise ("All human beings must eventually die") that the arguer simply assumes that anyone would accept. This classifies it as a syllogism; the arguer considers its premises true-by-definition and can abbreviate it regardless of the audience. Like all syllogisms, its purpose is to explain or demonstrate something to those who have accepted a certain set of conventions; it does not seek to persuade. Anyone who refused to accept that "All human beings must eventually die" would simply be refusing to enter the language game.

We must resist the temptation to claim that the premise is simply true. Many poems, novels, and religious beliefs deny universal human mortality. While this certainly does not invalidate the claim, it does reveal the existence of language games within which the premise does not apply. In the *Grammar of Assent*, Newman considers this premise and, quite straightforwardly, asks what it would say about Elijah! While we may claim general acceptance for analytic truths, we cannot claim universality. "General laws are not inviolable truths; much less are they necessary causes. Since, as a rule, men are rational, progressive, and social, there is a high probability of this rule being true in the case of a particular person; but we must know him to be sure of it."[42]

Enthymemes, on the other hand, deal with contingent statements about which we cannot even assume a high probability of general acceptance. Enthymemes may be abbreviated only under certain conditions—specifically, only when we have some reason to believe that the particular audience is already persuaded of, or is willing to supply, the missing premise. Thus, in our second example, the major premise— "All human beings are born in sin"—could be successfully omitted only if that audience were likely to accept it. "Aristotle instructs the speaker to abbreviate the enthymeme only when he knows that the listener will add the missing element on his own."[43]

We can now draw two conclusions. First, enthymematic reasoning can be very important for theological argumentation, because Christian theology deals with matters about which complete knowledge is impossible. Second, the question of whether or not an enthymeme can be abbreviated is a function of the relationship between the speaker and the audience. If the audience can be assumed to agree with the major premise, or if the audience can be expected to deduce the major premise on its own, then the enthymeme can be abbreviated. Otherwise, the speaker will have to state the premise explicitly (and perhaps even construct an additional argument) in order to persuade the audience to accept it. The enthymeme cannot be isolated from its rhetorical context; we may examine the enthymeme under the heading of *logos*, but its persuasive success depends primarily upon the speaker–audience relationship.

When abbreviated enthymemes are used in theology, they help to describe the speaker's construction of the audience. For example, consider an argument that develops the abbreviated enthymeme just described:

> We are all human beings; therefore,
> We are all born in sin.

This is a common theological argument; it appears, for example, in Romans 3:9 and in countless books, articles, sermons, and harangues. But this abbreviated form takes for granted the major premise: "All human beings are born in sin." Thus, the enthymematic argument tells us that the speaker has, wisely or unwisely, constructed an audience that already agrees with the omitted premise; otherwise, the speaker would have needed to state the premise explicitly, and perhaps have provided a further argument to justify its use.

At this point, the careful reader may object that even those who agree with the omitted major premise will not be persuaded, because no new information is presented here. We already know that we are human beings; thus, if we accept the major premise, we naturally accept the conclusion. How does this enthymeme "move" us, as all persuasive discourse claims to do? Why should we think or act any differently, once we have heard this argument? Are we not already persuaded?

This objection must be carefully considered, for it leads to an important amendment to Aristotle's account of rhetoric.

Admittedly, the members of an audience know that they are human beings. Moreover, if we assume for the moment that the particular audience accepts the major premise ("All human beings are born in sin"), then the audience already knows the conclusion. However, the persuasive force of an argument is not restricted to the creation of new knowledge in the mind of the listener. Sometimes an argument merely reminds the members of the audience of something of which they are already persuaded (or which they are already capable of deducing). This activity—making the members of an audience aware of that which they already know—has been treated extensively in the work of Chaïm Perelman, who names this activity *presencing*.[44]

Perelman claims that a persuasive argument often functions to make something present in the mind of the listener. Although the listener may already agree with the conclusion, such agreement is not always in the forefront of her or his memory or thought. In practice, human beings can only concentrate on a very small portion of their knowledge at any one time. This knowledge is only fully accessible if it is called into presence by an argument (whether initiated by others or by oneself).

We typically concentrate our attention on whatever is (physically) present in our immediate environment. Only when we perceive the intervention of an argument do we turn our thoughts to what is not physically present. "The techniques of presentation which create presence are essential above all when it is a question of evoking realities that are distant in time and space."[45] Thus, even an enthymeme that only reminds auditors of their own assumptions can still have a persuasive function. By making a particular matter present to the audience, the argument can still accomplish the traditional goals of rhetoric: to teach, to delight, and to move.

The example

Aristotle's second major argumentative structure is the example. While differing considerably in form from the enthymeme, the example requires a very similar process of reasoning. According to Aristotle, the example "does not concern the relation of part to whole nor of whole to part, but of part to part, of like to like. When two things fall under the same genus, but one of them is better known than the other, then the better-known one is the example."[46] Thus, the audience seems to be invited to make the application through an enthymematic form of reasoning: because such-and-such is the case in a particular instance, then it will also be the case in similar instances.

But again, the example cannot be divorced from the particular rhetorical context in which it is employed. The speaker who uses an example must make certain assumptions about how the audience will apply the example to other cases. Will the audience have the necessary knowledge to make the application that the speaker intends? Will counterexamples immediately spring to mind? Like the enthymeme, the example is not to be located only in some pure realm of *logos*, but at the intersection of *pathos*, *ēthos*, and *logos*—all three means of persuasion.

The use of example is commonly called *induction*, and is often assumed to be the only alternative to deduction as a mode of argumentation. Induction has often been attacked as an incomplete form of argument and was rejected by Hume for precisely this reason. Yet as Stephen Toulmin has noted, induction still plays a key role in the process of argumentation—even in the natural sciences. Induction provides the only way of moving from the seemingly random data of observation to general principles that can then be applied within deductive arguments in order to reach new conclusions.[47] Even formal deduction thus depends on induction for finding its first principles. This accords with Aristotle's notion that analytic modes of argument cannot discover their own first principles; this task can only be accomplished by beginning with common opinions. Inductive argumentation may, of course, be challenged by those who do not agree with the application of the example. Nevertheless, this argumentative structure is very commonly used and can often persuade an audience.

The argument by example is extremely common in Christian theology. Any time that a writer or speaker turns to a list of quotations from the Bible, the Creeds, or traditional dogma, the example is being employed. Similarly, one might list a variety of human experiences—an approach that often marks the theology of Karl Rahner. When Rahner wants to discuss the experience of God's grace, he does not provide an enthymeme as proof; instead, he offers a number of examples. He enumerates a wide variety of human experiences, including aloneness, responsibility, love, and death. He claims that through each of these experiences—albeit in a variety of different ways—God makes known to humanity the reality of grace.[48]

Of course, Rahner's list of experiences does not provide an exhaustive (or even conclusive) proof. Some readers will be unable or unwilling to identify with any of the experiences he cites; others may suggest that his categories are too abstract to be theologically meaningful. Yet the effectiveness of the example is determined precisely by its ability to account for its audience. To the extent that a member of the audience is able to identify with one or more of the examples, persuasion is possible. Hence, the example is very useful as a means of addressing heterogeneous audiences; while the variety of examples does not divide the audience into discrete sections, it can nevertheless appeal to a variety of auditors.

Additional argumentative structures

While Aristotle focused only on enthymeme and example as structures of rhetorical argumentation, recent theorists have further expanded the range of rhetoric to include a variety of additional structures. For example, Perelman and Olbrechts-Tyteca have described the use of the *illustration* and the *model* as closely related (but not identical) to the use of example. They also develop another category that helps to explain why many arguments seem to bear the marks of formal logic yet do not adhere to its canons of deduction. These "quasi-logical arguments" are able to "lay claim to a certain power of conviction, in the degree that they claim to be similar to the formal reasoning of logic or mathematics."[49] Quasi-logical arguments often make use of the vocabulary of logical analysis in order to make their appeal. Such arguments are often dominated by words such as *contradiction, tautology, identity,* and *analysis,* implying that the audience need only apply well-accepted logical rules in order to determine the conclusion. But because these words are used in contingent contexts, their necessity is based on persuasion, not on formal deduction.

As an example of these arguments, Perelman and Olbrechts-Tyteca cite the use of contradictions. If a system of assumption leads to contradictory conclusions, it is generally assumed to be unusable and therefore worthless. However, logical contradictions depend entirely on a fixed meaning for words and sentences. "When the statements are perfectly univocal, as is the case with formal systems, where the signs alone are sufficient, one can only bow to the evidence. But this is not the case with statements in ordinary language, whose terms can be interpreted in different ways."[50] Thus, while the use of the word *contradiction* may appeal to an audience's preference for clear-cut logical categories, the word does not thereby transform a contingent matter into a necessary one! When dealing with matters that could be otherwise, the terms employed are necessarily equivocal; and this insures that such arguments function persuasively rather than analytically.

The appeal to reject all contradiction is very common in theological argument, precisely because it seems to offer an ultimate reason (i.e., an analytic reason) for rejecting an opposing point of view. Consider, for example, the quasi-logical appeal to contradiction in the following rejection of the free-will defense in theodicy:

> The notion that man was at first spiritually and morally good, orientated in love towards his Maker, and free to express his flawless nature without even the hindrance of contrary temptations, and yet that he preferred to be evil and miserable, cannot be saved from the charge of self-contradiction and absurdity.[51]

Here, perfect freedom is declared to contradict any preference for evil and misery. But this depends on the covert introduction of a stipulation that is contingent—specifically, a definition of freedom that excludes any freedom to prefer evil. The supposed contradiction here is not a formal contradiction, because the terms employed (e.g., *freedom, preference, evil*) are not employed univocally. Nevertheless, the argument is persuasive to some precisely because of its implicit claim that contradiction must be resisted at any cost.

INFORMAL INFERENCE

While formal argumentative structures play a significant role in discourse, they do not exhaust the range of persuasive argument. Not all arguments can be reduced, without remainder, to one or another formal structure. Moreover, persuasion sometimes results from the gradual accumulation of formal structures. To the question, "Which of her arguments finally persuaded you?" an audience member might justifiably respond, "No particular one; all of them together."

In other words, persuasion is often a more organic and holistic endeavor than has been suggested thus far. To be sure, we have recognized the inadequacies of logic; but we have still tended to concentrate on the microstructure of argument and to investigate it apart from its overall rhetorical context. Were this the sum of our examination of *logos* as a means of persuasion, we would not have advanced far beyond the medieval and modern textbooks that simply sifted and categorized the various arguments. We would simply be producing an updated version of Whately's *Elements of Rhetoric*.

Whately's own pupil, John Henry Newman, was one of the first modern thinkers to recognize explicitly the insufficiency of a microstructural approach. In the *Grammar of Assent*, he explained:

> It is plain that formal logical sequence is not in fact the method by which we are enabled to become certain of what is concrete; and it is equally plain, from what has already been suggested, what the real and necessary method is. It is the cumulation of probabilities, independent of each other, arising out of the nature and circumstances of the particular case which is under review; probabilities too fine to avail separately, too subtle and circuitous to be convertible into syllogisms, too numerous and various for conversion, even were they convertible.[52]

Our mode of inference is frequently cumulative and organic; we do not normally sift arguments into syllogistic form in order to give our assent.

Newman emphasizes the inherently organic nature of persuasion through his comments about the "wholeness" of our apprehension. He objected to the common assumption that argumentation is a purely mental or rational endeavor: "After all, man is *not* a reasoning animal; he is a seeing, feeling, contemplating, acting animal."[53] Persuasion will not be effective if it concentrates only on moving the intellect, without regard to how, as Newman put it, "the whole man moves."[54]

In addition, persuasive speech is highly dependent on context. The speaker and audience are crucial; but the persuasive power of an argument may also vary according to its context among other arguments. This is why arrangement (*dispositio*) became such an essential aspect of rhetorical study, even though it receives excruciatingly brief treatment in Aristotle's *Rhetoric*. For example, we typically assume that the chronological treatment of a narrative would be the most effective sort of analysis; but countless novels and plays deliberately alter the temporal order of things, frequently with very positive results.[55] Thus, while the arrangement of arguments may affect their persuasive value, the variety of possible argumentative contexts makes the specification of such effects very difficult—another reminder of the cumulative and organic nature of persuasive argumentation.

The interaction of arguments is highly specific to the particular context, and often unpredictable. No longer can one assume that an argument has so thoroughly covered all possible objections that it can be capped with the words *quod erat demonstrandum*. By recognizing the role of informal inference in argumentation, we further emphasize the fragility and incompleteness of all persuasive discourse.

These issues have been taken up in detail by Wayne Booth, who discusses them with reference to an audience's judgments about literature. According to Booth, we evaluate literature (and people) "by experiencing them in an immeasurably rich context of others that are both like and unlike them."[56] In terms redolent of our earlier discussion of the complex relationship between speaker and audience, Booth recognizes that all argumentation demands a context.

> Judgment requires a community: no judge can operate outside a
> legal system; no just weighing can take place on scales not

calibrated with other scales; and nobody would trust a real estate
agent who lacked experience in comparing appraisals with other
agents. Perhaps the legal metaphor is least misleading, because it
reminds us that all judgment is pointless unless it can be shared
with other judges who rely in turn on their past experiences.[57]

Booth observes that such synthetic judgments are neither inductive nor deductive; in fact, we really have no name for this sort
of judgment-by-comparison. He thus calls it *coduction*—a process, he notes, that "is obviously about as different as possible
from what logicians claim to do before offering to share a universally valid proof."[58]

These varying approaches to informal inference have significant theological implications. While enthymematic reasoning
may have some applications in Christian theology, many theological concerns require a more organic approach—almost a
hermeneutics of argument, where the audience is asked to
interpret a vast field of evidence rather than to manipulate
highly structured claims. "In those complex and far-reaching
questions of value, belief, and faith, the real locus of persuasion
is not in the enthymeme *as such*, but in the multitude of details,
facts, and vaguely apprehended beliefs that the premises of
enthymemes only point to and inadequately represent."[59] The
significance of informal inference for theology can be measured
by the complex variety of sources on which the audience relies
in rendering judgment. I shall return to a discussion of these
sources in the latter part of this chapter. For now, I would simply summarize: Audiences judge not on the basis of deduction
alone, nor even on the basis of deduction accompanied by
induction, but, rather, according to their ability to synthesize
diverse information and to infer a conclusion from a wide range
of argumentative premises.

THE LINGUISTICALITY OF
THEOLOGICAL ARGUMENT

Thus far, we have explored formal and informal structures of
persuasive argument. But we have still not covered the entire
range of argumentation, which sometimes depends upon tracks

of thought and argument that cannot be described as any form of inference, whether formal or informal. For example, structures of inference cannot account for such common rhetorical devices as the use of a single word as an argument ("No!" "Rubbish!"); the repetition of an (apparently) nonargumentative discursive structure in ways that give it argumentative force; and the use of nondiscursive elements (gestures, tone of voice, and other signs) as supplements to discursive argument.

These additional argumentative features may be especially important in Christian theology. One might want to examine, for instance, how the language of liturgy persuades through repetition in a particular context (some elements of which are clearly nondiscursive). Similarly, one might ask how the Word of God persuades, even when that Word cannot be reduced to simple argumentative structures. How can we develop a category of *argumentation* that is broad enough to include the wide variety of persuasive language employed in Christian discourse?

Taking a clue from Aristotle's choice of terminology for "the arguments themselves" (*logos*), we should recognize that some arguments can simply be *words*—even words that neither create nor follow the inferential patterns explored above. The power of these words may be augmented by the use of nondiscursive devices. But whether supplemented or not, words are fundamental to all argumentation.

Language thus provides an excellent context within which the role of the arguments themselves can be understood and examined. Moreover, *language* is an especially appropriate category for understanding theological arguments. Theology and rhetoric alike concern themselves both with discourse and with the power of the spoken word: theology is discourse about God, whereas rhetoric is discourse about discourse itself. Both fields have a similarly linguistic orientation.

But so too any discipline: sociology is discourse about society; psychology is discourse about the psyche. These forms of discourse, or any other form, would also intersect with rhetoric. But Christian theology is more limited, in that it can speak truthfully about God only by analogy to those ways in which God has already spoken. This attention to the category of *revelation* requires theology to speak a word that is also God's

Word. As discourse about a self-revealing God, Christian theology must also be understood as discourse about Discourse— that is, as a word about the Word.

The close relationship between theology and language has been emphasized in the writings of Kenneth Burke, even as early as his *Rhetoric of Motives*. To offer but one example of many: "The end of rhetoric was 'to persuade with words' (*persuadere dicendo*); but the principle of Logos behind such purely human language was 'the Word' in another sense, a kind of Word that was identical with reality."[60] Burke later developed this insight, and others of the same sort, into a broader study of religious discourse. He understood this work as a study of words-about-words, and at the same time, a study of words-about-the-Word. He emphasized the self-referential linguisticality of this enterprise by naming his study *logology*.[61] Because theology concerns itself with matters of ultimacy and urgency, Burke believed that it could offer a paradigm for understanding persuasive language generally.

> Theological doctrine is a body of spoken or written *words*. Whatever else it may be, and wholly regardless of whether it be true or false, theology is preeminently *verbal*. It is "*words* about 'God.'"
>
> In being words about so "ultimate" or "radical" a subject, it almost necessarily becomes an example of words used with thoroughness. Since words-about-God would be as far reaching as words can be, the "rhetoric of religion" furnishes a good instance of terministic enterprise in general. Thus it is our "logological" thesis that, since the theological use of language is thorough, the close study of theology and its forms will provide us with good insight into the nature of language itself as a motive.[62]

By examining two theological texts—St. Augustine's *Confessions* and the first three chapters of Genesis—Burke developed a fascinating perspective on the ultimate human motive. He thereby made a significant addition to his own lifelong project: the compilation of a (highly unsystematic) catalogue of all the constituents of human relations. Here, we are interested not so much in that wider project as in Burke's more general observations on the paradigmatic function of theological language.

Language is a human means of communication. Similarly, theological language is not a divine dispensation, but a human attempt to communicate about first-order religious language. Nevertheless, language can be transformed when it is employed theologically. Burke claims that language that is taken up for specifically theological purposes tends to develop new, ultimate connotations that then find their way back into nontheological uses of the same language. He offers the examples of *grace* (meaning "for nothing," translated into the theological notion of God's free gift to humanity, and retranslated into an aesthetic indicator); and *create* (meaning "to make," used theologically to describe God's activity, and then suggesting human attempts to imitate nature). Such words return to the natural realm from the supernatural, but they have been changed—their meanings augmented—during their journey.[63]

Now Burke turns to a consideration of the use of the word *Word* (*logos, verbum*) in theology. He suggests that this theological usage provides an archetype to which all other uses of language may refer—the "master analogy" of logology. "What we say about *words*, in the empirical realm, will bear a notable likeness to what is said about God, in theology."[64] Burke then develops a number of additional analogies, all based on this master analogy.[65]

For example, one analogy between theology and language-in-general concerns what Burke calls the *negativity* of language. As language users, we are always tempted to confuse words with things; but we also realize that language usually works only by expressly denying this equivocation.

> We must remind ourselves that, whatever *correspondence* there is between a *word* and the *thing* it names, the word is *not* the thing. The *word* "tree" is *not* a tree. . . . But because these two realms coincide so usefully at certain points, we tend to overlook the areas where they radically diverge. We gravitate spontaneously towards naive verbal realism.[66]

We often comment on the nondiscursive; but we can do so only by using discourse. Thus we are forced to speak of things in terms of something that those things are not (that is, in *words*). This is more clearly so when we use irony or metaphor; however, insofar as we maintain a distinction between words and things, all language works in the same way.

The connection to theology is obvious enough—not only in the *via negativa* and the traditional negative attributes for God, but also in the negative moral command ("Thou shalt not") and in the ultimate human negation, death. As Burke suggests, "quite as language involves a principle of negativity in its very essence, so theology comes to an ultimate in 'negative theology,' since God, by being 'supernatural,' is *not* describable by the positives of nature."[67]

Another of Burke's analogies concerns the relationships between language and the doctrine of the Trinity. His description suggests that the first person of the Trinity is the thing itself, the fundament, which can be said to generate the Word who names it. The correspondence between the name and the thing is a *communion*—suggesting an analogy to the Holy Spirit, who (in Augustine's terms, at least) is sometimes understood as specifying the perfect communion between two persons.[68]

Here is fertile ground indeed. Burke has offered not only an analysis of the argumentative value of words; he has also helped to specify the important relationship between Christian theology and language in general. His comments help to describe how the whole range of theological language can become persuasive and thus rhetorical.

Too often, Burke has been quickly categorized as a critic of theology. Commentators claim to have seen, in his various forays into theological literature, an attempt to reduce all theology to mere verbiage. Consider, for example, the comment of John Freccero: "Burke's interest in theology is the reverse of the theologian's, and is essentially deconstructive of the theological edifices of the past."[69] But this analysis hinges on a weakened understanding of both language and theology. Certainly Burke himself had a higher vision of both, as is suggested especially by his comments on the *via negativa* (to which he alludes time and again, not only in *The Rhetoric of Religion* but also in *A Rhetoric of Motives*). Burke's program may indeed discredit a theology that embodies what Freccero later calls "the lust for unity";[70] but such a theology can and should be criticized on more general philosophical and theological grounds as well.

While Burke's writings develop analogies between theology and language in highly suggestive ways, his insights do not exhaust the relationship between the two. We can also point to a number of structural analogies, which can help to develop a notion of language as a model for theological argument. Here I use the word *model* in a somewhat technical sense—as an imaginative attempt to "regard one thing or state of affairs in terms of another."[71]

Language can serve as a model for understanding theology, for language and theology share a number of characteristics. Both provide a method for a particular group of individuals to communicate among themselves. On the one hand, we are all familiar with language; we use it every day. On the other hand, we do not claim to have any comprehensive knowledge about how language works; we depend on philosophers and scientists to explicate its inner machinations. So too with the method of argument in theology: those who talk about God find themselves using theological arguments regularly; yet they rarely pause to consider the structure and presuppositions of such arguments. If we think through the character of theological argumentation using the model of language in general, we can bring into high relief an "associative network"[72] of relationships and thereby improve our understanding of both theology and language. We shall then be able to speak, metaphorically, of the linguistic features of theological argumentation.

THE SOURCES OF CHRISTIAN THEOLOGY

In order to suggest how the considerations of this chapter might affect the practice of Christian theology, I want briefly to discuss various arguments that theologians have deployed concerning the sources of reflection on the Christian faith. Where do theologians turn for the raw material of their discipline? Do they attend primarily to written texts, to oral histories, or to more general accounts of the human condition?

Which texts are most important? Whose experiences are most relevant?

Theologians are frequently categorized according to the source(s) that they use most prominently in their work. This categorization has led to significant disputes over the relative merits of various sources, and even over the criteria to be used in evaluating theological sources. Some of these disputes have become intractable and have brought about or intensified a wide variety of denominational and academic schisms.

I want to suggest that many of these disputes can be traced to a process of classification that operates under a very limited notion of the nature of argument. If the range of argument were expanded, the entire discussion concerning the sources of Christian theology would take on a very different character. Specifically, by considering theological sources through the broader categories of *inference* and *linguisticality,* common classificatory systems begin to break down and lose their relevance. We may thereby come to understand the problem of sources in a less schematized and more organic form.

A descriptive analysis of the most common classificatory scheme for the sources of Christian theology will bring to light some inadequacies inherent in any typology of sources. A linguistic model for re-visioning theological sources, on the other hand, advocates a more organic understanding of the sources of reflection on the Christian faith.

A COMMON TYPOLOGY OF SOURCES

Many discussions of the sources of theology tend to construct a typology that classifies theologians according to their use of particular sources. By examining one of the more common schemes of classification, we will discover why it fails to provide an adequate account of the sources of Christian theology. Indeed, I would argue that *any* such typology tends to obscure the wide variety of ways in which theologians appropriate their source material.

The typology that I want to examine apportions the source material of Christian theology into the categories of *Scripture, tradition, reason,* and *experience.* Lest this fourfold schema be imagined to be merely a straw figure, I should emphasize that it has been employed by a number of different Christian ecclesial bodies and is often taken up by theologians as a starting point for reflection on the Christian faith. Of course, some observers might argue for more or for fewer categories, and others might draw the boundaries differently; but these alterations do not significantly affect my argument. Here, I am concerned not with a particular number or a precise specification of the categories, but with the more widespread tendency to divide theological sources into discrete groups. Some such categorization will be found among a wide range of commentators on theological method.

Rather than assigning specific labels to the various approaches considered under each category, I want to offer particular theologians as examples of each method. Unfortunately, my approach may tend to paint too tidy a picture of each theologian's project, for certainly, the writers mentioned here are considerably more complex than my sketch would suggest. Nevertheless, I believe that examples drawn from among *persons* (rather than ideas or abstract labels) can present a more concrete description of the variety of theological sources.

The Bible

While the Bible is almost universally accepted as a source for Christian theology, its use varies widely. At the outset, theologians have not even reached a consensus on the composition of the biblical canon; further disagreements arise over textual criticism and translation. But even when two interlocutors agree on the wording of a particular passage, they will employ the passage in a wide variety of ways.

At one end of the spectrum, the Bible is sometimes appropriated as an exclusive source, in an attempt to bring a final and definitive resolution to theological disputes. This approach usually understands interpretation as a scientific, rational procedure that follows certain laws and that, when correctly implemented, always produces correct results. This attitude toward the Bible allows no equivocation regarding the sources of theology; and so, at least theoretically, systematic theologies that embrace this approach should never disagree. Gordon Clark's contribution to this genre, for example, argues that Reformed theology has always turned to the Bible alone as a source for theological reflection. He argues that the best reason for taking Scripture literally is that the Bible tells us to do so: "Verbal and plenary inspiration, i.e., infallibility, inerrancy, is the claim the Bible makes for itself; and if the Bible does not correctly represent itself, there seems to be no good reason for taking it very seriously on any other point."[73] Here, Clark applies the canons of logic to the Bible. On his view, the Bible makes certain claims; these claims are univocal and are not subject to interpretation. One of the claims that the Bible makes, according to Clark, is that the biblical text itself never errs. Therefore, if the Bible is to play any role in Christian theology, it must play an absolute role.

The difficulty with this perspective, of course, is that it does not really depend on logic alone for its validity. It also depends on the notion that the Bible makes univocal claims, which are not subject to human interpretation. But this argument is rarely rendered explicit; thus, Clark's approach appears to rely on the Bible alone, while actually making a number of assumptions about the univocity of language. Nevertheless, the claim explicitly denies that biblical interpretation takes place within a specific rhetorical context.

The refusal to attend to argumentative context is mitigated somewhat among those who consider the Bible to be a primary (though not exclusive) source for Christian theology. On this view, the Bible outranks any other source to which the theologian might refer. This approach is exemplified by Dale Moody, who suggests that the Bible's superiority as a source is based on its primacy as the locus of revelation. Moody does not attempt to eliminate all considerations of interpretation and biblical criticism; nevertheless, he always returns to Scripture for the final word. "We are not saying that Scripture is the sole source of Christian faith. It is the supreme source, . . . but it surely is right to give attention to experience and revelation, culture, and reason also."[74] Moody's emphasis on the Bible does not make it the only source of reflection; nevertheless, the Bible may be relied on to adjudicate all claims. The Bible functions as the supreme arbiter of disputes, just as, in the paradigm of formal logic, the deductive argument can always be assumed to be decisive.

The uniqueness of the Bible is also stressed—in a very different way—among theologians who argue that the text must be recontextualized before it can be read. The difference between this approach and the previous two perspectives lies, not in the primacy of the source, but in the interpretive categories through which it is appropriated. Those who seek to recontextualize the Bible argue that readers who live in the modern age can comprehend ancient stories only when the narratives are placed in a more familiar context. The Bible provides a history of the origins of the faith and therefore should be treated as any other historical document would be. The Bible becomes the Christian equivalent of the histories of Herodotus and Thucydides; it will provide clues to the origins of Christianity, if only we can sort through its legends and ornamentations and get to the real history beneath the surface.

This view is illustrated in the work of Edward Schillebeeckx, in which the biblical text is appropriated through historical categories. "My purpose is to look for possible evidences in the picture of Jesus reconstructed by historical criticism. . . . Faith and historical criticism go hand in hand, therefore, on almost every page of this book."[75] For Schillebeeckx, the Bible remains an important source but seems to be a very different Bible from the one appropriated by Moody or Clark.

Clearly, then, those who appeal to the Bible as the initial source of theology do so from a very wide range of theological perspectives. The broad extent of variation raises questions about the usefulness of classifying particular theologians as using the Bible as their methodological point of entry.

Tradition

Obviously, the use of the tradition of the Church as a theological source does not exclude the use of Scripture; in fact, tradition widens the field of possible sources, making the Bible one source among several. But the very breadth of the category *tradition* makes it even more sweeping and inclusive than the first. Not only does the theologian's understanding of tradition vary according to hermeneutical models and overall under-standings of the enterprise of theology; it also differs with the theologian's particular tradition (or denomination) and with geography, intellectual climate, and historical period. A Reformed theologian will have another idea of what counts for tradition than will a Roman Catholic writer; the British will dif-fer from the Germans; and a theology written to justify secular authorities will not view tradition in the same way as a theol-ogy written at the risk of persecution.

The theologian who writes from (and to) a community with a clear understanding of its own traditions will write confidently and without much fear of opposition, because the community for whom the work is written provides the criteria for its sources. In Eastern Orthodoxy, for example, the question "What belongs to the tradition?" rarely becomes a controversial issue. The Church has a clearer sense of which historical fig-ures provide theological foundations worthy of emulation; and the community coheres, at least in part, through a fairly rigor-ous understanding of authority. These factors keep debates concerning sources to a minimum.

The confessional clarity of the Orthodox is embodied in John Meyendorff's work. In his discussion of ecclesiology, for example, he can point to a specific number of canonical sources that determine the proper approach to the governing of the Church.[76] He need not question, as theologians in other tradi-tions might, which canonical codes should be appropriated by the Church (and which should not).

On the other hand, a more eclectic theologian may have some difficulty in deciding how to appropriate the wide range of material produced throughout the history of the Church. If one sees oneself as belonging to a particular confessional stance, but as nevertheless willing to appropriate traditions of Chris-tianity from other confessions as well, the extent of potential sources can be enormous. For such theologians, any exclusions whatsoever would appear arbitrary or capricious. For example, the work of Avery Dulles represents an attempt to draw on *tradition* in the broadest possible sense of that term.

One can attempt to walk a middle path between these two extremes. For example, tradition plays a central role in Geoffrey Wainwright's *Doxology*, which attempts to place theology in the context of worship. This approach attends to a broad spectrum of traditions while allowing the liturgy itself to impose some limitations on the range of source material. However, such an approach can create certain tensions that may be difficult to maintain. On the one hand, if the liturgy is fixed, the system may fail to account for the great diversity of systematic approaches to the Christian faith and for the problem of doctrinal development. On the other hand, if the liturgy is subject to constant change, the systematic theology that is built upon it becomes highly dependent on the particularities under which the liturgy is recited (time, place, language, and denominational inflections). While Wainwright's approach does not favor either extreme, he clearly recognizes that he must work within the tensions they create. In a chapter entitled "Revision," these tensions manifest themselves in the polarities of "traditional and contemporary," "sacred and secular," "plural and common," and "fixed and free."[77]

In the end, an emphasis on tradition as a theological source can accommodate many different positions. The many strands of the tradition have grown and intertwined in such a way that no theologian can discern a completely coherent picture of the history of Christianity. Writers must pick and choose among many elements; and they will select the elements that are the most amenable to the denominational, geographical, and philosophical particularities of their own milieux.

Reason

This third major category in the traditional typology of sources includes theologians who believe that theology should begin with some particular philosophical framework—some particular plan for organizing our mental furniture. These writers admit that theology is properly talk about *God*; nevertheless, they hasten to add, only human beings can do the talking.

Thus, we must attempt to describe the faith in categories that we can understand. This philosophical approach may or may not consider the Bible and tradition as part of its source material. Other sources that are brought to bear on the theological system are typically interpreted according to a consistent philosophical principle that guides the writer.

Clearly, the spectrum for possible approaches in this category is even wider than in the previous two. Although the Bible and tradition both provide a great variety of material (which theologians may appropriate in highly idiosyncratic ways), both sources are circumscribed by their specifically Christian orientation. The category of *reason*, however, may reach well beyond the bounds of Christianity and thus into other traditions, sacred or secular.

The philosophical approach is exemplified in the work of John Macquarrie, whose theological method is informed by a number of twentieth-century philosophers and most prominently by Martin Heidegger. For example, the Heideggerian perspective gives Macquarrie a special view of the fallen state of humanity, which he paraphrases as "failure to attain, falling short of actualization, or falling away from authentic possibility, without of course implying that one had first arrived there, and then only subsequently fallen away."[78] Again, revelation can be understood in Heidegger's terms as "primordial thinking"—which, Macquarrie admits, "is a philosophical thinking, but it is described as a thinking which responds to the address of being, and is explicitly compared both to the insights of religion and to those of poetry."[79] For Macquarrie and for other theologians of a similarly philosophical orientation, the work of a secular philosopher becomes the prism through which traditional and biblical categories are reflected.

In contrast to Macquarrie's existentialist mode, a completely different approach is offered by Thomas Torrance, who uses more objectivistic philosophical categories. Torrance believes that theology can be made a *science,* in the popular understanding of that word—an objective enterprise that can avoid all presuppositions. "When we engage in theological thinking we are summoned to renounce all other presuppositions in concentration upon the object. This is thinking that freely refuses to be fettered by *a priori* dogmatisms drawn from anywhere outside of what is given to it."[80] Here Torrance clearly operates under his own set of presuppositions, which differ from those he denounces only in degree, not in kind. His presuppositions are those of the empiricist, who believes that we think most accurately when we clear away all our mental constructs: the emptier the mind, the better for the sake of objectivity.

Despite their wide divergences, however, Macquarrie and Torrance share many assumptions and would seem quite similar when set against certain other theologians. Much greater diversity could be demonstrated by analyzing the thought of writers who operate from very different confessional stances, cultural-linguistic backgrounds, or material conditions.

Experience

In the category of *experience*, diversity reaches its limit case; no two perspectives need be alike. Theologians are often classified here when they claim that a particular element of human experience provides the point of entry to the theological task. These writers believe that because theology deals with matters of such central concern, theological issues should be interpreted on the basis of the events which occur in our lives. Theology, says Theodore Jennings,

> is an inquiry into the meaning of human life pursued by fallible human beings for whom the meaning of their own lives and that of their neighbors is at stake. Theology, so long as it remains true to itself, is not concerned with endless quibbles having no relevance to the living and experiencing of life.[81]

Theology therefore must, according to this approach, take seriously the day-to-day experience of human beings. Nevertheless, as the quotation suggests, any appeal to experience (at least in this broad sense) will be tempted to describe human life in abstract and amorphous ways.[82]

Within this category, no particular example could provide a comprehensive paradigm. Each theologian determines which experiences seem, in his or her judgment, to be the important ones for the doing of theology. Many examples could be chosen; here, I hope to illustrate the wide range of this category by examining two perspectives and then showing how other approaches would be analogous. Specifically, a theologian may cite either human experience as a whole, or some very particular experience that some members of the audience may not have shared.

For example, Gordon Kaufman argues that all human beings experience themselves as historical beings, and therefore that Christianity—a historical faith—must be understood primarily through this category. He thus approaches the various sources of theology from a strictly historicist perspective: How much can be known? With what degree of certainty? Kaufman freely admits that a particular reconstruction of Christianity will depend completely on the perspective of the historian and the age in which he or she lives. "A particular event in human history can be affirmed to have happened if, and only if, memories, reports, and other documentary remains are available in the present, and careful critical analysis reveals them to be an adequate basis for historical reconstruction."[83] The human experience of history is, for Kaufman, the most essential factor in determining the adequacy of a theological position.

Kaufman's approach typifies a theological system that takes one particular aspect of universal human experience and makes it the criterion for theological understanding. By choosing instead the human experience of absolute dependence, Schleiermacher could construct a theological system that interpreted all theological sources through that specific experience. Again, by choosing the category of *ultimate concern* as central, Tillich created a theology grounded in that particular aspect of human experience. Clearly, no boundaries can contain the possible permutations of this approach.

On the other hand, the theologian may opt to choose an interpretive principle that is not a general condition of human experience, but a very specific one—experienced by a particular portion of the human race. Such an approach characterizes some feminist theology, which attempts to build a coherent system around women's experience of oppression. Rosemary Radford Ruether argues that a theological doctrine is truly tested only through its integration into human experience:

Even an Athanasius or a Leo I, who claim to be merely teaching what has always been taught, are in fact engaged in a constant process of revision of the symbolic pattern in a way that reflects their experience. Received ideas are tested by what "feels right," that is, illuminates the logic of the symbolic pattern in a way that speaks most satisfyingly to their own experience of redemption.[84]

Consequently, claims Ruether, modern theologians should also be willing to test ideas according to what "feels right." She thus deduces a critical principle: anything that devalues or oppresses women should be ignored, and anything that promotes the full humanity of women should be retained.[85]

Analogies to this use of theological sources are plentiful; any approach that recognizes a particular element of human experience as having some special validity also falls in this category. But the results are similarly diverse: Liberation theology comes into severe conflict with a theology of capitalism (Michael Novak et al.). African-American theology stands diametrically opposed to theologies of white supremacy. Each finds a certain human experience to be primary, but each can speak only to others with that same experience or with a strong sympathy for what that experience must be like.

The use of *experience* as a source of theology, then, creates the most diverse category of all. The most diametrically opposed positions seem to flourish under a single category. Indeed, certain troublesome features of this category, and of others, may start to cast doubt on the entire typology—and perhaps even of the whole enterprise of evaluating theological sources on the basis of a typology.

THE INADEQUACIES OF
THE STANDARD TYPOLOGY

The typology of sources that I have just described has already begun to display its own inadequacies. The categories are used to group widely varying perspectives, and often do so in ways that fail to do justice to the complexities among these variations. I want now to describe these problems in greater detail, in order to provide a clearing within which some possible alternatives may be considered.

First, theologians cannot limit their sources to any one of the categories described in the typology. Most do not claim to do so; but any attempt to classify theologians will necessarily suggest that one source can be primary (even if *primus inter pares*). The use of the Bible is inextricably tied to a worldview that makes assumptions about univocity and objectivity. Tradition can only be appropriated through specific philosophical categories, even when the theologian tries to prescind from such considerations. Some writers attempt to give equal weight to all four categories, or suggest the use of other sources as well. In each case, the theologian operates with a wide variety of source material; to attempt to classify theological approaches according to "one source" will result only in confusion and misunderstanding.

Second, the categories fail to distinguish among very different theological attitudes; they do not consider how a source is being used, but consider only the source itself. For example, theologians who attend primarily to the Bible do so with vastly differing assumptions. Significant differences are elided when, for example, Gordon Clark is grouped together with Edward Schillebeeckx, for these two theologians differ markedly in their hermeneutical, philosophical, and pastoral assumptions. These divergences suggest the inadequacy of speaking of, for instance, the Bible as the primary source for theological reflection.

A third difficulty (the converse of the second): the typology creates artificial distinctions among approaches that are actually very similar. Some theologians who rely primarily on the tradition of the Church must simultaneously take into account human experience—for example, the experience of the mystic who has since become a part of the tradition. Similarly, the separation of the Bible from tradition simply perpetuates the notion that the text of Scripture is somehow discernible without recourse to the tradition that has carried it from writer to reader.

Fourth, certain theologians simply cannot be adequately classified. Those who self-consciously attempt to balance their reflections by including some material from each of these sources simply cannot be accommodated—a problem illustrated by the work of Karl Rahner. While Rahner clearly wants to emphasize experience and tradition, he also takes cues from Heidegger and Kant. And although scriptural citations are not abundant in his work, he clearly recognizes the Bible as a primary source to which all churchly reflection must adhere. Similarly, Karl Barth would be difficult to place in the typology; although he clearly claims to eschew the last two categories, he never totally frees himself from their influence; and certainly both the Bible and tradition play important roles in his work. An even more complicated example is Eberhard Jüngel who, beginning with Barthian presuppositions, augments his list of sources through considerable dialogue with modern philosophy.

Fifth and finally, the categories provide no way of excluding any putative theology from the realm of theology properly so-called. What could possibly classify as an a-theology? Many theologians are quick to find candidates for this description, but their rationales tend to be based more often on disagreements about particular positions than on more general methodological questions. Certainly, no one should not be overly eager to withhold the label from any activity that claims to be theology—as though the name were a stamp of approval. Nevertheless, without some means of distinguishing theological investigations from any other sort, the whole enterprise of Christian theology begins to lose its identity.

Theologians who are typically placed in the category of *experience* offer the most examples of this problem. On what methodological grounds can the Black liberation theologian properly exclude the white racist "theologian"? How can the feminist exclude the chauvinist? How can the liberationist exclude the colonialist? Simply put, this typology does not allow room for the issues of political commitment discussed in chapters 2 and 3. As long as each participant in the debate can point to some vague form of human experience as a theological source, no *a priori* exclusions are possible.

BROADENING THE ARGUMENT

Discussions concerning the sources of Christian theology often seem fruitless and interminable, precisely because they operate with such a highly restricted notion of argument. When

limited to the categories of formal logic, arguments demand classification, precise discrimination of types, and—ultimately—a
decision in favor of one approach over the others, Too often, the
need to place a specific theological approach into one category
or another has overwhelmed our ability to understand the complexity of that theology's use of sources. I want to propose a
more organic understanding of the sources of theology, using
the expanded notion of argumentation developed above.
Recalling our examination of the symbiotic relationship
between theology and language, we may tentatively suggest
that theological argumentation may use *language* as a model
for its own self-understanding.

Here, this suggestion can be developed in only the most
schematic way. A linguistic model of theological argumentation
would eventually need to concern itself with all the elements of
language: vocabulary, grammar, and syntax, as well as some
finer points such as tropes, quotation, and indirect discourse.[86]
I will present some very tentative comments on grammar and
syntax in chapter 5. Here, by way of prolegomena, I offer a few
initial reflections on just one of the many aspects of a linguistic
model for theology. Specifically, I want to suggest that the
vocabulary of a language can serve as a model for describing
the sources of Christian theology.

We begin with a basic analogy: Theological sources perform
the same function for theology as a vocabulary does for a
language. In both, a group of smaller elements constitute parts
of a larger whole. I want to suggest that if we were to analyze
various theological approaches in terms of their vocabularies (as
opposed to their sources), a more refined view of their agreements and disagreements might be possible. Each vocabulary
would include a wide variety of linguistic elements that have
been appropriated in very different ways; no two approaches
would be identical. Nevertheless, the differences would not
prevent communication. In seeking to understand the specific
elements of a theologian's vocabulary, we might discover that
complex, highly unstable descriptions would replace neat and
tidy typologies.

Indeed, any discussion of a theological vocabulary should
not be understood simply as a new typology of sources to

replace the previous one, which would only perpetuate its in-adequacies in a different form. Instead, we need to look toward an approach to theological argument based, not upon content (biblical, philosophical, and so forth), but upon certain specific networks of associations that the model of a *vocabulary* evokes. If the use of this model succeeds, it will help us to understand more clearly the nature of theological argument and the sources on which it must draw.

What features of a vocabulary make it constitutive of the language by means of which we communicate? I want to suggest four primary features and examine each from both a linguistic and a theological perspective.

First: A vocabulary must provide clear and consistent limits to the words that may be used in any given language. Communication would be impossible if we thought we could add as many new words as we liked. For example, most audiences can survive the occasional use of a word from a foreign language; but a text that shifted constantly from one language to another would eventually exhaust all but the most patient of polyglots. Similarly, we can make sounds and write words which have no meaning in any language—nonsense words, arbitrary combinations of morphemes, and imitations of natural or artificial sounds. In order to communicate, we must circumscribe the realm of possible words; we can only communicate with those who agree to use primarily the words that reside within these limits.

In fact, only because of the limitation of our vocabulary can we ever learn a language—as Donald Davidson has noted.[87] If we had to try to learn an infinite number of words, or even sentence-parts (what Davidson calls "semantical primitives"), we would never learn the language. For then, Davidson argues, "no matter how many sentences a would-be speaker learns to produce and understand, there will remain others whose meanings are not given by the rules already mastered. It is natural to say such a language is *unlearnable*."[88]

Just as the range of possible words in a language's vocabulary must be limited, so too does theological argumentation require circumscription. We cannot expect conversation to occur if we allow every possible source to bear upon the theologies that we construct. All the sources examined in the typology described above can accommodate an almost unlimited range of material. For example, a particular experience could be claimed as a source for theological reflection as long as one human being is capable of such an experience. Similarly, when using philosophy or tradition as a source, the possible range of options is practically infinite. Even in the case of the Bible, many have argued for the inclusion of additional texts in the canon—for instance, works that were once excluded for what now appear to be unjustifiable reasons. Others have resisted these efforts; but even if we focus only on the traditional canon, the range of possible interpretations has no inherent limit.

However, if our model for the sources of theology is a *vocabulary* rather than a list of categories, then limitation becomes a natural part of communicative *praxis*. We can deploy only so many words—and, consequently, only so many arguments—at one time. As the authors of *The New Rhetoric* have observed, "by the very fact of selecting certain elements and presenting them to the audience, their importance and pertinency to the discussion are implied."[89] Just as we do not choose words without attending to the sentence that they will compose, we also do not select sources without attention to the particular argument that they will support and the auditors to whom they are addressed. Rather than classifying theologians into discrete categories and expecting them to justify their choice of source material, we need to be more attentive to the context within which particular sources are deployed. Their persuasive efforts succeed when they draw upon a coherent vocabulary that is sufficiently limited in scope.

We now consider a second feature of vocabularies: They must be appropriate to the language which they serve. Language functions by giving its users the tools they need to communicate with one another. This is less obvious in natural languages, since their domain is the entire range of communication. But in more limited linguistic domains (such as the artificial languages often employed within an academic discipline), the language must provide a vocabulary that allows its users to communicate about whatever they wish to discuss.

Similarly, a theological source must be appropriate to the theological argument that it serves. Thus, theologians will need to be familiar with the full range of sources that are necessary to communicate about the Christian faith. For example, as long as Christians continue to use the Bible in their worship and prayer life, theologians must also attend to the Bible in order to understand this faith. A theology that ignores those sources employed by at least some Christians necessarily ceases to address that portion of the audience.

Again, methodological questions begin to shift. We need not classify theologians according to the sources they use; we need not even ask which sources *should* be used. Instead, we need to ask: Given the sources that this theologian is using in this particular instance, what audience is being addressed? What kinds of appeals are being made? Has this theologian chosen sources that are appropriate to the audience and to the overall context of the argument? Did the choices result in persuasion? Or, was the audience completely unmoved?

In order to employ appropriate language, the speaker must maintain some respect for the general acceptance of words by the speakers of the language. This requirement suggests a third feature of vocabularies: A language can "work" if it is dependable; people expect the words that they use today to be understood tomorrow as well. In other words, a vocabulary has stability over time.[90] Admittedly, words can be added and subtracted; I will return to this point again, below. Nevertheless, communication depends on a vocabulary that retains a fairly high degree of consistency; for only a consistent vocabulary can gain the kind of widespread recognition required for communication across time and space. When words enter (or disappear from) the vocabulary, some speakers of the language will not be able to adapt to this change; consequently, communication may break down. Thus, when using a language, one must usually employ a vocabulary that has been very generally accepted over a long period of time.

In Christian theology, this means that a certain priority must be given to the sources that have traditionally been accepted by a wide range of the members of a particular audience.[91] Again, the precise specification of the sources will depend on the context of the argument. A dispute within a particular denomination may call for attention to a very limited number of sources. But disputes between confessions will be utterly unproductive if theologians ignore a source that is extremely important to the audience that they address.

As an example of this problem, consider a recent essay by Jürgen Moltmann on death and eternal life.[92] Moltmann rejects any notion of purgatory, partially on the grounds that,

> as Catholic theologians admit themselves, there is no scriptural proof for this notion. It originates from the ancestor cult of ancient religions. Moreover, it is not the Bible that is given as a basis but rather the early Christian practice of the cult of the dead and prayers for the dead. . . . But should religious practice really define Christian theology?[93]

Leaving aside the (almost unbelievable) closing question of Moltmann's comment, we need to observe that he simply ignores the sources that Roman Catholics would consider important in judging this argument. Moltmann is very well aware that Roman Catholics are not overly concerned that this doctrine cannot be proved from Scripture. We may conclude that either (1) Moltmann deliberately excluded Catholics from his audience (odd, since this paper originated at an ecumenical institute), or (2) he was unable to find any "catholic" means of persuading Catholics that the doctrine of purgatory should be rejected. Either way, he failed to employ a vocabulary that would be persuasive to those who held any position much different from his own.

Thus far, I have emphasized that sources (like a vocabulary) must be limited, appropriate, and accepted by a wide range of people over a long period of time. In other words, I have generally suggested only *restrictions* on the range of sources. But what happens when a language needs to expand? How can a vocabulary continue to provide the vehicle for human communication in a world for which it is no longer sufficiently nuanced?

These questions lead us to the fourth and final feature of vocabularies: They must be sufficiently flexible to allow new words to come into the language. According to Janet Soskice, this augmentation occurs in four basic ways: metaphorical catachresis, metonymy, parallel syntax, and neologism.[94] Catachresis occurs when a metaphor becomes a common word and thus fills a lexical gap (the "leg" of a table; the "stem" of a glass). In metonymy, a well-known word is appropriated as the name for a different object (as when a river, such as the Mosel, becomes the name for a particular wine). Extension by parallel syntax occurs when one grammatical form (often a noun) provides the model for the creation of a different form (thus the noun *facsimile* begets the verb *to fax*). Finally, neologism describes the creation of new words entirely; nevertheless, it usually draws on roots found in other languages.

When a vocabulary is extended, users of the language must be able to recognize some continuity between the new and the old. Even in the creation of a neologism, the existing elements of a vocabulary are often called upon to provide a basis for new elements. When we extend the range of possible words, we rely on the general acceptance of old words (or parts of words) in order to expect others to make sense of the new word. Thus, when theology needs to expand its vocabulary of sources, communication will be facilitated by the use of sources that have their roots in the standard theological vocabulary. So for instance, when attempting to incorporate events in the history of Christianity that had usually been brushed aside, the theologian could bring this source into the vocabulary by showing its close relationship to sources that have always been considered a part of the tradition. On the other hand, a new source that is simply dropped into the language might not be easily appropriated by other users of the language—even though they apparently speak the same language.

One method of extending a vocabulary cannot be built only on currently accepted words: the neologism. Here, the new word is often imported—a word that finds its roots not in the vocabulary of the language spoken, but in another language altogether. This too is possible in theology; theologians can use the terminology of other fields—history, anthropology, sociology, psychology—to express their understandings of the faith. But two provisions should be noted. First, the inventor of a neologism may have to make the case for its usage. In order for the word *television* to find a place in the English language, its Greek and Latin roots were probably explained to those who were unable to recognize the morphemes (just as those roots are still often explained when teaching someone the etymology of the word). Similarly, when arguing for the appropriation of rhetorical categories in theology, I must make my case by referring to parallel aspects in more traditional theological categories.

In addition, a coined word must pass the test of time. This provision, in fact, applies to all the modes of language extension—but especially to neologism, because it is often the most difficult for speakers of the language to incorporate into their vocabularies. In theology, a new source must be able to demonstrate its connection to other sources, and it must eventually gain general acceptance within the theological community. Only then can it become a generally accessible source on an equal footing with others.

These four features of a vocabulary are described here as an attempt to emphasize the linguisticality of theological argument. If theology is persuasive argument, then its ability to persuade rests on certain assumptions about language. The model of *language* provides us with a submodel, that of *vocabulary,* as a vehicle for examining the sources of theological argumentation. Four criteria have been suggested on the basis of this model: the sources of theology must cohere in some sort of unity; they must be appropriate to the religious practices that they seek to understand; they must command some degree of general acceptance before they can be depended on as sources; and, when new sources are developed, they must bear a family resemblance to sources that have already been in common use.

These criteria are derived neither from any peculiar theological perspective, nor from a preconceived notion that one source of theology is necessarily better than another. Interestingly enough, however, the four features outlined in this section bear a strong resemblance to another fourfold description—one with which Christians will already be familiar. We could say, I believe, that the sources of Christian theology must attend to the criteria of coherence (unity), religious appropriateness (holiness), widespread acceptance (catholicity), and change that respects the past (apostolicity). In other words, the basic features of the sources of Christian theology are the same features that, according to the Nicene Creed, have marked the Christian Church throughout its history.

This model presents a more organic understanding of the sources of theological reflection. It may also help us clarify theological arguments that involve the choice or specification of sources. Within such a model, the argumentative categories of informal inference, enthymeme, and example could operate comfortably, without recourse to the standards of formal logic.

This linguistic model for theological argument could be extended by examining other structures of language. For example, the *grammar* of a language might help identify the norms of theology; similarly, the *syntax* of that language might help to identify various theological methods. This extended linguistic model cannot be given a thorough treatment in the present work; nevertheless, in the following chapter, I shall offer a few indications of the forms it might take. But I want to postpone these comments for a few pages, because my suggestions about the grammatical and syntactical aspects of theology will require attention not only to language as *logos*, but also to a more complete appropriation of the specificity of rhetor and audience. Thus, I shall return to the linguistic analogy when I turn to the theme of *praxis*—that is, when I examine the symbiotic relationship among the three means of persuasion.

REVELATION AND PROCLAMATION AS RHETORICAL ACTIVITIES

This chapter has attempted to offer a rhetorical perspective on the word which theology speaks. I have suggested that this "word" should be understood chiefly in terms of persuasive argument. Theological arguments cannot be reduced to the categories of deductive logic; instead, they should be understood through the broader and more organic categories of informal inference and linguisticality. This approach to Christian theology can help to clarify some perennial debates, such as those concerning the sources of theological reflection.

But if these expanded categories of argument constitute the word which theology speaks, what does this imply for the more traditional understanding of the role of *Word* in theology? Certainly the word *logos* has a rich theological heritage, as has been recalled at various points in this analysis. In theology, *Word* signifies the Word of God, i.e., the word of revelation; it also signifies a human word, the word of proclamation.

These traditional theological uses of *word* are not supplanted by the notion of theology as argument. In fact, the analysis in this chapter suggests that all Christian theology is much more closely related to proclamation and to revelation than some theologians would like to believe. To understand theology as persuasion is to recognize that it is always an act of proclamation; and to understand theology as faithful persuasion is to recognize that its proclamation must be guided by God's revelation.

Revelation is the theological word that *God* can speak. It is ultimately persuasive, in the sense that it is authorized by God. God does not manipulate human beings; rather, God urges and persuades by means of the Word.[95] Yet this Word cannot always be precisely discerned, for it is not univocal—or, at any rate, it does not seem so to human beings. Christians do not dispute that revelation is persuasive; rather, they argue about precisely what counts as revelatory.

This "communicative" nature of revelation has been explored in the work of Ingolf Dalferth. While Dalferth does not label *revelation* a rhetorical category, his description clearly evokes the issues with which we have been concerned:

> Structurally, revelation is an activity that is (1) *relational*, (2) *directed* and (3) *effective*. (1) It is relational because in it God reveals himself to *someone*. (2) It is directed because this relation is asymmetrical (the revealer is logically prior to the receiver of revelation), irreflexive (the revealer and receiver of the revelation cannot be identical), and intransitive (if A reveals himself to B and B [reveals himself] to C, A has not revealed himself to C). . . . (3) Finally, revelation (but not proclamation) is effective, because it occurs only when it is received, and is known to have occurred, by at least one person.[96]

Dalferth then goes on to list other marks of revelation: it is interpersonal, direct, and particular; it is mediated and involves interpretation; it is belief-invoking and inexhaustible.[97]

Dalferth also emphasizes that revelation is an activity of *God*—not of human beings. When human beings communicate the Gospel to one another, they are engaging in the activity of proclamation, not revelation.[98] This important distinction can help us better understand the persuasive nature of theology. Specifically, while revelation can result from the rhetorical activity of God, proclamation can result from the rhetorical activity of humanity.

Proclamation can best be understood as the way in which a particular theological/political commitment (as discussed in chapter 2) can speak a particular word with authority (chapter 3). Its commitment and its authorization are welded together in the *Word* which theology speaks. Thus, proclamation must not be considered a theological sideshow, nor something that can only take place after the "real" theology is done. Rather, all Christian theology is proclamation. Homiletics and systematics differ from one another because of their audiences and the character by which they are authorized; but they are both acts of proclamation.

Finally, despite the important connections between the word *logos* and language, Christian proclamation is not limited to linguistic forms. Just as persuasion can take place without words, or through a combination of words and deeds, so too with proclamation. Thus, proclamation takes place, not only in the pulpit, but also at the altar; not only in acts of reading, but in acts of solidarity as well; not only in the Church, but throughout the world. As Rebecca Chopp has suggested, proclamation can take a wide variety of forms; but it is always committed and always authoritative.

> Proclamation must protest against oppressiveness and repressiveness through practices of insurrection, be they boycotts, prayers, fasts, alternative life-styles, legislative changes, or other forms of subversion. Issues such as nuclear destruction, depression, third world-first world relations, and aging all provide places to stand from which to capture a view of the social-symbolic order, places to render judgment in the midst of grace.[99]

Proclamation occurs whenever one human being seeks to persuade another in ways that are faithful to the Gospel of Jesus Christ.

God's rhetorical activity is revelation; human rhetorical activity is proclamation. The differences between the two categories are significant. But their differences should not distract us from the fact that they do intersect—at a single point. In one particular instance, the human word of proclamation and the divine word of revelation become one. Thus, the ultimate·rhetorical event in Christian theology, the ultimate word which theology speaks, is called, quite properly, the *Word*—who became flesh and dwelt among us, full of grace and truth.

5

Praxis
Theology
as Rhetoric

In the first four chapters, I have attempted to describe the usefulness of rhetoric as a methodological tool in Christian theology. Specifically, I have suggested that rhetorical analysis can help clarify theological disputes and thus make them more productive. As a result, speakers and audiences can better identify their agreements and disagreements, and can begin to recognize why theological positions will vary according to context. This process of clarification, I have claimed, results from close attention to the particular context of rhetor and auditor, and from an expanded notion of what counts for argument. Throughout the discussion, I have attempted to attend to concrete theological practices; however, because I have examined *pathos*, *ēthos*, and *logos* in separate chapters, I have not yet described how all three means of persuasion work in concert. This will be the goal of the present chapter.

The phrase *in concert* is carefully chosen; for the central metaphor of this chapter is a musical one. The theological enterprise requires us to listen to a variety of notes simultaneously, rather than to a single tone. Christian theology speaks, not in a unified voice, but through a complex counterpoint of harmonies and discords. Moreover, each voice—like a differentiated strand of a rich musical texture—achieves a high degree of independence, resounding with its own commitments and with its own assumptions about its audience. Yet too frequently, commentators have attempted to synthesize the Christian faith into a single refrain—thereby diluting and distorting its brilliant contrapuntal multiplicity.

My comments here draw upon the work of Mikhail Bakhtin, who distinguishes single-voiced, "monologic" discourse from multilayered, "polyphonic" discourse. Bakhtin attributes the significance of Dostoevsky's novels to the way in which readers find themselves striking up conversations with a multitude of different characters at once. "A plurality of independent and unmerged voices and consciousnesses, a genuine polyphony of fully valid voices is in fact the chief characteristic of Dostoevsky's novels."[1] According to Bakhtin, Dostoevsky's greatness lies precisely in his refusal to synthesize the complexity of human life into a facile and obvious "author's message."

In the modern age, Christian theologians have attempted too often to isolate a single "melody line"—to demonstrate the essential concept, to identify the golden thread that holds everything together. As methodologically tempting as this approach may be, its results are not always particularly pleasing to the ear. Bakhtin's praise of polyphony challenges us to speak about Christian theology in a way that does not reduce its multiform character to a tedious monotone. Here, the faculty of rhetoric can be of great assistance; for it underscores the complexity of all acts of human communication. Rhetoric can help us understand that Christian theology has neither a single essence nor a fixed form. Rather, theology bears a dynamic and polyphonic character: the character of faithful persuasion.

As we shall discover, the term *faithful persuasion* appropriately characterizes a number of significant theological endeavors, including the formulation of Christian doctrine, the interpretation of the biblical text, and the writing of Church history. Building on the linguistic analogy developed in chapter 4, I shall emphasize both the grammatical function of doctrine and the syntactical function of exegesis. Similarly, the rhetorical nature of theological historiography will become apparent when we examine the case history of a particular theological argument—namely, the debate among first-generation Reformers concerning the Eucharist. In a concluding section, I shall consider the implications of rhetoric for the future direction of Christian theology.

DOCTRINE AS
PERSUASIVE ARGUMENT

One of the most important theological tasks is the ongoing attempt to examine and reformulate Christian doctrine. While doctrines are usually stated as concisely and specifically as possible, they are neither final nor definitive. "Doctrine or dogma refers to official formulations of the faith which have become classical but which are conceivably not the only ways of stating the faith."[2] Unfortunately, the words *doctrine* and *dogma* have taken on pejorative connotations in the modern age, as suggested by cognates such as *doctrinaire* and *dogmatic*. These negative associations can be traced to the assumption that doctrine is somehow eternally fixed, and that it cannot change or develop. But doctrine must constantly be reformulated and reinterpreted, even if this process is understood only as translation into a modern language or idiom. As Karl Barth observed, all proclamation is composed of human words, and such words are equivocal; for this very reason, dogmatics is necessary.[3]

The examination and reformulation of doctrine is a complex process that can be understood in a wide variety of ways. The process raises large questions about identity and difference, continuity and change, stability and development.[4] Thus, Christian doctrine poses not only systematic questions, but a number of methodological and normative questions as well. Prior to the "remaking of doctrine," theologians must ask what they understand themselves to be doing.[5]

The nature and purpose of doctrinal formulation constitutes the problematic of the present section. A recent proposal by George Lindbeck concerning the nature of doctrine provides the melody, harmonized by the counterpoint of my own position: that Christian doctrine is best understood as persuasive argument. This rhetorical approach will suggest three new methodological features of the process of understanding and formulating Christian doctrine.

LINDBECK'S PROPOSAL AND
A SYMPATHETIC CRITIQUE

George Lindbeck has suggested that Christian doctrine has traditionally been understood in one of three ways: as a series of cognitive propositions; as expressions that reflect the experience of faith; or as some correlation of these two.[6] He offers a number of examples, ancient and modern, of each tendency; he also describes the inadequacies of each approach. He proposes as an alternative a cultural-linguistic paradigm, in which doctrine is understood as the grammar of religious belief. Specifically, he focuses on how doctrines are used, "not as expressive symbols or as truth claims, but as communally authoritative rules of discourse, attitude, and action."[7]

Lindbeck thus sees theology as an explicitly linguistic endeavor; doctrinal statements provide the grammatical rules that both shape and are shaped by theological activity. His rule-oriented approach to theology

> does not locate the abiding and doctrinally significant aspect of religion in propositionally formulated truths, much less in inner experiences, but in the story it tells and in the grammar that informs the way the story is told and used. From a cultural-linguistic perspective, it will be recalled, a religion is first of all a comprehensive interpretive medium or categorical framework within which one has certain kinds of experiences and makes certain kinds of affirmations. In the case of Christianity, the framework is supplied by the biblical narratives interrelated in certain specified ways (e.g., by Christ as center).[8]

Lindbeck thus offers a significant shift away from the two most common approaches to doctrine, which he labels *cognitive propositionalism* and *experiential expressivism*.

Lindbeck's proposal has received widespread attention, much of it positive.[9] Moreover, his perspective makes an important contribution to a growing body of literature on the grammatical nature of theology.[10] Although writing from a particular confessional stance, Lindbeck declares his motives to be ecumenical and conciliatory. In fact, judging by the sustained attention that the book has received among Protestants and

Roman Catholics alike,[11] he seems to have constructed his audience with considerable success—and thus to have discovered an effective way of breaking the deadlock over the nature of doctrine.

Lindbeck's cultural-linguistic model offers an excellent paradigm within which Christian theology can be understood and discussed. In fact, his approach has helped to break the ground for the rhetorical theology that I advocate. Moreover, Lindbeck's grammatical understanding of doctrine further develops the linguistic analogy that I presented in chapter 4. Doctrines provide the grammar of faith insofar as they provide community-based norms within which communication can occur.

Nevertheless, while I agree generally with Lindbeck's overall strategy, his specific proposals call for friendly revision—criticism *con amore*. I want to suggest that parallels between doctrine and grammar are not as straightforward as Lindbeck seems to assume. Specifically: Despite his attention to the cultural-linguistic location of theology, Lindbeck often ignores certain questions about context and commitment.

This failure is best exemplified in Lindbeck's taxonomy of doctrines.[12] Among practical doctrines, says Lindbeck, some may be unconditionally necessary, such as the law of love. Others may be conditionally essential, either permanent ("Feed the poor") or temporary; this latter group can be further classified as reversible (views on war) or irreversible (views on slavery).[13] Yet throughout this section, Lindbeck maintains silence as to *why* a particular doctrine falls into a particular category; it seems almost a matter of historical accident. That is: we just so happen to have changed our minds often about war (so this rule is reversible), whereas we seem to have come to a definitive assessment of slavery (so this rule is not). By what authority are doctrines understood under a particular category of rule? Lindbeck seems to ignore the ethical and political structures that shape these classifications. He does not mention, for example, that Christians often change their minds about war because their governments tell them they must. Neither does he consider the possible role that his own particular ecclesiological commitments may have played, consciously or otherwise, in his assessments. In any case, Lindbeck seems to assume—too optimistically, in my opinion—that doctrines can be adequately classified according to their historical sojourn.

Later in the book, another difficulty arises. Lindbeck claims that "it is self-evident" that rules "are separable from the forms in which they are articulated."[14] In his example (a pafient with jaundice), Lindbeck claims to separate a reality (the jaundice) from descriptions of it, e.g., by Galen (an imbalance of the humors) and by modern science (a viral infection). But what is "the jaundice" if not a description that is already linguistically informed? Here, Lindbeck's disjunction of *res* and *verbum* seems contrary to the general argument of his book—that theology is an essentially linguistic endeavor.[15] Rather than emphasizing the organic and polyphonic nature of language, he reintroduces a strict dichotomy of subject and object—and in a form particularly alien to Christian theology.[16] To be sure, Lindbeck recognizes that we cannot gain access to the *res* "independently" (extralinguistically). Yet he believes that the *verbum* somehow "points to" the *res* in a vaguely consequential sense; doctrines can be distinguished "from the concepts in which they are formulated" by stating them "in different terms that nevertheless have equivalent consequences."[17]

Such an enterprise will strike many readers as fraught with difficulties; their fears are confirmed a few paragraphs later, when Lindbeck performs this surgical technique on a particular doctrine. He claims to discover, encapsulated in the doctrine of the consubstantiality of the first and second persons of the Trinity, three regulative principles: monotheism (there is only one God), historical specificity (Jesus really lived), and "Christological maximalism" (which states that "every possible importance is to be ascribed to Jesus that is not inconsistent with the first rules").[18] Lindbeck admits that these rules, and especially the second and third ones, were not formulated as such by the early Church; but as rules governing the doctrine of consubstantiality, they are "self-evident," even "banal." And yet they are of decisive importance for Lindbeck, because he claims that the authority of a doctrine belongs not to its formulation (whether ancient or modern) but to the rules that it instantiates.

These rules, however, are rather less self-evident than Lindbeck suggests. Some theologians have indeed affirmed that monotheism is essential to a trinitarian doctrine of God; but others have argued that monotheism annuls the very possibility of a belief in God as Trinity.[19] In other words, the language of monotheism is no less malleable than that of consubstantiality. Similarly with regard to the historicity of Jesus: the reception of a proposition such as "Jesus really lived" depends largely on the listener's inclination (toward skepticism or toward assent). Finally, the rule of *Christological maximalism* is painfully ambiguous. What are we to make of the assertion that Jesus is to be ascribed every possible "importance"? Lindbeck seems to assume that it will be defined as "most like God" (or something very similar): Jesus is "the highest possible clue . . . within the space-time world of human experience to God, i.e., to what is of maximal importance."[20]

But the notion of maximal importance is equivocal; it depends (at least) on the predispositions of those who consider themselves constrained by the rule. This will vary widely, even among "mainstream" Christians: to the liberal, *importance* might signify "compassion"; to the conservative, "loyalty"; to the pacifist, "peace." To ascribe to Jesus "every possible importance" is, in effect, to make Jesus more like whatever it is that we already believe. The pluralist would like to make Jesus more tolerant; the fundamentalist would like to make him rather less tolerant. Many Christians might assume, with Lindbeck, that making Jesus "important" means emphasizing his divinity; but others might argue that what is "most important" is his essential humanity. And many theologians (including perhaps Lindbeck) might want to claim that we should be looking to Jesus to learn what God is like—not the other way around.

Throughout his book, Lindbeck stakes his approach to theological method on the notion of a rule, which he takes to provide a single-voiced, definite reference point—a moment of identity—for the ever-changing face of Christian doctrine. Yet his rules fail to act like rules, for the language in which they are expressed is necessarily equivocal and profoundly dynamic. These rules are open to wide-ranging interpretation, shaped much more by the character and predispositions of interpreter and audience than by an imagined univocal definition. The ambiguities mentioned here are merely specific instances of a more general problem. The analogy to rules might initially suggest something static and univocal; but theological "rules" must be expressed in such ambiguous language that they will often have no unifying function.

This problem may be clarified by an analogy. In baseball, the infield fly rule functions precisely because of a general agreement about the state of the game in which it is invoked: which bases must be occupied (and what it means to occupy a base); how many outs (and the definition of an *out*); and whether the ball is hit in the infield (and who will make that judgment). This rule is very different from the rules that Lindbeck discusses. A theological rule must use language about which there is no general agreement. Terms such as *monotheism, historical existence,* and *importance* are precisely the terms that are in dispute.

Moreover, rules operate in a great variety of ways, depending on both the context in which they are invoked and the consequences of their being broken. Breaking a rule in baseball may get a manager thrown out of the game; breaking a rule in the courtroom may land a witness in federal prison. Considerable formal and procedural differences separate the rules of chess from the rules of etiquette. Here again, Lindbeck fails to grapple with concrete specificity—with what might be called *the politics of doctrine.* The force of a doctrinal rule—indeed, the force of any rule—depends largely on the political and ethical authority under which it is invoked. Thus, doctrine is tied to the issues of political and ethical commitment that we investigated in chapters 2 and 3, as well as to the nuances of argumentation explored in chapter 4.

As I see it, the basic flaw in Lindbeck's approach is his tendency to assume that a *rule* is a definitive logical category that can provide a univocal (or at least unifying) description of doctrine. This is why the word *grammar* is frequently employed in describing his project; we have been taught to think of grammar in terms of univocal rules. But because rules must be expressed through language, they are subject to the same vicissitudes of reception as are the cognitive propositions (or experiential expressions) that they supposedly replace. Consequently, most rules—even in grammar—cannot function analytically; they are, at best, what Perelman calls "quasi-logical" arguments. They must be defined, redefined, and argued for; they are rarely "self-evident," and almost never "banal."

Lindbeck's understandable desire to unify the function of doctrine relapses into a method that we can only label *analytic.* He assumes that he can specify the content of a doctrine in ways that are not infected by the forms of language in which it is ensconced. This analytic urge is ironic in a work which advocates a cultural-linguistic approach to theology; for it is precisely the equivocal nature of language that argues for *dialectical,* rather than analytical, modes of inquiry. Just to the extent that Lindbeck's project is tied to a logical, analytical understanding of grammar, he underestimates the full potential of a grammatical approach to doctrine.

DOCTRINE AS RHETORIC

I want to suggest that doctrines do not follow the model of logical rules so much as the model of persuasive arguments. A doctrine describes how a speaker (often a doctrinal authority of some sort) attempts to persuade an audience (the faithful) of a particular way of understanding the faith. Thus, the doctrine of consubstantiality was, and continues to be, a description of one way in which Christians have been persuaded that they should think about Jesus in much the same way that they think about God. In coming to this belief, they may have considered and evaluated a number of arguments, both pro and con, concerning such a notion. These arguments might have included "God is one"; "The Word became flesh and dwelt among us"; or even "There was no time when he was not." The success of these arguments was not due to a discovery of the right instantiation of the right rules. Rather, believers have been persuaded by a complex combination of the moral authority of bishops and councils, the examples and enthymemes they offered, and perhaps even a general disposition to attribute divine qualities to one whom they called their Savior. Needless to say, some Christians may also have accepted the doctrine due to what Aristotle euphemistically calls "nonartistic proofs": laws, contracts, witnesses, tortures, and oaths. But to give too much weight to these more coercive instruments of conversion would be drastically to underestimate the persuasive power of word and deed throughout the history of Christianity.[21]

Let us consider another of Lindbeck's examples. The dogma of the Assumption is persuasive to some because of the moral character of those who promulgated it ("Pius XII was good, therefore this doctrine is sound"). Others may be persuaded because they consider themselves "good Catholics," and define a "good Catholic" as one who affirms Roman Catholic dogma. Others, including quite a large number of Christians who do not call themselves Roman Catholics, are persuaded to believe in the marian dogmas for other reasons—from their friendship with, and respect for, Roman Catholic believers, to their own spiritual experiences while praying the rosary.

This last point raises an additional concern about Lindbeck's proposal, a concern that would be addressed more fruitfully by a rhetorical understanding of doctrine. Certainly, Lindbeck stresses the degree to which religious practice shapes the reception of doctrine. But he does not always give adequate weight to the ways in which differences among Christian practices may radically revise the particular instantiation of a rule. For example, as James Buckley has suggested, Lindbeck's own assumptions about the priority of "the *viva vox evangelii* over sacramental enactment of the story"[22] may lead to difficulties when trying to transport Lindbeck's approach across confessional lines. Here we may recall the discussion in chapter 3, which suggested that audiences can be persuaded by nondiscursive as well as discursive arguments. Without seeking to privilege sacrament over word, we can suggest, with Buckley, that Lindbeck's horizon of what counts for "the Christian idiom" may need to be expanded.

> I am not claiming that [Lindbeck's] priorities are mistaken or that they are confessionally motivated. I am one of those Catholics who agree with Lindbeck's priorities, although I would locate the

paradigms of the Christian idiom not only intratextually but in the "heavily ritualized" use of the Gospel stories at the Lord's Supper.[23]

Buckley then goes on to suggest that the variety of accounts of "the Christian idiom" may cause Lindbeck's project to achieve the opposite effect from the one he had hoped for: that is, it may actually impair the process of doctrinal reconciliation.

This difficulty is at least partially ameliorated by a rhetorical understanding of doctrine. Rather than specifying in advance what counts for the Christian idiom (whether it be proclamation, adoration, communion, or discernment), a rhetorical approach would attend to the actual variety of practices among Christian believers. The rhetorical stress on *praxis* would insist on attention to both senses of the ancient Christian principle *lex orandi lex credendi*. Doctrine would be understood as a formulation of what Christians have been persuaded to believe.[24]

A rhetorical approach to doctrine pays close attention to the actual variety of practices among believers, rather than constructing theories about how doctrine might work in the abstract. Furthermore, it does not attempt to separate the rule-like language of a particular doctrine from the reality of which the language is an instantiation. Christians have changed their minds about war, but not because doctrines about war are temporary and conditional; they have changed their minds because they have been persuaded to do so. The means of persuasion may have included not only the moral authority of those who persuaded them (churches, governments, neighbors, soldiers), but also a personal knowledge of the conditions that they have come to describe as *war* and *peace*.

Thus, doctrine may have a grammatical function after all; but only if *grammar* encompasses more than the mere formulation of univocally conceived grammatical rules. The grammar of a language impinges much more broadly on how people live their lives. Recall Wittgenstein's remark: "The *speaking* of language is part of an activity, or of a form of life."[25] Grammar helps to describe not only how we speak, but also what we do—and, indeed, who we are.

Thus, if Christian theology is a grammatical endeavor, this is due, not to a notion of doctrines as rules, but to the ways in which language affects (and is affected by) everything we do.

This, too, was known to Wittgenstein, as exemplified by his cryptic parentheses in the *Investigations*: "(Theology as grammar)."[26] That fascinating epigram can lead to some very subtle and reflective insights, as Fergus Kerr has demonstrated.

> Theology as grammar is, then, the patient and painstaking description of how, when we have to, we speak of God. But why is it that we doubt it can be in mere words or signs or bodily activities that we discover anything interesting about our inner selves or about the divine? Why is it that we are so strongly tempted to turn away from what we say and do, as if these were not "significant" enough? Wittgenstein reminds us that we have no alternative to attending to the signs, the repertoire of gestures and so on that interweave our existence.[27]

Thus, the formulation of Christian doctrine is a grammatical activity—but not in the common, highly restricted sense of *grammar*. The category of *grammar* is appropriate here only insofar as it is taken as a way of understanding the entire scope of human thought and action. As I have attempted to suggest, this broad picture is well served by the expanded notion of argument supplied by the categories of rhetorical analysis.

Admittedly, a doctrine may persuade through arguments that seem very much like the formal argumentation of logic (e.g., syllogistic reasoning). For example, some Christians base their belief about the invocation of God's name on a simple practical enthymeme:

> Jesus called God "Father";
> I should imitate Jesus; therefore,
> I will call God "Father" as well.

However, because of the nonformal character of theological reflection, this argument is indeed an enthymeme, not a syllogism; thus, it cannot be judged by the canons of formal validity. Rather, the argument's persuasive force depends on a number of additional arguments—for example, that one should believe that Jesus did call God "Father"; that the English word *father* is an appropriately imitative translation for the Aramaic *abba*; that one should imitate Jesus; that imitation can be defined as repetition; and that historical changes since the time of Jesus do not necessitate a revision of this argument. Needless to say, these are not the sorts of arguments that can be resolved analytically, as though they were simple arithmetic problems. Their persuasiveness will depend on the particular rhetorical context in which they are employed: a confluence of character, disposition, time, and place.

THREE ASPECTS OF
RHETORICAL ANALYSIS

The advantages of this understanding of doctrine can be summarized by commenting on three methodological aspects of rhetorical analysis: *deconstruction, critique,* and *liberation.* These attributes are not consecutive, nor are they always even distinct from one another; they are simply part of the polyphony of a rhetorical approach to Christian doctrine. Working in concert, these three elements can help us identify the distinctive features of a rhetorical approach to doctrine, as well as providing an implicit argument in favor of that approach.

First, rhetorical method includes a deconstructive aspect. Here, *deconstruction* is not so much a *terminus technicus* as the identification of a methodological decision. Specifically, a rhetorical method seeks to identify the persuasive traces that inhabit theological discourse. Unlike much deconstructive criticism, a rhetorical deconstruction is never an end in itself. Its goal is the unmasking of persuasive appeals that operate covertly within any particular discourse concerning theological doctrine, and that have traditionally been shielded from a detailed investigation.

For example, in debates concerning the doctrine of the real presence in the Eucharist, arguments have traditionally centered on matters such as fidelity to Scripture and tradition, or adequacy to the believer's religious experience. Such matters are important; the moral authority of tradition, as well as the believer's receptivity, can help describe the persuasiveness of a doctrine. But a rhetorical deconstruction of eucharistic doctrine would attempt to identify additional factors affecting its persuasive appeal. For example: How did the doctrine of the real presence affect attitudes toward lay participation in communion? How have these attitudes shifted over time? How have political and theological power structures employed the "symbolic capital" of the real presence? The investigation of such questions can help develop a more nuanced description of theological arguments.[28]

The second aspect of rhetorical analysis is *critique*—an examination of the contextual appeal of theological doctrines. The focus of this critique is not limited to the logical structure of argument; it examines the entire rhetorical situation. What structures support the authority of the speaker for a particular audience? How thoroughly does the speaker understand the audience? How does she or he use this knowledge to construct a persuasive argument? How does the audience understand its own interests in the outcome of the argument? How is this self-understanding altered by the way in which the argument is presented?

For example, the role of suffering in Christology has traditionally been controlled by (among other things) a notion of divine impassibility. A critical rhetorical method will ask: Why was this notion persuasive? Whose interests were served by its general acceptance? What arguments were used by theologians who sought to reassert a notion of divine suffering? Whose interests were served by this counterargument? To mention a specific instance: Does Moltmann's emphasis on "the crucified God" stand in the service of, or in isolation from, those who suffer in the present? Or does his position even underwrite a certain natural order to relationships of dominance and oppression?[29]

The third aspect of rhetorical analysis is *human liberation*. The affirmation of this aspect requires a particular political commitment; but as I suggested in chapter 2, such commitment is an important part of both rhetoric and theology. Thus, a rhetorical approach to doctrine should attempt to reveal concrete political interests, unmasking those which support the structures of human subjugation. It should also trace the effective-history of the arguments that undergird a particular doctrinal position, thus identifying its relationship to structures of power and influence. Of course, the mere identification of unjust power relationships in no way guarantees their demise; a method cannot single-handedly bring about human liberation. Still, by putting ethical and political assumptions in the forefront, rhetorical analysis can play a liberative role. For example, it can help indicate when a theologian, though actually allied against the interests of a marginalized people, nevertheless claims to speak on their behalf.

Such a claim is made, for example, by Michael Novak, much of whose work advocates a theological doctrine of democratic capitalism as the best way to help the poor. Novak's arguments are quite vulnerable to critique on more traditional grounds, e.g., his tendency to abstraction and over-generalization.[30] But a rhetorical critique would not stop here; it would identify the structural alignments that lead some people to find Novak's argument persuasive. Exemplary in this respect is the approach of Lee Cormie who, in a review of Novak's *Will it Liberate?* notes that

> the tone of this book is one of respectful, scholarly dialogue about complicated issues. But it must also be noted that the forces Novak identifies with and supports, such as large corporations and the United States government in its policies in Latin America, are militantly committed to snuffing out dialogue over political and economic alternatives, to silencing the critics of capitalist development, to reducing alternatives to the single option of the "free market" and its frequent servant, the military government, which relies on policies of terror, disappearances, torture, and murder to maintain "peace and order."[31]

Cormie's method of analysis here can be called rhetorical insofar as it identifies the specific interests that define a writer's political and ethical authority. A full-fledged rhetorical analysis of Novak's work would go still further—for example, identifying the economic and political interests of Novak's constructed audience (i.e., first-world Christians) and comparing these to the interests of the Latin American poor.

Again, such analysis cannot ensure progress in the cause of human liberation. But it can clarify arguments about liberation by describing the relationship between an author's doctrinal approach and its practical consequences. A rhetorical method assumes that theories are already embodied in concrete practices; for example, a theoretical appeal for more capitalism in Latin America is not just a theory but grows from the practices in which the author and the audience are already intimately involved. This analysis helps reveal the interests that underlie the persuasive appeal of discourse—which, in turn, helps to predict how power would be redistributed if a particular theory were implemented in practice.

These three aspects of rhetorical analysis—deconstruction, critique, and liberation—point to some of the practical consequences of understanding doctrine as persuasive argument. This approach would provide a concrete means of implementing the best theoretical insights of a number of recent commentators on the postmodern condition. Theologians have often sought to employ the work of literary critics, sociologists, and philosophers; but rarely are these insights developed as a coherent method. (While theology should maintain a certain playful randomness, too sweeping an eclecticism has a tendency "to reduce great thinkers to characters in a farce, their ideas to slogans.")[32] A rhetorical method can provide a means of integrating, in a manner attentive to concrete *praxis*, a wide variety of recent insights in literary analysis, critical theory, and political hermeneutics.

These insights will take on greater significance as I turn now to a more self-consciously hermeneutical element of the theological task: biblical exegesis. In examining how theologians use the Bible, we will discover that the range of rhetoric in theology is not limited to its application to doctrinal reformulation alone.

BIBLICAL EXEGESIS AS
PERSUASIVE ARGUMENT

Biblical interpretation is a central task of Christian theology.[33] Unfortunately, theologians have too often delegated the interpretive task to others, assuming that biblical scholars can determine "what the text means," so that theologians may then apply it in doctrinal and ethical reflection. This division of labor, however, leads to some unfortunate results. Separating exegesis from theology suggests that the essence of Scripture somehow resides among the highly codified marks on a page of text. This would assume that technical experts could be assigned the task of breaking the code, and that their results could be appropriated by those who need the encoded information.[34]

Needless to say, this hermeneutical model leaves much to be desired. It tends to ignore—too easily—the role of the reader in determining the meaning of a text. This model also suggests that textual meanings can be transferred, like so much iron ore, from the biblical scholar's mine to the theologian's smelting factory. Willingly or unwillingly, theologians also interpret the Bible: even by appropriating the work of one particular biblical scholar instead of another, a theologian makes concrete hermeneutical choices.[35]

I want to suggest that biblical exegesis can best be understood as persuasive argument. Regardless of the method being used, theologians who turn to the text of Scripture do so in order to make a particular argument; and these arguments arise not from some inherent structure of the text, but from the commitments—religious, ethical, political, cultural—with which a particular theologian approaches the exegetical task.

The methodological problems associated with biblical exegesis can be clarified only after tracing their pre-history through three stages: the development of traditional modes of biblical interpretation, the scrutiny of such modes by historical criticism, and the subsequent critique of historical criticism in contemporary hermeneutics. My own alternative position will indicate why exegesis should instead be understood as persuasive argument—a view that will be supported by examining the wide range of argumentative contexts in which one particular New Testament text has been employed.

THE VARIETIES OF BIBLICAL EXEGESIS[36]

Traditionally, the "fourfold sense of Scripture" played an important role in biblical exegesis. However, the weight given to the various senses has varied greatly. The four senses—literal, allegorical, tropological, and anagogical—are often summed up in a simple Latin rhyme, usually attributed to Nicholas of Lyra:

> Littera gesta docet
> Quid credas allegoria
> Moralis quid agas
> Quo tendas anagogia.

This verse reminds us that the literal sense could describe "what happened" but could not exhaust the Bible's meaning. The text also helped Christians understand what they believed, what they should do, and where they were headed.

The fourfold sense has often been accused—unjustly, in my view—of leading commentators to use Scripture in wildly arbitrary ways. Prescinding from the difficulty of establishing criteria for determining "wild arbitrariness," we should note that a quite opposite tendency was more often in evidence. As David Steinmetz has pointed out, far from letting "their exegetical imaginations run amok," medieval commentators actually exercised considerable restraint in their investigation of a text.[37] This restraint was due in part to the structural boundaries of the fourfold sense, which limited interpretations to the allegorical, moral, and anagogical senses of Scripture, all of which were understood to rise out of the primary sense, the literal.[38] Yet the literal meaning was not an exclusive meaning, especially in the realm of theological application.

> Medieval theologians defended the proposition, so alien to modern biblical studies, that the meaning of Scripture in the mind of the prophet who first uttered it is only one of its possible meanings and may not, in certain circumstances, even be its primary or most important meaning.[39]

The medieval tradition is thus strangely contemporary; it dovetails nicely with recent discussions of the intentional fallacy.[40] Traditional commentators admitted that they were less concerned about what an author intended than about how the text could be applied to particular circumstances.

The same interpretive framework informs the exegesis of the Reformation. Despite its occasional claims to novelty, the Reformation emphasis on *sola scriptura* does not denote a major methodological shift in exegesis. If Luther's interpretations (or Calvin's, or even Zwingli's) differed considerably from those of Thomas and Augustine, the difference was due primarily to the contexts in which they interpreted the Bible, rather than to a change in method. Luther, for example, is just as capable as his predecessors of using Scripture to make moral, doctrinal, or teleological arguments.[41]

A much more significant turn in the history of exegetical method resulted from the rise of historical consciousness during the Enlightenment. This shift encouraged historical criticism of the biblical text—a method that sought to recover, as accurately as possible, the actual historical events to which the Bible bears witness. On this view, the interpreter is concerned not with what the text says, but with the events that lie behind the text—the events as they might have been experienced by eye-witnesses.

Historical criticism marks a true watershed in the history of exegetical method, for it advocates a shift from polysemy to univocity. In place of the fourfold sense of Scripture, the search for a single meaning dominates historical criticism. This very desire for univocity prompted Schleiermacher to turn to authorial intention as an ultimate criterion of meaning.[42] The same motivation led Benjamin Jowett to declare that "Scripture has one meaning—the meaning which it had to the mind of the prophet or evangelist who first uttered or wrote, to the hearers or readers who first received it."[43] (Jowett's turn of phrase already suggests a subtle tension between the *writer's* meaning and that of the *reader*, this will concern us again shortly.)

In some hermeneutical quarters, Jowett's dictum retains an unquestioned positive status. For instance, Dennis Nineham claims that twentieth-century readers are bound by the same hermeneutical principle that motivated Jowett a century ago. He believes that these modern readers "will seek, with the aid of all the historical and critical enlightenment they can get, to grasp the meaning of the Gospel considered as a spiritual message *addressed to the church for which it was originally written*, and only then will they expect to be able to find in it a spiritual message for the Church of today."[44] Like many modern commentators on the Bible, Nineham believes that we understand the text only if we can somehow get into the author's mind, and see the picture as the author (and/or the original audience) would have seen it. On this view, historical criticism becomes closely associated with the skeptical approach to history that informed both the rationalism of Descartes and the empiricism of Hume. Because the biblical authors were seeking converts to the faith rather than historical veracity, their witness could not be taken at face value. Historical criticism instead advocated a critical, even suspicious, scrutiny of the text—attempting to determine *wie es eigentlich gewesen ist.*[45]

Throughout the early part of this century, the historical-critical method dominated the study of the Bible. Despite the protestations of neo-orthodox critics, and despite the intermittent flourishing of the biblical theology movement, the books of the Bible were generally understood as historical documents. As such, argued the historical critics, they should be sifted, sorted, and categorized. More recently, the historical-critical approach has come under fire.[46] Critics have argued that while historical criticism ostensibly operated without presuppositions, it actually depended very heavily on the particular philosophical framework of Enlightenment rationalism and empiricism. That very framework is being questioned—not only in theology, but also in philosophy, literary criticism, political science, and even the natural sciences.

The critique of historical criticism has generated a number of very different methods of approaching the biblical text. Among these are literary criticism of all types, including structuralist and deconstructionist techniques; appeals to the *sensus plenior* of Scripture; and studies that operate within the givenness of the biblical canon (sometimes called canonical criticism). These widely varying exegetical techniques find some common ground in their assertion that the Bible is more than history—i.e., that *history* is an insufficient category to describe its impact.

The Bible is full of history; religious history, literary history, cultural history, world history, and human history of every sort. A picture full of animation and color is unrolled before all who approach the Bible with open eyes. But the pleasure is short-lived: the picture, on closer inspection, proves quite incomprehensible and flat, if it is meant only for history. The man who is looking for history or for stories will be glad after a little to turn from the Bible to the morning paper or to other books. . . . The Bible meets the lover of history with silences quite unparalleled.[47]

That is, the Bible is not a history book if *history* is understood in the Enlightenment sense—a chronicle of what actually happened, a documentation of the *res gestae*. As an alternative to the historical-critical hermeneutics of suspicion, other approaches are commonly grouped together and designated as a *hermeneutics of consent*.[48]

Of course, this approach has come under fire as well. Historians charge that it opens the door not only to subjectivism but also to relativism; it allows interpreters to manipulate the text in any way they see fit.[49] In an extreme form, it would underwrite a rampant authoritarianism, that very reign of tyranny over which the Enlightenment had hoped to triumph. Armed with these arguments, historical critics have continued to do battle against those advocating an approach based on consent, with no cessation of hostilities in sight.

EXEGESIS AS PERSUASIVE DISCOURSE

I want to argue that the juxtaposition of these two approaches to exegesis is misleading at best. Their apparent opposition is merely one more manifestation of the philosophical oppositions that plague us: scientism versus emotivism, objectivism versus subjectivism, empiricism versus idealism. As an alternative to the similar dualism of suspicion versus consent, I want to suggest that biblical exegesis is simply a form of persuasive argument.

The argumentative use of the Bible in Christian theology has been explored at some length by David Kelsey.[50] Following the work of Stephen Toulmin, Kelsey suggests that the use of Scripture often bears an "argumentative" structure, which he exemplifies through the use of Toulmin's model of the layout of arguments.[51]

Kelsey's use of this model helps to highlight the syntactical nature of the interpretive task. While neither he nor Toulmin employ the term *syntax*, the role of the so-called Toulmin model in argument is precisely the role of syntax in language: it demonstrates how constituent parts are connected to one another and how they depend on one another. As suggested at the end of chapter 4, exegetical method could be considered one example of the syntax of theology, in that it describes how the various elements of a theologian's vocabulary can be connected and structured in ways that allow communication to occur.

Unfortunately, however, Kelsey's approach fails to account for the full range of syntax, in the same way that Lindbeck's work operates with a too-limited notion of grammar. Specifically, Kelsey seems to restrict argument to the logical categories that were criticized in chapter 4. By focusing narrowly on Toulmin's model and by appropriating it in a quasi-logical way, Kelsey fails to make any significant progress toward widening the range of argumentation.

I would want to suggest that the syntactical elements of Christian theology—of which exegesis is but one example—depend much more on context, and on the specific commitments of theologian and audience, than Kelsey's approach acknowledges. In essence, Kelsey does not recognize that arguments about the use of Scripture are not analytic deductions, but rhetorical (and thus persuasive) arguments. Arguments about exegesis depend on the particular speaker and audience, and on the whole range of formal and informal inference. Only by emphasizing the persuasive character of exegesis can we begin to forge a path through the disabling—and potentially endless—methodological oppositions in the history of biblical interpretation.

When theologians interpret the Bible, they engage in a rhetorical activity. They are faced with a particular audience, and they attempt to persuade that audience of the significance of a text for the argument at hand. This process of persuasion does not depend on inherent structures in the text, but on the interpreter's commitments, the audience's willingness to listen, and the skill with which the arguments are constructed.

Of course, this process does not imply a complete relativizing of textual meaning, for any completely outrageous interpretation will find few adherents. For example, I may choose to argue that John 11:35 ("Jesus wept") actually means that Jesus smiled and laughed, and then did a little jig. At this point, my argument would not attract much of an audience; after all, anyone can make silly assertions. But what if I then continued my argument along quite sophisticated lines? Suppose, for example, that I pointed out that the Greek word for "wept" in this passage, *dakruō*, is unique in the New Testament (which, in fact, it is; all other instances of the verb "to weep" are some form of the verb *klaiō*). At this point, an audience might begin to gather—an audience which included those who found my knowledge of Greek to be a sign of erudition, as well as those who were simply fond of novel interpretations. I might then argue that parallel instances of the verb *dakruō* in Philo of Alexandria and Josephus suggest a different sense; there, *dakruō* means only to *pretend* to weep, while actually experiencing great joy. Now I might have quite a large audience, due to the originality of my insight. However, if I were to make this last argument, I would, of course, be relying on sheer fabrication. I would soon be indicted by every classics scholar in the country, convicted of impudence, and sentenced to retranslate the entire *Loeb Classical Library*.

Arguments about interpretation rely heavily on their context; and this contextualization eliminates the possibility of the complete relativism so widely feared by textual realists. In fact, my wildly arbitrary reading of John 11:35 depended on a number of assumptions about the interpretive community of which my own constructed audience is a part: assumptions about knowledge of Greek, about the nature of commentaries on the Greek text of the New Testament, and about Josephus and Philo. As Stanley Fish has suggested, we all depend on the existence of such interpretive communities in order for interpretation (and debates about interpretation) to occur at all.[52]

On this view, historical criticism is but one attempt among many to persuade an audience to adopt a particular reading of a text. It happens to have been a phenomenally successful one, if success be measured by the publication of new biblical commentaries during the twentieth century. Historical criticism relies on a number of rhetorical strategies, a few of which deserve our attention here.

First, historical criticism appeals to the (implicitly) superior status of scientific language. By concentrating on philological arguments, source material, and categories of classification, historical criticism appeals to the discourses of rationalism and empiricism so popular in the period from Darwin to Einstein and beyond. Consider, once again, the language of Benjamin Jowett:

> It may be laid down that Scripture has one meaning—the meaning which it had to the mind of the prophet or evangelist who first uttered or wrote, to the hearers or readers who first received it. Another view may be easier or more familiar to us, seeming to receive a light and interest from the circumstances of our own age. But such accommodation of the text must be laid aside by the interpreter, whose business is to place himself as nearly as possible in the position of the sacred writer.[53]

Gently rebuking the reader who would choose the "easier" or "more familiar" route, Jowett advocates a more rigorous and businesslike (one senses that he almost wants to say: "manly"!) method of historical analysis. He casts aspersions on any temptation to "accommodation," which only "seems" to offer "light and interest." Finally, Jowett concludes by sanctifying the method of historical science, praising the "sacred" writer. That writer's intentions must be respected, if the interpreter is correctly going about his "business." Jowett's rhetorical *coup* has been echoed for a century; we are inundated with appeals to intellectual honesty, rigorous methods of interpretation, and the willingness to submit all interpretations to testing.

A second appeal employed by historical criticism is its call to marshall a last line of defense against tyranny and authoritarianism. This appeal is exemplified in a commonly used theological textbook:

> We are able to acknowledge that scriptural authority, while it may be in some sense indispensable to Christian theology, also has a dark underside in its potentiality for obscurantism, resistance to science, authoritarianism, and "book religion"—veneration of the "the book" [*sic*] as a holy object. . . . We seem to be passing through a new wave of critical consciousness in which all authorities are

being questioned, especially those associated with the dominant Western cultural and religious tradition.[54]

This argument gains much of its persuasiveness by appearing on the first page of the chapter on "Scripture and Tradition" in a book that is very widely used in the classroom.[55] The book's argumentative appeals are clear; for example, the authors are opposed to "darkness" (apparently, they have no taste for "the dark night of the soul"). They are also opposed to "veneration of the book"; they are in favor of "science." They exclude from their audience those who, for example, believe that the Bible should be venerated as a holy object, thereby excluding those Christians for whom the Bible has traditionally been an object of veneration.

> In the Byzantine liturgy, the "lesser entrance" with the book of the gospel for reading is made with a dignity second only to the "greater entrance" with the bread and wine prepared for the eucharist. In the Roman Catholic mass, the gospel may be censed and kissed at its reading. In the Reformed tradition, the bringing of the Bible into the church may constitute the ceremonial beginning of the service, though it is also a common custom to leave an open Bible on the Lord's table at all times. In all churches, the scriptures are read with solemnity.[56]

Despite the historical-critical effort to vilify any veneration of the Bible as a holy book, it retains a sacred character through a variety of Christian practices.

Finally, historical criticism appeals to the need to save the biblical text from irrelevance. By claiming that the Bible is meaningless to the modern reader, historical critics create a market for themselves as expert interpreters of an otherwise useless text. While this argument has been enormously successful among editors and publishers, its larger impact on Christian biblical interpretation is now being called into serious question. As Janet Soskice has observed,

> If it is true that Biblical imagery is lifeless to modern man (and it is not obvious that this is so), this is more likely to be the legacy of historical criticism, of the search for the historical Jesus, and of attempts

made by Christians both liberal and conservative to salvage his exact words and acts from the dross of allusion and interpretation with which the gospel writers surrounded them. It is the legacy of a literalism which equates religious truth with historical facts, whatever these might be.[57]

The privileging of these "historical facts" is inherent in the rhetorical strategy of historical-critical approaches to the Bible.

In order to summarize the difference between historical criticism and more traditional uses of the Bible, I want to return to Mikhail Bakhtin's distinction between polyphonic and mono-logic discourse. Traditional biblical exegesis was polyphonic, to the extent that it encouraged its readers and auditors to hear multiple voices in the biblical text. This multiplicity has been viewed by many modern commentators as inconsistent and chaotic—an indictment strikingly similar to one leveled against the work of Dostoevsky. But as Bakhtin notes, the chaos is only apparent; on closer inspection, one can "begin to understand the profound organic cohesion, consistency and wholeness of Dostoevsky's poetics."[58] A similar degree of underlying cohesion and organic wholeness can be found in traditional biblical interpretation and in its postmodern revival.

On the other hand, most forms of historical criticism (and, in fact, some forms of a consent-oriented hermeneutic as well) are typically monologic. Like the monologic literature that Bakhtin castigated, monologic forms of biblical interpretation have only two poles of decision.

In the monologic world, *tertium non datur:* a thought is either affirmed or repudiated; otherwise it simply ceases to be a fully valid thought. An unaffirmed thought, if it is to enter into the artis-tic structure, must be deprived in general of its power to mean, must become a psychical fact. . . . Ideological monologism found its clearest and theoretically most precise expression in idealistic philosophy. The monistic principle, that is, the affirmation of the unity of *existence*, is, in idealism, transformed into the unity of the *consciousness*.[59]

Historical criticism privileges this "unity of the consciousness" by seeking the definitive meaning of a biblical text.

My lengthy diatribe against historical criticism is not without its own rhetorical purpose. I believe that, as long as we understand biblical exegesis to be defined by a single, monologic method, we shall fail to recognize the function of exegesis as persuasive argument. Instead, we shall wrongly assume that historical criticism is some form of apodictic demonstration—like a geometry proof. But once we understand exegesis as characterized by multiplicity and polyphony, we can much more easily discern its persuasive aspects.

ARGUMENTATIVE EXEGESIS IN PRACTICE

The wide variety of ways in which biblical interpretation has been employed as persuasive argument can be demonstrated by examining the exegetical history of a single verse of Scripture. Consider the following text:

> Foxes have holes, and birds of the air have nests; but the Son of Man has nowhere to lay his head. (Matt. 8:20 = Luke 9:58)

This passage has been of considerable interest, whether the commentator was searching for the single meaning of the text, or for a multiplicity of applications. This investigation should help us establish how the text has been used—that is, the history of its effects.[60]

As I selectively canvassed the literature on this text, I expected to find the verse employed in only two contexts: a pastoral one, mostly by ancient commentators; and a historical one, mostly by moderns. Some such pattern was faintly discernible; but as my research continued, greater diversity became the norm. Indeed, I discovered at least nine different arguments that this text had been called upon to support. The diversity of the arguments reminds us of the specificity of the rhetorical situations in which they have been used.

Pastoral concern

A number of commentators use the passage as an opportunity to denounce the anxieties that arise out of worldliness and to offer consolation in a time of trial. Jerome, for example, uses it to remind his audience that Christ, too, faced many difficulties and bore them well: "The foxes have holes, and the birds of the air nests, but the Son of Man has nowhere to lay his head—that you might not be sorrowful when in straitened circumstances."[61] Similarly, Chrysostom counsels against worry about the future; "nothing so pains the soul," he says, "as carefulness and anxiety."[62] He couples Matt. 8:20 with other sayings on this theme, including Matt. 6:34 ("Do not worry about tomorrow") and Matt. 10:9–10 ("Take no gold, or silver, or copper in your belts, no bag for your journey"). Likewise, Cyprian includes these same verses—and many others—under a general heading that reads: "That he who has attained to trust, having put off the former man, ought to regard only celestial and spiritual things, and to give no heed to the world which he has already renounced."[63]

Humility and Discipleship

The same passage is also used to denounce those who seek glory in this world and those who are puffed up with pride. Again, Jerome provides a typical instance. In his letter to the monk Heliodorus, he enjoins a life of discipline:

> The Son of Man has nowhere to lay his head, and do you measure out wide porticoes and buildings of great extent? Do you, a joint heir with Christ, expect an inheritance in this world? Translate the word "monk": that's your proper title. What are you, a "Solitary," doing in a crowd?[64]

This approach is also a favorite of Augustine's, who counsels his readers not to use their status as disciples in order to seek their own glorification. Augustine notices the context of this saying; Jesus is answering a would-be disciple. Augustine makes use of the words *foxes* and *birds*, subtly denouncing the person who claims to intend to follow Jesus: "in your heart foxes have holes, you are full of guile; in your heart birds of the air have nests, you are too high-flown [*elatus te*]. Being full of guile and self-elation as you are, you shall not follow me. How can a guileful man follow simplicity?"[65] Chrysostom picks up the same themes, suggesting that this would-be follower was

much like others of little faith: like those who did not believe
John the Baptist because he "did no sign," like the Corinthians
who were severed from one another, and like the Romans who
were carried away with pride. "Each of these, one aiming at the
wealth, another at the glory, which the miracles bring, fell away
and perished. But care of practice, and love of virtue, so far from
generating such a desire, even takes it away when it exists."[66]

Nor is this theme restricted to ancient commentators. Cox
(1952) entitles this whole section of Matthew's gospel "The Cost
of Discipleship."[67] Similarly, Kirk and Obach (1978) suggest that
"to follow Jesus means both renunciation as well as the acceptance of certain joy or happiness in living that no possessions
can give."[68] And Daniel Patte's structuralist commentary points
out that "following Jesus means sharing his condition."[69]

Certainly, not all commentators use this passages to exhort
or reprove. Indeed, the more common usage is a christological
one; writers believe that this verse gives us added insight into
the person and nature of Jesus Christ. However, the christological arguments that they offer vary widely, as the next several
uses of this text will demonstrate.

The origins of "Son of Man"

This is the first occurrence of the phrase *Son of Man* in the gospel of Matthew. As a result, most modern commentaries take this
opportunity to describe, sometimes in great detail, the possible
Aramaic origins of this term. Was it used as a self-reference? As a
messianic title? Some commentators venture definitive answers
to these questions, while others remain cautious. In a number of
modern commentaries, this is practically the only comment on
the verse.[70]

The humanity of Christ

In other commentaries, the phrase *Son of Man* makes the
passage useful for emphasizing Jesus' humanity. Augustine
says that Jesus often applies this title to himself, "thereby
commending to our notice what in his compassion he has con-
descended to be on our behalf."[71] The humanity of Jesus is also

taken up by Luther, who often reminds his audience how difficult it is to accept a savior who is all-too-human:

> His majesty is concealed in humanity. He does not appear on the scene amid lightning and thunder and in the company of angels, but as the Son of a poor virgin . . . we say: "Bah, the man who does not even have a place to lay his head is supposed to be the Messiah!"[72]

The same theme is explored by Karl Barth. Barth cites the present text alongside Philippians 2, the Lucan infancy narratives, the language of *flesh* in John's gospel, and the Passion narratives. All these passages, Barth says, must remind us of the genuine humanity of Christ. He sums up this exegetical excursus with the following admonition:

> Exegetes old and new have been right in their references and comments when they have seen this and tried to consider the deity of Jesus Christ in the light of it. On the other hand, it has always led and always does lead to confusion where this more precise understanding of the human being of God and the divine being of the man Jesus is disregarded or weakened or not taken as the starting-point for all further discussion.[73]

Thus, Barth uses the passage (and others like it) to argue that Jesus Christ must be understood to be human as well as divine.

The weakness and humility of Christ

The verse is also used as the basis for a more specific christological argument—namely, that Jesus was not merely a human being, but one who lived a humble and lowly life. In one of his many homiletical exhortations on the theme, John Chrysostom reminds his flock that Jesus "needs nothing of the human wares; . . . For this cause he does not choose for himself so much as a house; for 'the Son of Man,' he says, 'has nowhere to lay his head.'"[74] Similarly, Karl Barth couples the text with Matt. 11:29 ("I am gentle and lowly in heart") and, again, with the infancy and Passion narratives, in order to stress Jesus' role as servant—even in the midst of his kingship.

The royal man shares as such the strange destiny which falls on God in His people and the world—to be the one who is ignored and forgotten and despised and discounted by men. . . . His kingdom has neither the pomp nor the power, the extent nor the continuance, of even the smallest of the human kingdoms which all the same it overshadows and questions.[75]

Barth provides an excellent example of how a text that some might find innocuous can be appropriated in rhetorically powerful ways.

The poverty of Jesus

Again, the christological argument becomes more precise. Jesus was not only a humble human being; he was also poor in a very material sense. For Tertullian, Matt. 8:20 provides a way of emphasizing the poverty, humility, and obscurity of Jesus. The text is marshaled, along with others, as an argument against ostentatious dress and ornamentation.[76] The same usage can be found in John Chrysostom, who stresses Christ's earthly poverty. (In fact, Chrysostom's opposition to the extravagance of Empress Eudoxia led to his own exile—a good example of persuasion by means of *ēthos!*) His sermons on Lazarus and the Rich Man provide one of early Christianity's most impassioned pleas for earthly poverty.[77] He argues that Matt. 8:20 should remind us that Jesus "had neither table nor dwelling nor anything else of that kind: not because He was at a loss to obtain them, but because he was instructing people to go in that path."[78]

Christ's poverty is also emphasized by Thomas Aquinas, for whom the point of disputation is "Whether Christ should have led a life of poverty in this world."[79] One might argue that Christ should have "embraced the most eligible form of life"[80]—which, for those predisposed to accept Aristotle's understanding of the virtues, would be a life of moderation, not a life of extreme poverty (or of extreme wealth). Thomas begins the *sed contra* of the question with a quotation of Matt. 8:20 and then continues by quoting Jerome: "Why would you follow me for the sake of riches and worldly gain; since I am so poor that I have not even a small dwelling-place, and I am sheltered by a roof that is not my own?"[81] Thomas offers a number of reasons for Christ's worldly poverty, most of which center on his prophetic office. After all, had Christ's apostles been wealthy, "they would have seemed to preach for profit, not for the salvation of humanity."[82]

Similarly, John Calvin uses Matt. 8:20 both to comment on Jesus' poverty and to enjoin others to discipleship. Calvin's treatment of the text provides a good example of an argument by means of *pathos*; he recognizes that his Genevan audience will be surprised by the inhospitality that this passage seems to imply:

> God's Son reveals the conditions of His own life, while He lived on earth, and further prescribes for all His disciples the pattern of living by which they should learn. It is only surprising that Christ says He has no foot of earth on which to lay His head, while He had many godly and kindly men, who would readily have given Him hospitality. But note that this was said as a warning that the scribe should not look for an ample and wealthy reward, as from a master of great means, since the master himself lived a precarious existence in other people's homes.[83]

The Passion

The same passage became, for Martin Luther, an argument for the connection between Jesus' earthly poverty and his eventual crucifixion. In fact, Luther employed the text in a variety of ways, showing little concern as to whether his argument was somehow contained in the text. Instead, he saw the passage as argument for the *theologia crucis.*

> But what are the garments of Christ, who "had not where to lay His head"? In the whole earth He did not have a single foot of space which he could call His own, or on which He might die, but He died high in the air. So it is an adornment different from that of the world. As if with most beautiful gold, the head of Christians is adorned with the crown of faith and with hope, love, patience, and other gifts of the Holy Spirit.[84]

When he was crucified, Jesus truly had "no place to lay his head." This connection fascinates Luther; he returns to it frequently. It provides him with a means of contrasting Christ's poverty with the wealth of nations:

> In his own kingdom he was so miserable and poor that he had no place where he could lay his head. No crown, royal adornment, or pomp could be seen about him—nothing but cross, nails, and blood. There He hung, unable to touch either heaven or earth and unable to stand up on His feet.[85]

As his career progressed, Luther became increasingly specific about just who was at fault in the failure of Christians to follow Christ's example of poverty.

> We do not know of a single city today that provides for its preachers. . . . While [Christ] lived on earth, He had nowhere to lay His head. . . . No, our preachers are being provided for from donations given to the pope in exchange for the abominations of suppressing the Gospel, teaching human traditions, and establishing wicked forms of worship.[86]

Luther thus found a number of different argumentative uses for this passage; it served both as a general pointer to the cross of Christ, and as an argument against the practices of the Roman church. Luther did not seem concerned that it could be employed in such a wide variety of ways.

Possible contradictions

Several commentators make no attempt to develop the passage as an ethical or christological argument, instead dwelling on the degree to which the passage seems to conflict with other passages in the gospel. Why, for example, does Jesus speak of having no place to lay his head? Georges Gander claims that

> we should interpret the expression "nowhere to lay his head" in a figurative sense. The Lord cannot have meant it in the strict sense of "having no home." For we know, according to the evangelist himself, that the Master of the Twelve did indeed have a legal domicile—his own lodging or room. It was at Capernaum.[87]

Similarly, R. T. France argues that, at the very least, Jesus' homelessness must have been "a matter of choice, not of necessity."

He even makes the unusual claim that "Jesus' family was probably a comfortable, if not affluent, 'middle-class' one."[88]

A proverb in search of a source

Finally, a large number of modern commentaries attempt to locate a source for this saying, and especially for the use of *foxes* and *birds*. John Fenton argues that the birds may refer to gentiles and foxes to Herod.[89] Green, on the other hand, is more general, arguing that the text "has a proverbial ring, though no parallel to it has been discovered. Possibly a saying first spoken of hunted humankind in general was obliquely and ironically applied to Jesus himself."[90] Finally, some commentaries find a possible parallel in Plutarch.[91]

The wide variety of interpretations of this verse helps to demonstrate that exegetes have not sought simply to *find* meaning in a text. Instead, commentators have used the text as a basis for argument; and their arguments have been addressed to a wide range of differing contexts. Some commentators urge the audience to adopt a particular ethical or doctrinal position; others attempt to convince the audience to investigate the relationships among various parts of the biblical text. Still other writers use the text as a way of discussing the phrase *Son of Man*; and this discussion may include anything from comments on semitic etymology to the humanity of Christ. In each instance, the precise form of the argument is controlled by its genre, its constructed audience, and the character of the writer—rather than by any objective reference to "the text itself."

This experiment could be applied, *mutatis mutandis*, to almost any text from the Bible. We would discover, for each passage, that commentators have derived from it a great variety of meanings—and have employed it in an almost infinite array of arguments. While this widely varying usage might offend our modern sensibilities, it did not seem to have caused much anxiety among our predecessors. The commentators cited in this section all knew that their own perspective on a text might well differ from the positions of other commentators and, indeed, even from a view that they themselves had held at another time or place. Undoubtedly, each theologian believed in the appropriateness and accuracy of a particular interpretation; but each commentator also knew that interpretations can change under changing circumstances. Consequently, these exegetes wisely avoided coercing their audiences by claiming the achievement of some objective insight into *the* meaning of the text. Instead, the interpreters sought to persuade their listeners that a particular use of the text was appropriate in a particular context— supplementing these interpretations with other appeals and making use of those means of persuasion that we have called *pathos*, *ēthos*, and *logos*.

RHETORICAL HISTORY AND CHRISTIAN THEOLOGY

The rhetorical nature of both doctrinal formulation and biblical exegesis suggests that many commonly held assumptions about Christian theology need to be reconsidered. Such a reformulation of the theological task will require that the history of theological disputes be reexamined, this time with attention to contextual issues which traditional histories have often failed to make salient. This process may help us better understand the nature of arguments and may thereby contribute to the ongoing challenge of clarifying theological discourse.

After a brief methodological skirmish, I offer here an extended example of a specific theological argument—the exegetical and doctrinal controversy surrounding Martin Luther's understanding of the Eucharist. My account will emphasize the evolution of Luther's views during the course of a highly contextualized argument. This analysis will provide some interesting perspectives—both on the particular theological issues with which Luther wrestled, and on theological method in general.

WRITING RHETORICAL HISTORIES

In examining the history of discursive theological practices, we need to attend more carefully both to the general context in which these practices occur and to the nondiscursive practices that accompany them. The historian should raise questions about the ecclesiological, cultural, and political commitments of the writer or speaker; about the assumptions and commitments of the audience; and about the structure and impact of the arguments. Such questions will not always lend themselves to a final answer. Instead, they will raise issues about—rather than attempting a complete description of—the circumstances in which a particular argument was deployed. Nevertheless, the essential incompleteness of such investigations should not be considered a liability; the goal of historical theology should not be to present *the history of doctrine* or *the history of exegesis* in the traditional sense of those terms. In fact, such conventional histories have often obscured the most important features of theological disputes.[92]

Specifically, traditional approaches to the history of doctrine or exegesis have too often treated their constitutive discursive events as discrete monads. For example, a doctrine is stated, perhaps by quoting it from the *Enchiridion Symbolorum*, and then is analyzed—in an attempt to discover what the doctrine means. This approach does not address the circumstances in which the doctrine was promulgated, its constructed audience, and the interaction of its constituent arguments—a failure that obscures the relationship of theological discourse to the political, economic, and cultural life of the Church and the world.

Similar obfuscations have been noted within the discipline of literary criticism. For example, the traditional approach to the history of interpretation typically focuses on isolated texts and abstract ideas. Commenting on histories of literary study in the United States, Steven Mailloux notes that "traditional histories tended to minimize the importance of social, political, and economic factors in the development of American literary study; the focus was almost exclusively on abstract intellectual history."[93] Mailloux seeks to correct this tendency by writing the history of literary criticism as *rhetorical history*.

The notion of a rhetorical history is derived from the work of twentieth-century communication theorists, who usually describe it as the investigation of historical movements through rhetorical categories.[94] When appropriated in the field of literary criticism, rhetorical history becomes a way of disclosing the assumptions, strategies, and power relationships that operate within particular approaches to the task of interpretation. As Mailloux understands it, rhetorical history can provide a way through the impasse between (what he calls) "textual realism" and "readerly idealism." He asks literary theorists to

> provide histories of how particular theoretical and critical discourses have evolved. Why? Because acts of persuasion always take place against an ever-changing background of shared and disputed assumptions, questions, assertions, and so forth. Any full rhetorical analysis of interpretation must therefore describe this tradition of discursive practices in which acts of interpretive persuasion are embedded.[95]

In order to understand how a specific discursive practice persuaded an audience (or failed to do so), we need to examine the context in which it took place.

The writing of rhetorical histories will also be of importance to Christian theology. Such histories can attend to the argumentative nature of theology and thereby help theologians to begin to acknowledge their own work as persuasive argument. Thus, in the remainder of this section, I want to make an initial attempt to write Church history as rhetorical history. Needless to say, I cannot begin to offer the sort of detailed, painstaking analysis of discursive practice recently offered by writers such as Pierre Bourdieu, Michel Foucault, and Mailloux himself.[96] Nevertheless, in my description of Martin Luther's argumentative strategies, I hope to exemplify the primary purpose of rhetorical history: the analysis of the concrete situation in which arguments are developed and deployed.

LUTHER'S ARGUMENTATIVE STRATEGIES

Traditional histories of Luther's controversial theology tend to make broad claims about his commitment to a particular logical or hermeneutical principle. For example, Heinrich Bornkamm believes that Luther is the first great objective historian—a man who "freed himself from earlier attempts to find a superhistory or metahistory behind the actual events, and, through his exegesis, strove to appreciate only that which actually happened."[97]

But according to other commentators, Luther is the opposite of a modern historian. Instead, he is a precursor of New Criticism—attending only to the text itself. This is the view of Mark Ellingsen, who claims that, according to Luther, "there is no critical judgement about Scripture's subject matter to be made apart from the grammatical meaning. One's use of or reaction to a text has no effect on the text's meaning. Thus a text means what it says."[98] So for Ellingsen, at least some aspects of Luther's theological method are marked by their literary-critical character.

These two verdicts on Luther differ markedly, but they share a very important assumption: that Luther's theological method can be abstracted from particular argumentative contexts and be assigned a nonrhetorical classification. Bornkamm and Ellingsen share a commitment to write Church history in a way that quickly glosses over the subtleties of Luther's own commitments, audiences, and argumentative strategies. These contextual features become much more salient when Luther is studied as a rhetorician. By studying Luther's exegesis, we can identify his rhetorical strategies—three of which will be explored here: his commitment to seek certitude; his appeals to the abilities of his audience; and his implicit ethical appeals.

The search for certitude

Luther's theological method grew out of a very traditional conviction: like his contemporaries, he recognized a fundamental difference between God and humanity. Indeed, Luther felt this gap to be so vast that it could never be overcome by human power. During his time as an Augustinian friar, he nearly lost sight of God on account of that infinite distance. "The terror of the Holy, the horror of Infinitude, smote him like a new lightning bolt, and only through a fearful restraint could he hold himself at the altar to the end."[99] Luther described his terror as *Anfechtung*, which Bainton translates roughly as "all the doubt, turmoil, pang, tremor, panic, despair, desolation, and desperation which invade the spirit of man."[100]

This *Anfechtung* has been widely recognized as an important aspect of Luther's character. Viewed from a rhetorical perspective, this insight also helps us understand some of his argumentative strategies. For example, Luther's early works against scholastic theology focused primarily on human beings' inability to reach God by an act of will. He claims that "human nature is evil and vitiated naturally and inevitably,"[101] and that "natural man possesses neither a sound reason nor a good will."[102] At Heidelberg, Luther argues that if God's law cannot justify humanity, "how much less can the works of man bring him to righteousness, done as they are time and time again and aided and abetted by the dictates of the natural man."[103] In sum, Luther believes that "man is flesh. This includes the fact that he can neither escape from his mortal condition nor overcome it by his natural powers."[104] The need to differentiate God from humanity had always been recognized in Christian theology; but for Luther, the disjunction became an almost unbridgeable chasm.

This commitment effectively foreordained Luther's argumentative strategy. Convinced that human knowledge of God could come from God alone, Luther insists that the only reliable source of revelation is the one that comes directly from God: Holy Scripture. But the Bible could assuage Luther's terror only if it offered a final, definitive answer, rather than an answer subject to human mediation. Thus, Luther supported his thesis by claiming that the interpretation of Scripture required only that its true message be allowed to shine through. Although he lived a century before Descartes, Luther was motivated by the same anxious quest for a sure foundation. To him, the magisterium of the Church was a willow—bending to and fro at the whim of whatever tyrant was in charge. Similarly, medieval Scholasticism had sought its proof in an all-too-human source; Aristotle was just as prone to error as the rest of us. Scripture, on the other hand, provided certainty. As David Steinmetz has argued, "For a brief period of time, Protestants thought it would be possible to write a theology which was wholly biblical and excluded all philosophical and speculative questions."[105]

Appeals to the audience

Over time, Luther's arguments grew more rhetorically sensitive to his audience. He came to recognize the intuitive appeal of a theology that encouraged individual members of the audience to adjudicate methodological questions. This had not been the case at the beginning of his career, when Luther was quite willing to shape his theology in accordance with the tradition. For example, he ends his 1517 "Disputation against Scholastic Theology" with the motto

> In these theses we wish to say nothing
> Nor do we believe we have said anything,
> which is not in accordance with the
> catholic church and the ancient doctors
> of the church.[106]

But Luther soon discovered that the appeal to tradition was not only unnecessary; it was actually much less persuasive than an appeal to the judgment of the common, ordinary person. The same appeal had been successful for William of Ockham, who had confidently declared that the mission of the Church should be determined, not by the ecclesiastical or civil authorities, but by the Scripture, interpreted by "the discretion and counsel of the wisest men sincerely zealous for justice without respect to persons, if such can be found—whether they be poor or rich, subjects or rulers."[107]

Thus, at Leipzig in 1519, Luther claimed that Scripture weighed more heavily in the balance than did the authority of tradition.[108] The tradition, after all, is composed of a series of individual attempts to interpret Scripture correctly, and the individuals who made those attempts were fallible. "Luther was willing to accuse even his favorite among them, St. Augustine, of sometimes having failed to grasp the full implications of the Biblical doctrine of grace and thus of falling into a moralistic distortion of the gospel."[109]

Luther's strategy was to free his audience to adhere to an interpretation different from the ones offered by the Roman Church. But if Christians are able to read the Bible without any reliance on experts, then the Bible must be a clear and perspicacious book. Accordingly, Luther strongly objects to Erasmus's contention[110] that Scripture is an obscure book that cannot be easily comprehended. If Scripture seems unclear to us, Luther argues, then we have not listened carefully enough.[111] In his reply to Erasmus, Luther says that "it ought above all to be settled and established among Christians that the Holy Scriptures are a spiritual light far brighter than the sun itself, especially in things that are necessary to salvation."[112]

By implication, the only possible guide to Scripture would be Scripture itself. Because Luther constructs an audience that refuses to rely on the Church or the tradition of interpretation, he must advocate the principle that "Scripture is its own interpreter" (*scriptura sui ipsius interpres*). Again, this position is necessitated by Luther's argumentative strategy. He wants to claim that ordinary Christian believers are just as skilled at biblical interpretation as are priests and doctors of the Church. Ironically, Luther constructed his own audience so as to exclude many believers— women, for example. Nevertheless, he claims to be offering to *all* believers those privileges of interpretation which the Church had sought to reserve for a chosen few.

> If some other authority would explain the Scripture, then it would also validate it. Thereby, however, Scripture would lose its character as the final authority. Its self-validation necessarily includes its self-interpretation. . . . Luther uses self-interpretation of the Scripture and interpretation through the Holy Spirit as a pair of synonymous expressions.[113]

The appeal to the self-validating text is an excellent example of an appeal to the audience, since it claims to remove the speaker from the interpretive process. That is, by claiming that Scripture is clear and perspicacious (and that it interprets itself), Luther was able to appeal to his auditors' sense of their own ability to listen to the voice of the text. He constructed an audience whose members would claim to avoid any merely human attempt to talk about God—whether through the living of saintly lives, through the ancient traditions of the Church, or through the Church's teaching office. The only legitimate interpreters of Scripture would be the auditors themselves. In an age when ecclesiastical authorities were becoming increasingly coercive and oppressive, this strategy would probably have had considerable appeal.

Ethical appeals

Yet Luther's advocacy of his audience's competence to interpret Scripture did not deter him from an occasional appeal to *ethos*. In fact, he frequently claims that particular passages in the Bible gain their significance from the character of the writer. "I do not ask myself what Bede says, or what any man says. I ask what they ought to say. One must look at God's Scripture only, and not simply what is said but who says it."[114] Similarly, Luther claims that his opponents "flee to the glosses and distinctions of the Fathers. They have prevailed to such an extent that the voice of Paul is silenced throughout the world."[115] By appealing directly to the character of St. Paul, Luther is able effectively to strengthen his own position, which relied heavily on the Pauline epistles.

Moreover, by emphasizing the priority of Scripture, Luther simultaneously appealed to the character of Jesus. As David Lotz has argued,[116] the principle of *sola scriptura* was necessarily an appeal to *solus Christus*. The Bible is understood as the only path whereby God in Christ can speak directly to human beings; consequently, an appeal to Scripture is an appeal to the *ēthos* of Jesus Christ.

Finally, Luther's appeal to the Bible is at the same time an appeal to his own character as an interpreter. While all previous interpreters had failed to let the Scripture speak, Luther claimed to provide a distortion-free channel for the reception of true doctrine. As we shall discover shortly, this claim was difficult for Luther to sustain over the course of his career. Nevertheless, the claim provided an implicit (and modestly veiled) argument for Luther's own superiority as an exegete. In his claim to surrender to the text, Luther appeared to deprecate himself; but he was implicitly promoting his own exegesis over that of interpreters past.

LUTHER ON THE EUCHARIST

When employed in actual practice, Luther's argumentative strategies did not always remain fully intact—as can be illustrated by examining Luther's arguments concerning the doctrine of the Eucharist. In the course of the dispute, Luther discovered that the appeals that had worked so well against Rome did not always work against Zurich. He thus found himself forced to make certain adjustments in his strategy, in order to meet the changing circumstances of the conflict. By examining how Luther reacted to the changing focus of this particular debate, we shall gain a clearer sense of the highly contextual nature of theological argumentation in general.

Luther's arguments concerning the Eucharist frequently hinge on interpretations of the sixth chapter of the gospel of John. In this passage, Jesus declares, "I am the bread of life" (John 6:35,48), associating this bread with his flesh (John 6:51) and with the flesh and blood of the Son of Man (John 6:53). Jesus also promises that "those who eat this bread will live forever" (John 6:58; cf. 6:54, 56). Throughout the history of the Church, these rich associations have frequently been employed by theologians to support doctrines concerning the Eucharist.

However, despite its long-standing history, this usage of John 6 troubled Luther. Too often, he believed, the passage had been used by the Church to endow the Eucharist with a deep, mysterious power, urgently connected to the salvation of one's soul. This meant that certain representatives of the institutional structures of the Church could withhold the Eucharist as a means of coercing particular behaviors on the part of believers. After all, if the faithful could not receive the "life-giving bread," their souls would be in peril. As Jaroslav Pelikan notes, the eucharistic use of John 6 "was an exegesis which had led Christian theologians since the second century to speak of the Lord's Supper as a 'medicine of immortality.'"[117] This interpretation had become the basis for what Luther felt had been violent abuses of the Eucharist by the medieval Church.

Thus, from early in his career, Luther fought to dissociate the doctrine of the Eucharist from any reference to John 6. In *The Babylonian Captivity of the Church*, he states that

> the sixth chapter of John must be entirely excluded from this discussion, since it does not refer to the sacrament in a single syllable. Not only because the sacrament was not yet instituted, but even more because the passage itself and the sentences following

plainly show, as I have already stated, that Christ is speaking of faith in the incarnate word.[118]

Luther goes on to explain that the passage refers only to spiritual eating and drinking, which gives rise to the Jews' misgivings as related in the passage (John 6:41, 52). Only such a spiritual eating and drinking can give life, Luther says; a sacramental eating cannot, because many eat unworthily.[119]

However, *The Babylonian Captivity* had been written against the position of the Roman Church; and now, Luther was coming under attack by very different adversaries. From the perspective of the radical Reformers, Luther had not gone far enough; he had clung to the Roman doctrine of the real presence in the Eucharist. Nevertheless, against these new opponents, Luther saw no reason to change his strategy; he still claimed that John 6 had nothing to do with the Eucharist. In his first work directed against the teachings of the Sacramentarians—a series of sermons published in 1526—he does not even mention the sixth chapter of John.[120] And when Luther does bring the passage into the argument a year later,[121] he sometimes seems to restrict its use to a description of the spiritual body of Christ, just as he had done in *The Babylonian Captivity*. Christ's flesh, he says, "is not of flesh, or fleshly, but spiritual; therefore it cannot be consumed, digested, and transformed, for it is imperishable as is all that is of the Spirit, a food of an entirely different kind from perishable food."[122]

Clearly, Luther had a strong interest in eliminating the possibility of using John 6 as a eucharistic text. Doing so provided him with a useful argument on both fronts of the battle he was fighting. By avoiding the text, he strengthened his position against Rome; he was able to argue that the laity should receive the sacrament in both kinds and that it should not become a "magic potion" which the Church could use as an instrument of coercion. Similarly improved was his stance against the Sacramentarians, who had used John 6:63 ("The Spirit gives life; the flesh profits nothing") in support of their "spiritualized" understanding of the Eucharist.

But Luther is in a bind here, for this very passage—John 6— supplies some of his most valuable texts for a related (but very different) argument. Specifically, portions of the sixth chapter of John were needed in order to support the claim that Christ is really present in the Eucharist. For the most part, Luther seems willing to forgo the opportunity to use these texts, relying instead on the synoptic institution narratives and Paul's description of them (Matt. 26:26 par.; 1 Cor. 11:24). In these passages, the bread is referred to as Christ's body (*sōma*). In John 6, however, the word is flesh (*sarx*). How should Luther treat the relationship between these two words, if he wants to maintain his position against both Rome and the radical Reformers?

When Luther comments on the use of *sarx* in John 6:63, he wants to avoid associating it with the word with *soma*. To conflate the two words would be to support the Sacramentarians, who employed John 6:63 in order to argue that "the flesh" (that is, the real presence) "profits nothing." But Luther would like to treat *sōma* and *sarx* as synonyms when he turns to John 6:51, "whoever eats of this bread will live forever; and the bread that I will give for the life of the world is my flesh [*sarx*]." How can Luther distinguish between the two passages, in order to claim that in one instance *sōma* and *sarx* mean the same thing, while in the other, they do not?

This argumentative quandary calls for the rhetorical strategy of "the dissociation of ideas"[123]—which is exactly what Luther employs. He notes that, whenever Jesus is speaking of his own flesh (that flesh which is present in the Eucharist), he uses the possessive pronoun: "those who eat *my* flesh" (John 6:54, 56). But in John 6:63, the possessive pronoun is absent. In that instance, argues Luther, Christ is speaking of flesh in general— that is, humanity in all its sinfulness and weakness. "One can irrefutably testify against you that as often as Christ speaks in the Scriptures of his flesh or body, he adds the word 'my,' saying, 'my flesh,' 'my body,' as he says in the same chapter, John 6, 'My flesh is food indeed.'"[124]

In order to support this distinction, Luther turns to the Fathers of the Church. He quotes Irenaeus, for instance, who uses John 6:55 and 6:58 to argue that Jesus "speaks of physical eating when he says that our bodies receive the sacrament. . . . This, of course, can be nothing but the body of Christ, of which he speaks in John 6."[125] Luther then offers similar examples from Hilary, Cyprian, and Augustine.[126] Thus, when arguing against the Sacramentarians, Luther appeals to the authority of the interpretations offered by the Church Fathers—the very authority that he had explicitly rejected at Leipzig.

Indeed, in this new dispute, Luther changed not only his exegetical principles but his doctrinal stance as well. By using part of John 6 as a eucharistic text, Luther was basically adopting a view of the sacrament that he had rejected in 1520. In attempting to address the arguments of a very different adversary, Luther was now bordering on an exegesis of John 6 that suggested that the Eucharist somehow magically transforms us and creates the possibility of resurrection. He had rejected this view in *The Babylonian Captivity*; but, by the year 1527, he was able to state flatly that

> the mouth, the throat, the body, which eats Christ's body, will also have its benefit in that it will live forever and arise on the Last Day to eternal salvation. This is the secret power and benefit which flows from the body of Christ in the Supper into our body, for it must be useful, and cannot be present in vain.[127]

Here Luther makes an explicit connection between the eucharistic meal and the "spiritual eating" of John 6.

Now Luther seemed to be back on the side of Rome—as Zwingli was quick to point out.[128] Luther had to fight to defuse this objection. In the end, he seems to have decided that the usefulness of John 6 as an argument for the real presence was not sufficient to outweigh the pastoral and political difficulties in which it had embroiled him. In his 1528 work on the subject—the "Confession Concerning Christ's Supper"[129]—Luther seems to have dropped completely the use of John 6 to point to the resurrection of the body. Rather, he simply states that "the sixth chapter of John does not refer at all to the Supper."[130] He relies on the institution narratives alone for his eucharistic theology.[131]

Similarly, the various accounts of the Marburg Colloquy (1529) show Luther at pains to forgo any appeal to John 6. Zwingli fought hard, but without success, to convince Luther that the passage was worth considering with regard to the Eucharist.[132] Much of the colloquy thus degenerated into a debate over which text to use, rather than a discussion about the meaning of any particular text.[133] Marburg provided a clear indication that agreement on the principle of *sola scriptura* did not necessarily lead to agreement on dogmatic issues.

In summary, then, Luther's use of John 6 varied considerably during his polemical exchanges on the Eucharist. Against Rome, he had sought to exclude it entirely, because of its magical connotations. But against the Sacramentarians, he believed John 6 would prove useful in support of the real presence. He even found a useful device for dissociating these arguments from the spiritualizing tendency of John 6:63. This strategy worked only too well against the left wing, who felt that Luther had capitulated back to Rome. Thus, in his later writings and at Marburg, Luther drops the use of John 6 altogether.

Indeed, Luther's encounter with the radical Reformers forced him to rethink not only his usage of particular texts of Scripture, but also his more general statements on the doctrine of the Eucharist. Much later, in his "Brief Confession" of 1544, he even suggested that had he known that the eucharistic doctrine would be so harshly attacked from the Protestant side, he would have retained even the elevation of the host.[134] Here, Luther shows himself fully aware of the importance of context in all theological argumentation.

LUTHER AS RHETORICAL THEOLOGIAN

Most modern studies of Luther's exegetical method focus primarily on the category of *sola scriptura*. Luther is frequently claimed to have had a single, definitive, unifying approach to the task of theology. But his so-called unambiguous exegetical principles did not survive the Reformation intact. They had not been formulated to fight the "enthusiasts"; they had been formulated to fight the abuses of the medieval Church. Thus, Luther soon found himself undertaking some difficult rearguard actions to prevent his own radical reliance on Scripture from swallowing the whole of what he had come to understand as the Christian faith. He thus felt compelled to shift his methodological position according to the context in which he deployed his arguments.

But this willingness to shift should not be seen as a fault. In fact, precisely because of his willingness to reformulate his argument according to the context, Luther was often successful in persuading his various audiences to agree with his position. At first, he had hoped that a turn to *sola scriptura* would mean an end to the vicissitudes of human intervention and a definitive foundation for doctrine. But his encounter with the radical Reformers made it clear that such a hope could not be realized. He was therefore willing to modify his methodology in order to address the new situation.

This brief exercise in rhetorical history leads to three conclusions. First, theological claims are highly context-dependent. They depend on the commitments of the theologians who present them, on the predilections of the audience to which they are addressed, and on the arguments that are being deployed by those who hold different assumptions. Thus, a particular theology cannot be easily distilled into a single method, without regard to differences imposed by the various contexts in which arguments are deployed.

Second, anything resembling theological objectivity is a fairly elusive goal. The Reformers (especially Luther and Calvin) are often considered great masters of objectivity, breaking the subjective corruption into which medieval Christianity had fallen. This is, for example, the view of Thomas Torrance:

> It is once again to the Reformation that we must turn for the modern emphasis upon unbiased and disinterested truth, which arose particularly in the conflict between Reformed theology and Roman tradition. . . . This was a passion for the truth from the side of the object which inculcated a repentant readiness to rethink all preconceptions and presuppositions.[135]

This appeal to objectivity is itself an argumentative strategy, of which Torrance is certainly one of the reigning masters. But the rhetorical tradition urges us to evaluate the appeal to objectivity in the same way that we would evaluate any other philosophical appeal. Moreover, the actual rhetorical practices of the Reformers do not seem to support classifying them as objective interpreters.

Third, and finally, the absolute certainty toward which human beings often feel driven simply cannot be obtained in the realm of theology. Luther's attempt to ground all authority in *sola scriptura*—like so many analogous attempts throughout the ages—all come to grief on the essential brokenness of human existence. Argument is endemic to the human condition in general, and to the context of Christian theology in particular. "The ubiquity of rhetoric, indeed, is unlimited."[136]

Rhetoric's ubiquity implies that human thought and action are inherently fragile—that we must always dwell in regions of uncertainty, or even in the borderlands of chaos. This is difficult to accept and must be learned again and anew in every generation. Our modern unwillingness to dwell in the midst of uncertainty can be traced in part to the Reformation itself, whose heirs "remained optimistic about the clarity of Scripture and the simplicity and persuasive power of the truth which it contained."[137] The Reformation inspired a new hope for the discovery of some final, definitive resting-place that could provide security in a fundamentally unstable world. But the Reformers and their heirs eventually discovered what we are all continually in the process of discovering: the final security that we seek is offered neither by the exegesis of Scripture, nor by the reformulation of doctrine, nor by the recitation of history, nor by any other aspect of the theological task. For in spite of the efforts of theologians, historians, and exegetes, the Christian faith knows only one true source of security: "Our hearts can find no rest, until they rest in Thee."[138]

CHRISTIAN THEOLOGY AS A RHETORICAL ACTIVITY

This chapter has described some of the practical effects of a rhetorical approach to Christian theology. I now want to conclude with some brief reflections on the wider implications of this proposal for the theological task. Specifically, I want to suggest that rhetoric points us back to some traditional theological *loci*, endowing them with new meaning and new life. These traditional categories include anthropology, ecclesiology, and Christology, as well as the Christian doctrine of the triune God.

Here, I can offer only the briefest sketch of how these four
loci might be affected by a rhetoric of Christian theology.
Clearly, each one could become the basis for an entire volume
of reflection—or more. I hope to take them up in greater detail
in future works. Meanwhile, I can only hope to whet the reader's
appetite by offering some preliminary musings on Christian
theology as a rhetorical activity.

A rhetorical theology must develop a new understanding of
theological anthropology. Because the audience plays such a
vital role in the rhetorical situation, theologians must attempt to
understand what it is to be human. But this will need to be a
very different enterprise from the abstract commentary on
human experience that typically characterizes discussions of
theological anthropology. A rhetorical theology would not
operate with totalizing and universalizing assumptions, but
would instead attend to specific situations; thus, its anthropology will need to become more nuanced and more specific to a
particular time and place. The world to which theology speaks
in the poorest quarters of Rio de Janeiro differs markedly from
that in the hotels and salons along Lake Geneva. Any theological attempt to analyze the human situation must pay close
attention to these differences.

Secondly, a rhetorical method must also come to terms with
the question of ecclesiology. Rhetoric flourished in ancient
Greece because people could make certain assumptions
about the life of the community in which they lived. Today,
these structures of community are more difficult to find; persuasion is thus made much more complex. If Christian theology hopes to be persuasive, it must reexamine the role of the
believing community. To what extent is this community
defined by traditional or contemporary understandings of the
Church? How does this community come to evaluate a theological argument? The character *with* which theology speaks
is evaluated by the community *to* which it speaks. This calls
for a more complete investigation into how a community
judges character—and thus, an investigation into the roles
played by narrative, by the virtues, and by formation of (and
in) moral judgment.

A rhetorical theology must pay close attention to Christology as well. In Christianity, the ultimate appeal to *ēthos* is

the appeal to the authority of Christ. Whenever this appeal is misunderstood, communication (and thus, persuasion) will break down. Thus, Christian theology must participate in an ongoing attempt to describe the person and work of Christ, as understood in the particular place and time in which the theology is being done. This will not be another quest for the historical Jesus; it will be an attempt to articulate the specific ways in which the character of Jesus Christ is used to authorize theological reflection—so that Christ can be claimed, authentically, as the Word which theology speaks.

Finally, and perhaps most urgently, a rhetorical theology must seek to articulate its understanding of God as Trinity. As briefly noted in chapter 1, rhetoric is itself a trinitarian activity, in that it seeks to move away from a monistic or dualistic approach and toward a triangular mode instead. But it also seeks to understand how speaker, audience, and argument operate as an organic process of communication—that is, to understand the mystery of how these Three are also One. Rhetorical theology is trinitarian theology, in this sense at least: it withdraws from any easy synthesis into universality, and also from the antinomies of an endless dualism. The precise specification of Christian theology's threeness-in-unity will be (appropriately enough) a matter for *argument*. But the simultaneity of threeness and oneness will remain essential for a Christian theology that understands itself through rhetorical categories.

These comments remind us that the present work consists only of prolegomena. The full development of a rhetorical theology will be a lengthy and complex undertaking, without much hope of coming to any definitive conclusions. In fact, as we have discovered, the absence of such conclusiveness is a feature common to both ancient rhetoric and Christian theology. For this reason, a rhetorical theology must always be marked by a willingness to return, time and again, to the actual, concrete practices of the faith. This I shall attempt to do in the few pages that remain.

Unconcluding Rhetorical Postscript

Theology as
Faithful Persuasion

As readers come to the close a lengthy treatise in theological method, they deserve some relief: relief from the constant barrage of claim and counterclaim, the endless citation of academic authorities, and the pretensions to clever analysis and brilliant insight that such treatises so frequently comprise. Thus, my closing remarks are reflective, rather than constructive; I offer them in the mode of doxology, rather than critique.

I believe that doxological language is especially appropriate in a theological treatise, especially as it draws to a close. Doxology is an essential aspect of reflection on the Christian faith and has played an important role in the life and work of theologians, ancient and modern. A closing doxology may take the form of a hymn, a poem, or a prayer; but regardless of its particular shape, it should give the reader some clue to the theologian's religious vision. It is the theological equivalent of the *peroration* of a speech—in which the argument is summarized and its significance is heightened. In Greek, this summary was called the *anakephalaiosis*—a word of theological significance, which St. Paul uses to describe the uniting of all things in Christ (Eph. 1:10).

Among contemporary theologians, one of the great masters of this closing doxological in-gathering is Nicholas Lash. Near the end of his treatise on human experience and the knowledge of God, *Easter in Ordinary*, Lash seeks to offer an explanation of the book's title. He first quotes a sonnet by George Herbert that speaks of prayer as "heaven in ordinarie." He then quotes a poem of Gerard Manley Hopkins, which includes the phrase, "Let him easter in us." Finally, Lash closes his book with a passage which must itself rank among the finest pieces of religious writing in recent years. This passage has, in many ways, guided my own theological reflections; and it provides a fine example of faithful persuasion.

> I do not know of a better way of ending than with the conjunction of Herbert's "heaven in ordinarie" and Hopkins's use of "easter" as a verb. Living in relation, in the way that we do, to the unknown God, we do not possess, nor do we need to know, more of the form which the fullness of his eastering in all our ordinariness may take.

We do not possess, nor do we need to know: here is perhaps the most significant insight of Christian theology.

Thus, we are led back to the same place from which we took our departure in the introduction. We have once again reached the point of the *via negativa*: the conviction that theology offers no certainty or security, but only an ongoing series of questions into the mystery of God. Have we simply gone in a circle? Probably so. But circular journeys—ceaseless explorations—are not always for naught: " . . . the end of all our exploring / Will be to arrive where we started / And know the place for the first time."[2]

A well-worn excerpt, to be sure. But an appropriate one for theological reflection, because this is all we can do: we can journey and return, seeking to "know the place for the first time." Indeed, all our travels are very little else than an attempt to come to know the place that we ought never to leave. The psalmist knew it well:

> Lord, you have been our dwelling place
>   in all generations.
> Before the mountains were brought forth,
>   or ever you had formed
>   the earth and the world,

> from everlasting to everlasting
> you are God. (Psalm 90:1–2)

And yet we do leave our dwelling place—and return—time and again.

In this work, I have attempted to articulate the nature of our explorations. I believe they are best understood as attempts at persuading others of the Christian faith. Persuasion cannot guarantee truth—and appropriately so for the work of Christian theology, which should always acknowledge that God alone embodies the fullness of truth. Needless to say, theological authorities of all sorts have often claimed to speak "the truth"; however, on occasion, they have also admitted—rather more wisely—that even their most definitive statements must finally submit to the authority and the mystery of the triune God.

The theological task is a yearning for truth, a longing for truth; but this side of the beatific vision, theology discovers ultimate truth to be elusive. Truth is not the special province of theologians but, rather, an eschatological reality; truth is the final object of the Christian hope. In this time between the times, we ought not seek to declare our meager theological accomplishments to be true. Until we are able to see "face to face," all judgments of truth must rest with God alone.

In the meantime, however, we can seek to persuade others of the Gospel—and, in fact, to persuade ourselves as well. We all do so, each in various ways. Rather than constantly trying to deny that we engage in this activity, I believe we should embrace it. Doing so involves considerable risk, for it means taking responsibility for the commitments with which we theologize. We cannot evade, or even lighten, this burden by declaring that we are constrained by particular denominational guidelines, or by academically approved methods, or even by politically enforced regulations. Christian theology is a religious activity, and those who engage in it do so under the judgment of God. Doing theology would be a much easier task if we knew the criteria by which we are being judged; but we do not know. So all we can do is to desire that our most successful moments of persuasion will be moments of *faithful* persuasion—moments of persuasion for the sake of the God of Jesus Christ, in whom we live and move and have our being.

Thus, the concluding word of this book is no conclusion at all, but, instead, a frank admission of insecurity and fragility. Any further specifications of what might constitute faithful persuasion would have to be phrased in language closer to the language of prayer than to that of an academic treatise. But such admixtures of language are not unprecedented. One of my teachers, Nicholas Lash, closed his inaugural lecture at Cambridge with a prayer of St. Thomas Aquinas. My doctoral advisor, Geoffrey Wainwright, closed the last session of his divinity school seminars with a prayer. And most significantly of all, St. Gregory of Nazianzus closed his final theological oration[3] with the following words:

> Finally, then, it seems best to me to let the images and the shadows go, as being deceitful and very far short of the truth; and clinging myself to the more reverent conception, and resting upon few words, using the guidance of the Holy Spirit, keeping to the end as my genuine comrade and companion the enlightenment which I have received from the same Spirit, and passing through this world to *persuade all others* also to the best of my power to worship Father, Son, and Holy Spirit, the one Godhead and power. To God belongs all glory and honor and might forever and ever. Amen.

Notes

Throughout the notes, whenever an abbreviated citation is given, the chapter and note number of the first (and full) citation of a work is given in square brackets, using a capital roman number for the chapter number and an arabic numeral for note number—e.g., [II/32] refers to the work cited in note 32 of chapter 2.

All references to classical, patristic, and medieval works are cited by their standard abbreviations, which may be found in *The Oxford Classical Dictionary,* ed. N. G. L. Hammond and H. H. Scullard, 2nd ed. (Oxford: Clarendon Press, 1970).

INTRODUCTION

1. Kenneth Burke, *The Philosophy of Literary Form,* 3rd ed. (Berkeley: University of California Press, 1973), 110–11.

2. St. Gregory of Nazianzus, "Second Theological Oration," trans. Charles Gordon Browne and James Edward Swallow, in *Christology of the Later Fathers,* ed. Edward Rochie Hardy and Cyril C. Richardson, Library of Christian Classics, vol. 3 (Philadelphia: Westminster Press, 1954), 138.

3. Vladimir Lossky, *The Mystical Theology of the Eastern Church,* trans. Fellowship of St. Alban and St. Sergius (Crestwood, N.Y.: St. Vladimir's Seminary Press, 1976), 35.

4. The phrase, which is W. B. Gallie's, is developed in interesting ways in Stephen Sykes, *The Identity of Christianity* (London: SPCK, 1984), 251–61.

259

5. Ray L. Hart, *Unfinished Man and the Imagination: Toward an Ontology and a Rhetoric of Revelation,* with an introduction by Mark C. Taylor (New York: Herder and Herder, 1968; reprint, Atlanta: Scholars Press, 1985), 40.

6. See, *inter alia,* Jacques Derrida, *Writing and Difference,* trans. with an introduction by Alan Bass (Chicago: University of Chicago Press, 1978); Walter J. Ong, *Orality and Literacy: The Technologizing of the Word,* New Accents (London: Methuen, 1982); and Paul Ricoeur, *Interpretation Theory: Discourse and the Surplus of Meaning* (Fort Worth: Texas Christian University Press, 1976).

1. *THEŌRIA*

1. The Greek notion of *theōria* serves as a reminder that certain aspects of the process of theorizing have been overlooked in recent efforts to discredit theory. See, e.g., Steven Knapp and Walter Benn Michaels, "Against Theory," *Critical Inquiry* 8 (Summer 1982): 723–42; reprinted in *Against Theory: Literary Studies and the New Pragmatism,* ed. W. J. T. Mitchell (Chicago: University of Chicago Press, 1985), 11–30.

2. James L. Golden, Goodwin F. Berquist, and William E. Coleman, *The Rhetoric of Western Thought,* 2nd ed. (Dubuque, Iowa: Kendall/ Hunt, 1978), 3.

3. Plato *Protag.* 315c.

4. Renato Barilli, *Rhetoric,* trans. Giuliana Menozzi, Theory and History of Literature, vol. 63 (Minneapolis: University of Minnesota Press, 1989), 3–4.

5. See the comments in Martin Heidegger, *An Introduction to Metaphysics,* trans. Ralph Manheim (New Haven: Yale University Press, 1959), 61–69.

6. Kenneth Burke, *A Rhetoric of Motives* (1950; reprint, Berkeley: University of California Press, 1969), 50.

7. *Doxa* is related to *dokei moi,* which might be translated as "it seems to me." (Compare the use of *edoxen* in Acts 15:28: "it has seemed good to the Holy Spirit and to us.") Similarly, *eikos* is closely related to *eika,* which is the word that Socrates frequently uses to begin his statements in the Platonic dialogues (often translated "it seems"—to me, or, to us). See the clarifying comments by Lawrence W. Rosenfield, "An Autopsy of the Rhetorical Tradition," in *The Prospect of Rhetoric: Report of the National Development Project,*

ed. Lloyd F. Bitzer and Edwin Black, Prentice Hall Speech Communication Series (Englewood Cliffs, N.J.: Prentice Hall, 1971), 65.

8. See, for example, Jean-François Lyotard, "De la force des faibles," *L'Arc* 64 (1976): 4–12; Larry Arnhart, *Aristotle on Political Reasoning: A Commentary on the Rhetoric* (DeKalb: Northern Illinois University Press, 1981), ch. 2 *passim*.

9. George A. Kennedy, *Classical Rhetoric and Its Christian and Secular Tradition from Ancient to Modern Times* (Chapel Hill: University of North Carolina Press, 1980), 32.

10. I make no attempt to adjudicate arguments concerning the proper distinctions between the views of Plato and Socrates, or between Socrates himself and Socrates as portrayed by Plato. I simply refer to the dialogues, in the form in which we have received them, as Plato's.

11. Plato's views on rhetoric have been interpreted in a variety of ways. For the position advocated here, see Kennedy, *Classical Rhetoric* [I/9], 42–60; see also Brian Vickers, *In Defense of Rhetoric* (New York: Oxford University Press; Oxford: Clarendon Press, 1988), 83–177. For a different view, see Robert E. Cushman, *Therapeia: Plato's Conception of Philosophy* (Chapel Hill: University of North Carolina Press, 1958), 212–41.

12. Plato *Gorg.* 463a.

13. A number of commentators have undertaken analyses of Plato's own rhetoric; for example, Jane V. Curran, "The Rhetorical Technique of Plato's *Phaedrus,*" *Philosophy and Rhetoric* 19, no. 1 (1986): 66–72.

14. James S. Murray, "Disputation, Deception, and Dialectic: Plato on the True Rhetoric (*Phaedrus* 261–266)," *Philosophy and Rhetoric* 21, no. 4 (1988): 280.

15. Rosemary Radford Ruether, *Gregory of Nazianzus: Rhetor and Philosopher* (Oxford: Clarendon Press, 1969), 3.

16. Kennedy, *Classical Rhetoric* [I/9], 59.

17. Quintilian *Inst. Orat.* 2.15.34–38.

18. Kennedy, *Classical Rhetoric* [I/9], 102.

19. For example, it determines the overall structure of Josef Martin, *Antike Rhetorik: Technik und Methode*, Handbuch der Altertumswissenschaft (Munich: C. H. Beck, 1974).

20. Gerhard Ebeling, *Introduction to a Theological Theory of Language*, trans. R. A. Wilson (London: William Collins and Sons, 1973), 143.

21. Here, the opportunity for terminological confusion is great. For Aristotle, "common opinion" (*doxa*) can allow us to achieve interesting

philosophical insights, whereas "science" (*epistēmē*) is rather mundane. For Plato, in contrast, only *epistēmē* could be philosophy; *doxa* was a distraction. In fact, much of Plato's dialectic is, in Aristotelian terms, a thoroughly analytic endeavor. In the present work, all further uses of the terms *analytic* and *dialectic* refer to Aristotle's distinction.

22. Chaïm Perelman, *The Realm of Rhetoric*, trans. William Kluback, with an introduction by Carroll C. Arnold (Notre Dame, Ind.: University of Notre Dame Press, 1982), 1.

23. Barilli, *Rhetoric* [I/4], 82.

24. Cf. the helpful comments in Arnhart, *Aristotle on Political Reasoning [I/8]*, 18.

25. Aristotle *Rh.* 1354a1. I have attended to the Greek text of Aristotle's *Rhetoric* throughout, using a number of different English translations for guidance. The conversational style of the translation by Lane Cooper (Englewood Cliffs, N.J.: Prentice Hall, 1960) is bought at a price; see Thomas M. Conley, "The Greekless Reader and Aristotle's *Rhetoric,*" *Quarterly Journal of Speech* 65 (1979) 74–79. The standard translations are John Henry Freese, *The "Art" of Rhetoric*, Loeb Classical Library, vol. 193 (Cambridge: Harvard University Press, 1926); and W. Rhys Roberts, in *The Works of Aristotle*, ed. W. D. Ross, vol. 11 (Oxford: Clarendon Press, 1946). I am also indebted to two commentaries on the *Rhetoric*: William M. A. Grimaldi, S.J., *Aristotle, Rhetoric I: A Commentary* (New York: Fordham University Press, 1980); and Arnhart, *Aristotle on Political Reasoning* [I/8].

26. As noted in Arnhart, *Aristotle on Political Reasoning* [I/8], 14.

27. Aristotle *Rh.* 1355a14–18; cf. *Top.* 100a18–21; *Soph. El.* 183a37–183b1.

28. Aristotle *Rh.* 1357a7.

29. According to Aristotelian psychology, such changes require more than mere rational decisions; they require desire or striving (*orexis*).

30. Aristotle *Rh.* 1355b26.

31. For example, Charles Sears Baldwin, *Medieval Rhetoric and Poetic* (New York: Macmillan, 1928; reprint, Gloucester, Mass.: Peter Smith, 1959).

32. Some scholars have emphasized the roots of Descartes's philosophy in earlier metaphysical systems and especially in nominalism. See, for example, Michael Allen Gillespie, *Hegel, Heidegger, and the Ground of History* (Chicago: University of Chicago Press, 1984), 125. Here, I focus on Descartes not because of his originality, but because his work illustrates nicely the conflict between rhetoric and rationalism.

33. Richard J. Bernstein, *Beyond Objectivism and Relativism* (Oxford: Basil Blackwell, 1983), 18.

34. See, *inter alia*, Eberhard Jüngel, *God as the Mystery of the World*, trans. Darrell L. Guder (Grand Rapids, Mich.: William B. Eerdmans, 1983), *passim*.

35. René Descartes, *Meditations on First Philosophy* (1641), trans. Donald A. Cress (Indianapolis: Hackett, 1979), 24.

36. For an extensive study of this revival, see Ernesto Grassi, *Rhetoric as Philosophy: The Humanist Tradition* (University Park: The Pennsylvania State University Press, 1980).

37. Ernesto Grassi, "Humanistic Rhetorical Philosophizing: Giovanni Pontano's Theory of the Unity of Poetry, Rhetoric, and History," *Philosophy and Rhetoric* 17, no. 3 (1984): 138.

38. The definitive modern work on Ramus is that of Walter J. Ong, S.J., *Ramus, Method, and the Decay of Dialogue* (Cambridge: Harvard University Press, 1958).

39. Richard A. Lanham, "The 'Q' Question," *South Atlantic Quarterly* 87, no. 4 (Fall 1988): 656.

40. Peter Ramus, *Arguments in Rhetoric against Quintilian,* trans. Carole Newlands, with an introduction by James J. Murphy (DeKalb: Northern Illinois University Press, 1986), 99.

41. See the instructive comments on Vico's notion of the *sensus communis* in Hans-Georg Gadamer, *Truth and Method*, trans. William Glen-Doepel, 2nd ed. (London: Sheed and Ward, 1979), 19–23.

42. Richard Harvey Brown, *Society as Text: Essays on Rhetoric, Reason, and Reality* (Chicago: University of Chicago Press, 1987), 67.

43. The point is elaborated in Barilli, *Rhetoric* [I/4], 83.

44. Kant does reinstate the role of the *sensus communis* in his discussion of aesthetic judgments in the Third Critique. See Immanuel Kant, *Critique of Judgement,* trans. J. H. Bernard (New York: Hafner, 1951), 135–38. Nevertheless, as Gadamer and others have noted, Kant here employs a very diluted notion of the *sensus communis* (see *Truth and Method* [I/41], 30–39).

45. Sabina Lovibond, *Realism and Imagination in Ethics* (Minneapolis: University of Minnesota Press, 1983), 22–23.

46. Kennedy, *Classical Rhetoric* [I/9], 227.

47. Noted in Kennedy, *Classical Rhetoric* [I/9], 230.

48. Immanuel Kant, *Critique of Pure Reason,* trans. Norman Kemp Smith, 2nd ed. (New York: Macmillan, 1933), 645 (A:820; B:848).

49. This shift has been expertly documented in Gadamer, *Truth and Method* [I/41], 5–73; 153–214.

50. John Henry Newman, *Newman's University Sermons: Fifteen Sermons Preached before the University of Oxford, 1826–43,* with an introduction by Donald M. MacKinnon and J. D. Holmes, 3rd ed. (London: SPCK, 1970).

51. John Henry Newman, *An Essay in Aid of a Grammar of Assent* (London, 1870; reprint, with an introduction by Nicholas Lash, Notre Dame, Ind.: University of Notre Dame Press, 1979).

52. Walter Jost, *Rhetorical Thought in John Henry Newman* (Columbia: University of South Carolina Press, 1989). This book is a historical study of Newman's contribution to the rhetorical tradition. (Jost teaches rhetoric; he is not a theologian.) Nevertheless, given Newman's status as one of the most important theologians of the nineteenth century, Jost's book also confirms the general argument of the present work: theology and rhetoric are methodologically complementary enterprises.

53. Jost, *Rhetorical Thought in Newman* [I/52], 8.

54. Ibid., 21.

55. Chaïm Perelman and Lucie Olbrechts-Tyteca, *The New Rhetoric: A Treatise on Argumentation,* trans. John Wilkinson and Purcell Weaver (Notre Dame, Ind.: University of Notre Dame Press, 1969), 1.

56. Bernstein, *Beyond Objectivism and Relativism* [I/33], 19.

57. Perelman and Olbrechts-Tyteca, *The New Rhetoric* [I/55], 3 (entire passage emphasized in the original).

58. Frank Lentricchia, *Criticism and Social Change* (Chicago: University of Chicago Press, 1983), 138–39.

59. Jost, *Rhetorical Thought in Newman* [I/52], 25.

60. Robert L. Scott, "On Viewing Rhetoric as Epistemic," *Central States Speech Journal* 18 (February 1967): 9–17.

61. Ibid., 15.

62. See Scott's follow-up article: Robert L. Scott, "On Viewing Rhetoric as Epistemic: Ten Years Later," *Central States Speech Journal* 27 (1976): 258–66. Since these early articles, studies of the epistemic function of rhetoric have mushroomed. See, for example, Richard A. Cherwitz and James W. Hikins, *Communication and Knowledge: An Investigation in Rhetorical Epistemology* (Columbia: University of South Carolina Press, 1986); Walter R. Fisher, "Narration as a Human Communication Paradigm: The Case of Public Moral Argument," *Communication Monographs* 51 (March 1984): 1–22; Richard B. Gregg, *Symbolic Inducement and Knowing: A Study in the Foundations of Rhetoric* (Columbia: University of South Carolina Press, 1984). A review essay on this last book provides a good summary of the *status quaestionis*: Walter M. Carleton, "On Rhetorical Knowing," *Quarterly Journal of Speech* 71 (May 1985): 227–37.

63. Stephen Toulmin, *The Uses of Argument* (Cambridge: Cambridge University Press, 1958), 231.

64. Brown, *Society as Text* [I/42], 85.

65. Burke, *A Rhetoric of Motives* [I/6], 101.

66. Ludwig Wittgenstein, *Philosophical Investigations,* trans. G. E. M. Anscombe, 3rd ed. (New York: Macmillian, 1953), sec. 257, p. 92.

67. A well-known recent example is that of E. D. Hirsch, Jr., *Validity in Interpretation* (New Haven: Yale University Press, 1967). Hirsch's position will be criticized in chapter 3.

68. Hans-Georg Gadamer, "On the Scope and Function of Hermeneutical Reflection," 1967, in *Philosophical Hermeneutics,* trans. David E. Linge (Berkeley: University of California Press, 1976), 21.

69. Aristotle *Rh.* 1359b13–15.

70. For example, despite its suggestive subtitle, Ray Hart's book, *Unfinished Man and the Imagination: Toward an Ontology and a Rhetoric of Revelation* [Intro./5], focuses more generally on the theological problems raised by what has come to be called *postmodernism.* A very abbreviated treatment of rhetoric is found in David Tracy, *Plurality and Ambiguity: Hermeneutics, Religion, Hope* (San Francisco: Harper and Row, 1987), ch. 1. A more detailed study has been undertaken by one of Tracy's students, who has helped initiate a series of books on rhetoric and theology: Stephen H. Webb, *Re-Figuring Theology: The Rhetoric of Karl Barth,* SUNY Series in Rhetoric and Theology, ed. David Tracy and Stephen H. Webb (Albany: State University of New York Press, 1991).

71. This method is described in, for example, Edwin Black, *Rhetorical Criticism: A Study in Method* (New York: Macmillan, 1965; reprint, Madison: University of Wisconsin Press, 1978).

72. See, for example, David Klemm, "Toward a Rhetoric of Postmodern Theology: Through Barth and Heidegger," *Journal of the American Academy of Religion* 55, no. 3 (Fall 1987): 443–69.

73. Franz Josef van Beeck, S.J., *Christ Proclaimed: Christology as Rhetoric,* Theological Inquiries, ed. Lawrence Boadt, C.S.P. (Ramsey, N.J.: Paulist Press, 1979).

74. This claim is explored with intelligence and rigor in John Milbank, *Theology and Social Theory: Beyond Secular Reason,* Signposts in Theology (Oxford: Basil Blackwell, 1990).

75. Kennedy, *Classical Rhetoric* [I/9], 121.

76. The pioneering work in this field is George A. Kennedy, *New Testament Interpretation through Rhetorical Criticism* (Chapel Hill: University of North Carolina Press, 1984). For a review of the short

history of this study and its future prospects, see Wilhelm Wuellner, "Where is Rhetorical Criticism Taking Us?" *Catholic Biblical Quarterly* 49, no. 3 (1987): 448–63.

77. Some of the rhetorical implications of these *loci* have been mentioned by theologians to whose work I will again refer. For revelation: Ingolf U. Dalferth, *Theology and Philosophy*, Signposts in Theology, ed. Kenneth Surin (Oxford: Basil Blackwell, 1988); and Hart, *Unfinished Man* [Intro./5]. For proclamation: Beeck, *Christ Proclaimed* [I/73]; Rebecca S. Chopp, *The Power to Speak: Feminism, Language, God* (New York: Crossroad, 1989).

78. Used as an epigraph in Kennedy, *New Testament Interpretation through Rhetorical Criticism* [I/76], 1.

79. Robert Dick Sider, *Ancient Rhetoric and the Art of Tertullian*, Oxford Theological Monographs (Oxford: Oxford University Press, 1971), 9–10.

80. The definitive study in English is that by Rosemary Radford Ruether, *Gregory of Nazianzus: Rhetor and Philosopher* [I/15]. See also Marcel Guignet, *Saint Grégoire de Nazianze et la rhétorique* (Paris: Picard, 1911).

81. For one thoroughly enjoyable example, see Kenneth Burke, *The Rhetoric of Religion: Studies in Logology* (Boston: Beacon Press, 1961; reprint, Berkeley: University of California Press, 1970), 43–171.

82. Augustine *Conf.* 1.16.26, as cited and translated in Peter Brown, *Augustine of Hippo* (London: Faber and Faber, 1967), 36.

83. Cf. Burke, *A Rhetoric of Motives* [I/6], 49–50.

84. Augustine *De doct. Chr.* (trans. D. W. Robertson, Jr. [New York: Liberal Arts Press, 1958]) 4.12 (emphasis mine).

85. Burke, *A Rhetoric of Motives* [I/6], 53.

86. Gerald S. Vigna, *The Influence of Epideictic Rhetoric on Eusebius of Caesarea's Political Theology* (Ph.D. diss., Northwestern University, 1980); James M. Campbell, *The Influence of the Second Sophistic on the Style of the Sermons of St. Basil the Great* (Washington, D.C.: The Catholic University of America Press, 1922); Louis Méridier, *L'influence de la seconde sophistique sur l'oeuvre de Grégoire de Nysse* (Paris: Hachette, 1906); T. E. Ameringer, *The Stylistic Influence of the Second Sophistic on the Panegyrical Sermons of St. John Chrysostom* (Washington, D.C.: The Catholic University of America Press, 1921); William J. Bouwsma et al., *Calvinism as Theologia Rhetorica* (Berkeley: Center for Hermeneutical Studies in Hellenistic and Modern Culture, 1987); John Campbell-Nelson, *Kierkegaard's Christian Rhetoric* (Ph.D. diss.,

School of Theology at Claremont, 1982); Jost, *Rhetorical Thought in Newman* [I/52].

87. Elisabeth Schüssler Fiorenza, "The Ethics of Interpretation: De-Centering Biblical Scholarship," *Journal of Biblical Literature* 107, no. 1 (March 1988): 13–14.

88. Rebecca Chopp, "Theological Persuasion: Rhetoric, Warrants, and Suffering," in *Worldviews and Warrants: Plurality and Authority in Theology,* ed. William Schweiker (Lanham, Md.: University Press of America, 1987), 18.

89. Ibid., 20.

90. I take this remark from a slightly different context in Nicholas Lash, *Easter in Ordinary: Reflections on Human Experience and the Knowledge of God* (Charlottesville: The University Press of Virginia, 1988), 13.

91. Additional relevant commentary on this passage may be found in Ebeling, *Theological Theory of Language* [I/20], 97–99.

92. Augustine *De doc. Chr.* 4.2.

93. Ignatius, Ephesians (trans. Maxwell Staniforth [Harmondsworth: Penguin, 1968]) 15:2.

94. I appropriate this term from Ray Hart, *Unfinished Man and the Imagination* [Intro./5], 40.

95. With all due respect for the fragility of such comparisons, similarities among the derivations of words often point to more substantial relationships that should not be ignored.

96. Burke, *A Rhetoric of Motives* [I/6], 52.

97. James L. Kinneavy, *Greek Rhetorical Origins of Christian Faith* (New York: Oxford University Press, 1987).

98. John Milbank, "The Second Difference: For a Trinitarianism without Reserve," *Modern Theology* 2, no. 3 (April 1986): 230.

99. Hans-Georg Gadamer, "The Relevance of the Beautiful: Art as Symbol, Play, and Festival," in *The Relevance of the Beautiful and Other Essays,* ed. Robert Bernasconi, trans. Nicholas Walker (Cambridge: Cambridge University Press, 1986), 5.

100. Lash, *Easter in Ordinary* [I/90], 131–32.

101. Wittgenstein, *Philosophical Investigations* [I/66], sec. 325, p. 106e.

102. John D. Zizioulas, *Being as Communion: Studies in Personhood and the Church* (Crestwood, N.Y.: St. Vladimir's Seminary Press, 1985), 122.

103. Jüngel, *God as the Mystery of the World* [I/34], 196.

104. Lash, *Easter in Ordinary* [I/90], 216.

2. PATHOS

1. Aristotle *Rh.* 1356a3.
2. Ibid., 1356a14.
3. Lentricchia, *Criticism and Social Change* [I/58], 92.
4. Ibid.
5. Jost, *Rhetorical Thought in John Henry Newman* [I/52], 78–79.
6. Aristotle *Rh.* 1384a10–12.
7. Ibid., 1377b21.
8. See the discussion of the demise of rhetoric in chapter 1.
9. Wittgenstein, *Philosophical Investigations* [I/66], sec. 1.
10. Some commentators believe that certain aspects of Wittgenstein's thought can be traced to the work of Mikhail Bakhtin, to whom I shall return in the third section of this chapter. See Terry Eagleton, "Wittgenstein's Friends," *New Left Review* no. 135 (September-October 1982); reprinted in *Against the Grain: Selected Essays* (London: Verso, 1986), 99–130.
11. Perelman and Olbrechts-Tyteca, *The New Rhetoric* [I/55], 17.
12. "All disagreement is based on agreement": this is a standard dictum of argumentation theory.
13. Burke, *A Rhetoric of Motives* [I/6], 55.
14. Ibid., 56.
15. Ibid., 58.
16. Plato *Rep.* (trans. Allan Bloom [New York: Basic Books, 1968]) 331c, 331e, 336e, 338a. While we have often been taught to understand such passages as moments of Socratic irony, this does not alter their rhetorical usefulness in Plato's dialogues. Clearly, they allow Socrates to urge his interlocutors to listen to him.
17. Donald Davidson, "On the Very Idea of a Conceptual Scheme," *Proceedings of the American Philosophical Association* 47 (1974); reprinted in *Inquiries into Truth and Interpretation* (Oxford: Clarendon Press, 1984), 196.
18. *The Fragment of Muratori*, in J. Stevenson, ed., *A New Eusebius* (London: SPCK, 1957), 145.
19. See, e.g., the hostile remarks in Eusebius *Hist. Eccl.* 4.29.6–7.
20. Kennedy, *New Testament Interpretation* [I/76], 98–101.
21. For this, and for the example that follows in the text, see Kennedy, *New Testament Interpretation* [I/76], 116–40.
22. Hans von Campenhausen, *The Fathers of the Latin Church*, trans. Manfred Hoffmann (London: Adam and Charles Black, 1964), 8.
23. Augustine *De doct. Chr.* 4.13.
24. Ibid. 4.9.

25. As Richard J. Bernstein has noted, this is one aspect of "the Enlightenment project which itself needs to be reclaimed and preserved. . . . For we do a grave injustice to the Enlightenment if we fail to appreciate the extent to which it was a legitimate protest against hypocrisy and injustice" ("Nietzsche or Aristotle? Reflections on Alasdair MacIntyre's *After Virtue,*" *Soundings* 67 [Spring 1984]: 24).

26. An analogous (though markedly different) investigation into the audiences of narrative fiction is developed in Peter J. Rabinowitz, "Truth in Fiction: A Reexamination of Audiences," *Critical Inquiry* 4 (Autumn 1977): 121–41.

27. Perelman and Olbrechts-Tyteca, *The New Rhetoric* [I/55], 19.

28. For example, Tübingen theologian Ingolf Dalferth dramatically increased the size of his expected audience for his 1988 book *Theology and Philosophy* [I/77] without having to face the problem of securing a translator: he simply wrote it in English.

29. For an analysis of how details surrounding a book's publication can become a source of "capital," see Pierre Bourdieu, *Homo Academicus,* trans. Peter Collier (Stanford: Stanford University Press, 1988), especially ch. 2–3.

30. Karl Barth, *Church Dogmatics,* ed. and trans. G. W. Bromiley and T. F. Torrance, 4 vols. in 14 pts. (Edinburgh: T. and T. Clark, 1958–75), I/2:825.

31. Ibid., 827.

32. See, for example, Hans Urs von Balthasar, *The Glory of the Lord: A Theological Aesthetics,* 7 vols. (San Francisco: Ignatius Press, 1982–89); Walter Kasper, *The God of Jesus Christ,* trans. Matthew J. O'Connell (London: SCM Press, 1983); Hans Küng, *Justification: The Doctrine of Karl Barth and a Catholic Reflection,* trans. Thomas Collins, rev. ed. (London: Burnes and Oates, 1981); and Nicholas Lash, *Theology on Dover Beach* (London: Darton, Longman, and Todd, 1979).

33. The reception of Barth among English-speaking theologians is chronicled in Stephen W. Sykes, "The Study of Barth," in *Karl Barth: Studies of His Theological Method,* ed. Stephen W. Sykes (Oxford: Clarendon Press, 1979), 9–10.

34. Roland Bainton, *Here I Stand* (Nashville: Abingdon Press, 1950), 281.

35. Additional arguments against hermeneutical intentionalism will be developed in chapter 3.

36. Perelman and Olbrechts-Tyteca, *The New Rhetoric* [I/55], 19.

37. Robert N. Bellah, Richard Madsen, William M. Sullivan, Ann Swidler, and Steven M. Tipton, *Habits of the Heart: Individualism*

and Commitment in American Life (San Francisco: Harper and Row, 1986).

38. Ibid., 234.

39. Ibid., 219.

40. Vincent Harding, "Toward a Darkly Radiant Vision of America's Truth: A Letter of Concern, an Invitation to Re-Creation," in *Community in America: The Challenge of Habits of the Heart,* ed. Charles H. Reynolds and Ralph V. Norman (Berkeley: University of California Press, 1988), 67–83.

41. Lanham, "The 'Q' Question" [I/39], 692.

42. Avery Dulles, S.J., *Models of the Church* (Garden City, N.Y.: Doubleday, 1974); idem, *Models of Revelation* (1983; reprint, New York: Doubleday, 1985).

43. Dulles, *Models of the Church,* 203.

44. This problem would be even more salient in the case of Dulles's *Models of Revelation,* in which the various models seem even more mutually exclusive than those in Models of the Church.

45. Perelman and Olbrechts-Tyteca, *The New Rhetoric* [I/55], 31 (emphasis mine).

46. See the summary of this debate in James L. Golden, "The Universal Audience Revisited," in *Practical Reasoning in Human Affairs: Studies in Honor of Chaïm Perelman,* ed. James L. Golden and Joseph J. Pilotta (Dordrecht: D. Reidel, 1986), 287–304.

47. Perelman and Olbrechts-Tyteca, *The New Rhetoric* [I/55], 31.

48. This is clearly how the universal audience was first understood by Henry W. Johnstone, Jr.—who claimed to find in *The New Rhetoric* an argument "that there are arguments addressed to mankind as a whole; to wit, the ones employed by the philosopher" ("Persuasion and Validity in Philosophy," in *Philosophy, Rhetoric, and Argumentation,* ed. Maurice Natanson and Henry W. Johnstone, Jr., with a foreword by Robert T. Oliver [University Park: Pennsylvania State University Press, 1965], 147). Similarly, see the idealist interpretation offered by James Crosswhite, "Universality in Rhetoric: Perelman's Universal Audience," *Philosophy and Rhetoric* 22, no. 3 (1989): 157–73.

49. This is the force of the argument in John W. Ray, "Perelman's Universal Audience," *Quarterly Journal of Speech* 64 (1978): 361–75.

50. The connection between Perelman and Habermas is made in Crosswhite, "Universality in Rhetoric" [II/48], 160–61.

51. Jürgen Habermas, *Philosophical-Political Profiles* (Cambridge: Harvard University Press, 1984), 158. See Crosswhite, "Universality in Rhetoric" [II/48], 172.

52. Paul Tillich, *Systematic Theology*, vol. 1 (Chicago: University of Chicago Press, 1951), 3–4.

53. As I revise this manuscript, the Iraqi invasion of Kuwait—with subsequent U.S. military involvement—has altered most public references to the Middle East; the *situation* has become a *crisis*. As U.S. troops are withdrawn from the area, I expect that the word *situation* will regain its previous currency—despite the lack of any corresponding improvement in the daily lives of most people in the region.

54. David Tracy, *The Analogical Imagination: Christian Theology and the Culture of Pluralism* (New York: Crossroad, 1981), 4.

55. Ibid., 28.

56. Ibid., 5.

57. Ibid., 69–79.

58. Ibid., 5.

59. Tracy seems to be aware of this, insofar as he admits that "a sociology of theology remains beyond my competence and distinct from the central task of the present work" (ibid., 4). Yet even this comment seems to suggest that such an enterprise might be possible, even desirable.

60. Ibid., 21.

61. See the comments on *appropriateness* and *intelligibility* (ibid., 238–41). One may legitimately ask whether these categories are anything more substantial than simply "a way of dividing-and-conquering certain vexing questions." See David S. Cunningham, "Clodovis Boff on the Discipline of Theology," *Modern Theology* 6, no. 2 (January 1990): 147.

62. Tracy, *The Analogical Imagination* [II/54], 9.

63. For the term *symbolic capital*, which is Pierre Bourdieu's, cf. Rogers Brubaker, "Rethinking Classical Theory: The Sociological Vision of Pierre Bourdieu," *Theory and Society* 14 (1985): 754–58.

64. Tracy, *The Analogical Imagination* [II/54], 5–6.

65. Ibid., 28.

66. Cf. the critique in Ong, *Orality and Literacy* [Intro./6], 175–77.

67. Perelman and Olbrechts-Tyteca, *The New Rhetoric* [I/55], 19.

68. Ibid., 20.

69. Cf. Walter J. Ong, S.J., "The Writer's Audience Is Always a Fiction," *PMLA* 90 (1975): 9–22; reprinted in *Interfaces of the Word: Studies in the Evolution of Consciousness and Culture* (Ithaca, N.Y.: Cornell University Press, 1977), 53–81.

70. Terry Eagleton, *Literary Theory: An Introduction* (Minneapolis: University of Minnesota Press, 1983), 84.

71. Edward W. Said, "Opponents, Audiences, Constituencies, and Community," in *The Politics of Interpretation,* ed. W. J. T. Mitchell (Chicago: University of Chicago Press, 1983), 9.

72. Wolfgang Iser, *The Act of Reading: A Theory of Aesthetic Response* (Baltimore: Johns Hopkins University Press, 1978), 34.

73. Iser's emphasis on text (over author) is starker than might initially be apparent. *Implied* at least suggests that someone must be doing the implying. But "the implied reader" is a translation (Iser's own) of the original title of the book, *Der implizite Leser.* By suggesting that the reader is implicit in the text itself, Iser gives insufficient attention to the role of the author. See Wolfgang Iser, *The Implied Reader: Patterns of Communication in Prose Fiction from Bunyan to Beckett* (Baltimore: Johns Hopkins University Press, 1974).

74. Wayne C. Booth, *The Rhetoric of Fiction,* 2nd ed. (Chicago: University of Chicago Press, 1983), 397–98.

75. Barth, *Church Dogmatics* [II/30], I/2:827.

76. Ong, "The Writer's Audience" [II/69], 60.

77. M. M. Bakhtin, "The Problem of Speech Genres" (1953), in *Speech Genres and Other Late Essays,* ed. Caryl Emerson and Michael Holquist, trans. Vern W. McGee (Austin: University of Texas Press, 1986), 71.

78. Chaïm Perelman, "The New Rhetoric and the Rhetoricians: Remembrances and Comments," *Quarterly Journal of Speech* 70 (1984): 191.

79. Ong, "The Writer's Audience" [II/69], 76.

80. Ibid.

81. Burke, *A Rhetoric of Motives* [I/6], 28.

82. Lentricchia, *Criticism and Social Change* [I/58], 88.

83. Steven Mailloux, *Rhetorical Power* (Ithaca, N.Y.: Cornell University Press, 1989), xii.

84. Eagleton, *Literary Theory* [II/70], 207.

85. Cf. the critique of the "commitment to pluralism" in Ellen Rooney, *Seductive Reasoning: Pluralism as the Problematic of Contemporary Literary Theory* (Ithaca, N.Y.: Cornell University Press, 1989).

86. Tracy, *The Analogical Imagination* [II/54], 99.

87. See, for example, the insightful comments on David Tracy's political commitments by Sharon D. Welch in her review of his *Plurality and Ambiguity: Hermeneutics, Religion, Hope,* in *Theology Today* 44, no. 4 (January 1988): 509–13. For another example of the rhetorical criticism of theological politics, see David S.

Cunningham, "Structures of Interest, Structures of Love: A Response to Michael Novak," *America* 160, no. 15 (22 April 1989): 369–71.

88. Matthew L. Lamb, *Solidarity with Victims: Toward a Theology of Social Transformation* (New York: Crossroad, 1982).

89. Justo L. González, *Christian Thought Revisited: Three Types of Theology* (Nashville: Abingdon Press, 1989), 78.

90. Clodovis Boff, O.S.M., *Theology and Praxis: Epistemological Foundations*, trans. Robert R. Barr (Maryknoll, N.Y.: Orbis Books, 1987), 43.

91. Schüssler Fiorenza, "The Ethics of Interpretation" [I/87], 11–12.

92. Arnhart, *Aristotle on Political Reasoning* [I/8], 114.

93. See, for example, Lovibond, *Realism and Imagination in Ethics* [I/45]; Diane Tennis, *Is God the Only Reliable Father?* (Philadelphia: Westminster Press, 1985); Wayne C. Booth, *The Company We Keep: An Ethics of Fiction* (Berkeley: University of California Press, 1988); idem, *A Rhetoric of Fiction* [II/74].

94. Wayne C. Booth, *Modern Dogma and the Rhetoric of Assent* (Chicago: University of Chicago Press, 1974), 163.

95. Jost, *Rhetorical Thought in Newman* [I/52], 60.

96. John Henry Newman, "The Tamworth Reading Room," in *Discussions and Arguments* (London: Longmans, Green, and Co., 1872), 295. See also Jost, *Rhetorical Thought in Newman* [I/52], 2.

97. Lovibond, *Realism and Imagination in Ethics* [I/45], 1. This is not Lovibond's own position, but rather a position that the argument of her book effectively demolishes.

98. Eagleton, *Literary Theory* [II/70], 13.

99. Perelman and Olbrechts-Tyteca, *The New Rhetoric* [I/55], 150, n. 20.

100. Rowan Williams, *Resurrection: Interpreting the Easter Gospel* (London: Darton, Longman, and Todd, 1982), 119–20.

101. For example: Perelman and Olbrechts-Tyteca, *The New Rhetoric* [I/55], 169.

102. Ibid., 169–70.

103. Janet Martin Soskice, *Metaphor and Religious Language* (Oxford: Clarendon Press, 1985), 89.

104. I return to a more detailed discussion of the theological role of allegory in chapter 5.

105. See, for example, David B. Burrell, C.S.C., *Aquinas: God and Action* (Notre Dame, Ind.: University of Notre Dame Press, 1979), 12–14. See also Nicholas Lash, "Ideology, Metaphor, and Analogy," in *The Philosophical Frontiers of Christian Theology: Essays Presented to D. M. MacKinnon,* ed. Brian Hebblethwaite and Stewart R. Sutherland

(Cambridge: Cambridge University Press, 1982), 183–98; reprinted in Nicholas Lash, *Theology on the Way to Emmaus* (London: SCM Press, 1986), 95–119.

106. Cf. Giambattista Vico, *Selected Writings*, ed. and trans. Leon Pompa (Cambridge: Cambridge University Press, 1982), 163.

107. Chopp, *The Power to Speak* [I/77], 91–92.

108. Kenneth Burke, *A Grammar of Motives* (New York: Prentice Hall, 1945; reprint, Berkeley: University of California Press, 1969), 6–7.

109. Ibid., 7 (emphasis mine).

110. Gadamer, *Truth and Method* [I/41], 271.

111. Nicholas Lash, "What Authority Has Our Past?" in *Theology on the Way to Emmaus* [II/105], 57.

112. See, for example, Gadamer, "On Scope and Function" [I/68], 29.

113. Gadamer's position has been criticized for employing a notion of tradition that assumes too great a degree of universality and continuity; see, for example, Eagleton, *Literary Theory* [II/70], 72. This critique has particular force when applied to Gadamer's extended metaphor (the "fusion of horizons"), which may indeed be too static and abstract a notion. All the same, the simple metaphor of *horizon* can point to both mobility and finitude. An audience can be bounded by a particular horizon and still be *moved*—that is, persuaded.

114. Lentricchia, *Criticism and Social Change* [I/58], 142.

115. Schubert M. Ogden, "Theology and Religious Studies: Their Difference and the Difference It Makes," in *On Theology* (San Francisco: Harper and Row, 1986), 118.

116. See, for example, the work of Stanley Hauerwas and James McClendon. A more critical perspective on MacIntyre's notion of practices is developed in L. Gregory Jones, *Transformed Judgment: Toward a Trinitarian Account of the Moral Life* (Notre Dame, Ind.: University of Notre Dame Press, 1990).

117. Alasdair MacIntyre, *After Virtue: A Study in Moral Theory*, 2nd ed. (Notre Dame, Ind.: University of Notre Dame Press, 1984), 187. MacIntyre's slight revisions of this definition, found on pp. 273–76 in his "Postscript to the Second Edition," do not affect my argument in this section.

118. Ibid., 188.

119. Ibid.

120. Pente is played by two players who alternately place one of their own pieces on the intersections of the lines of a grid. The game

is won by placing five such pieces in a row in any direction, or by capturing five pairs of the opponent's pieces by surrounding them on both sides with one's own pieces.

121. Newman, *Oxford University Sermons* [I/50], 227. See Jost, *Rhetorical Thought in Newman* [I/52], 37–38.

122. Chopp, *The Power to Speak* [I/77], 95.

123. Peggy L. Shriver, "The Paradox of Inclusiveness-That-Divides," *Christian Century* 101, no. 6 (February 22, 1984): 195.

124. Cf. Ong, "The Writer's Audience" [II/69], 60.

125. Reported by the *Boston Globe*, 8 May 1989; quoted by Martin E. Marty, "Not Dumb Persons," *Christian Century* 106, no. 18 (24–31 May 1989): 575.

3. ĒTHOS

1. Aristotle *Rh.* 1356a4–13.

2. Martin Heidegger, "Letter on Humanism" (1947), in *Basic Writings,* ed. David Farrell Krell (New York: Harper and Row, 1977), 233.

3. This is the case even when the book is edited by theorists who recognize the contextual nature of argument—e.g., Stephen Toulmin, Richard Rieke, and Allan Janik, *An Introduction to Reasoning* (London: Collier; New York: Macmillan, 1979).

4. Cf. Quintilian *Inst. Orat.* 3.8.12. The interrelationships among the terms *author, character,* and *authority* have been explored by a number of communication theorists; see, e.g., Kinneavy, *Greek Rhetorical Origins* [I/97], 47.

5. Ebeling, *Theological Theory of Language* [I/20], 168.

6. Perelman and Olbrechts-Tyteca, *The New Rhetoric* [I/55], 317.

7. Newman, *Grammar of Assent* [I/51], 240.

8. Kennedy, *Classical Rhetoric* [I/9], 121–22.

9. Cf. the discussion in Kennedy, *Classical Rhetoric* [I/9], 120–25.

10. This claim is studied at length in John Howard Schütz, *Paul and the Anatomy of Apostolic Authority* (Cambridge: Cambridge University Press, 1975).

11. St. Gregory of Nazianzus, "Second Theological Oration," in *Christology of the Later Fathers* [Intro./2], 129.

12. Ibid., 136.

13. Ibid., 136–37.

14. Consider, for example, recent discussions of abusive sexual relationships perpetrated by members of the clergy: e.g. Ann-Janine

Morey, "Blaming Women for the Sexually Abusive Male Pastor," *Christian Century* 105, no. 28 (5 October 1988): 866–69; Marie M. Fortune, *Is Nothing Sacred? When Sex Invades the Pastoral Relationship* (San Francisco: Harper and Row, 1989).

15. See the interesting remarks on this matter by Nicholas Lash, "Can a Theologian Keep the Faith?" in *Theology on Dover Beach* [II/32], 45–59.

16. The significance of this shift is explored in John C. Briggs, *Francis Bacon and the Rhetoric of Nature* (Cambridge: Harvard University Press, 1989).

17. See Lovibond, *Realism and Imagination in Ethics* [I/45]; Booth, *Modern Dogma and the Rhetoric of Assent* [II/94]; and the discussion in chapter 2, above.

18. Booth, *The Company We Keep* [II/93], 26–27.

19. William K. Wimsatt and Monroe C. Beardsley, "The Intentional Fallacy," in *The Verbal Icon* (Lexington: University of Kentucky Press, 1954), 3–18.

20. This claim was nuanced differently among various New Critics. Some argued that an author's intentions can never be recovered; others suggested that intentions are recoverable in principle but are not terribly useful for the critical task.

21. One claim to possess this insight may be found in Hirsch, *Validity in Interpretation* [I/67]. Hirsch's position has been attacked by a wide range of literary critics; only a few of their arguments are explored here.

22. Eagleton, *Literary Theory* [II/70], 68–69.

23. As noted in Lentricchia, *Criticism and Social Change* [I/58], 138.

24. Michel Foucault, "What Is an Author?" (1969), in *Language, Counter-memory, Practice*, ed. Donald F. Bouchard, trans. Donald F. Bouchard and Sherry Smith (Ithaca, N.Y.: Cornell University Press, 1977), 138.

25. Calvin O. Schrag, *Communicative Praxis and the Space of Subjectivity* (Bloomington: Indiana University Press, 1986), 127.

26. Perelman and Olbrechts-Tyteca, *The New Rhetoric* [I/55], 317.

27. Foucault, "What Is an Author?" [III/24], 137–38.

28. These include Eastern Orthodox writers such as Alexander Schmemann and John Zizioulas; feminists such as Anne Carr, Rebecca Chopp, and Letty Russell; liberation theologians such as Clodovis Boff and Leonardo Boff; and a number of writers who take up the postmodern critique within the classical Western tradition of Christian theology—for example, L. Gregory Jones, Nicholas Lash, John Milbank,

and Rowan Williams.

29. Schrag, *Communicative Praxis* [III/25], 148.

30. Ibid., 148–49.

31. For a somewhat different argument against relying on the concept of meaning, see Jeffrey Stout, "What Is the Meaning of a Text?" *New Literary History* 14, no. 1 (Autumn 1982): 1–12.

32. Aristotle *Rh.* 1367a28–30.

33. Cf. the related comments in Burke, *A Rhetoric of Motives* [I/6], 56.

34. Schrag, *Communicative Praxis* [III/25], 201. Cf. also the descriptions of the devaluation of value in Lovibond, *Realism and Imagination in Ethics* [I/45], 1–23; and MacIntyre, *After Virtue* [II/117], 11–35.

35. Stanley Hauerwas, "From System to Story: An Alternative Pattern for Rationality in Ethics," in *Truthfulness and Tragedy: Further Investigations in Christian Ethics,* by Stanley Hauerwas, with Richard Bondi and David Burrell (Notre Dame, Ind.: University of Notre Dame Press, 1977), 29.

36. In addition to a great many works cited elsewhere in this study, one could mention Walter Benjamin, *Illuminations,* ed. Hannah Arendt, trans. Harry Zohn (New York: Schocken Books, 1969); Walter R. Fisher, *Human Communication as Narration: Toward a Philosophy of Reason, Value, and Action* (Columbia: University of South Carolina Press, 1987); and Martha C. Nussbaum, *The Fragility of Goodness: Luck and Ethics in Greek Tragedy and Philosophy* (Cambridge: Cambridge University Press, 1986).

37. See especially the essays collected in *Why Narrative? Readings in Narrative Theology,* ed. Stanley Hauerwas and L. Gregory Jones (Grand Rapids, Mich.: William B. Eerdmans, 1989).

38. Schrag, *Communicative Praxis* [III/25], 123.

39. Thomas S. Frentz, "Rhetorical Conversation, Time, and Moral Action," *Quarterly Journal of Speech* 71, no. 1 (1985): 4.

40. Ibid., 14.

41. The implications of this problem for a different theological issue (the study of comparative religion) are discussed in Nicholas Lash, "How Large is a 'Language Game'?" *Theology* 87 (January 1984): 19–28.

42. This movement—once advocated by such writers as John Erskine, Robert Maynard Hutchins, Mortimer Adler, and Daniel Bell— seemed to die out in the 1960s and 1970s. Recent attempts to resuscitate it have met with mixed reviews: see, e.g., Allan Bloom, *The Closing of the American Mind,* with a foreword by Saul Bellow (New

York: Simon and Schuster, 1987); E. D. Hirsch, Jr., *Cultural Literacy: What Every American Needs to Know*, rev. ed. (New York: Random House, Vintage Books, 1988).

43. Such positions involve a view of ancient civilizations that is romantically naïve at best and, at worst, tyrannical. They have been subjected to penetrating critiques, based on their apotheosis of Platonism, their cultural and economic imperialism, and their incipient sexism, racism, and classism. See the critiques offered, for example, in Eagleton, *Literary Theory* [II/70], 1–16; Lanham, "The 'Q' Question" [I/39], 677–81; and Lentricchia, *Criticism and Social Change* [I/58], 123–32.

44. Perelman and Olbrechts-Tyteca, *The New Rhetoric* [I/55], 320.

45. Technology, and especially information-oriented technology, can fundamentally alter these relationships. The relationship between technology and communication, which cannot be taken up here, is the subject of an ever-expanding range of studies. See the work of Walter J. Ong, S.J., especially *Rhetoric, Romance, and Technology* (Ithaca, N.Y.: Cornell University Press, 1971). For a general overview, see Michael J. Hyde, ed., *Communication Philosophy and the Technological Age* (Tuscaloosa: University of Alabama Press, 1982).

46. Henry W. Johnstone, Jr., "'Philosophy and *Argumentum ad Hominem*' Revisited," in *Validity and Rhetoric in Philosophical Argumentation: An Outlook in Transition* (University Park, Pa.: Dialogue Press of Man and World, 1978), 55–56.

47. Henry W. Johnstone, Jr., "Truth, Communication, and Rhetoric in Philosophy," in *Validity and Rhetoric* [III/46], 76.

48. Henry W. Johnstone, Jr., "Rationality and Rhetoric in Philosophy," in *Validity and Rhetoric* [III/46], 84.

49. Aristotle *Rh.* 1378a9.

50. Perelman and Olbrechts-Tyteca, *The New Rhetoric* [I/55], 323–24.

51. Perelman and Olbrechts-Tyteca seem to recognize this, and even describe how these shifts can be effected. See their extended comments on techniques of severance and restraint in *The New Rhetoric* [I/55], 324–27.

52. Perelman and Olbrechts-Tyteca, *The New Rhetoric* [I/55], 319.

53. Cf. Schrag, *Communicative Praxis* [III/25], 155.

54. See, *inter alia*, Lash, "Performing the Scriptures," in *Theology on the Way to Emmaus* [II/32], 37–46; Alexander Schmemann, *For the Life of the World: Sacraments and Orthodoxy*, 2nd ed. (Crestwood, N.Y.: St. Vladimir's Seminary Press, 1973); and Geoffrey Wainwright, *Doxology: The Praise of God in Worship, Doctrine, and Life* (Oxford: Oxford University Press, 1980). I shall return to this point in chapter 5.

55. See Stanley Fish, "What Is Stylistics and Why Are They Saying Such Terrible Things About It?" (1973), in *Is There a Text in This Class? The Authority of Interpretive Communities* (Cambridge: Harvard University Press, 1980), 68–96.

56. Friedrich Nietzsche, *The Gay Science, with a Prelude in Rhymes and an Appendix of Songs*, trans. Walter Kaufmann (New York: Random House, Vintage Books, 1974), sec. 290, p. 232.

57. Eagleton, *Literary Theory* [II/70], 208.

58. Richard Weaver, "Ultimate Terms in Contemporary Rhetoric," ch. 9 in *The Ethics of Rhetoric* (South Bend, Ind.: Regnery/Gateway, 1953), 211.

59. Barth, *Church Dogmatics*, IV/3/2:518.

60. S. W. Sykes, "The Study of Barth" [II/33], 2–3.

61. John Macquarrie, *Principles of Christian Theology*, 2nd ed. (New York: Charles Scribner's Sons, 1977), 464.

62. Notice, for example, how Christianity appears comfortably balanced between the contrasting extremes of other religions (diagram, ibid., 167).

63. Melchior Hofmann, *The Ordinance of God* (1530), in *Spiritual and Anabaptist Writers,* ed. George H. Williams and Angel M. Mergal, Library of Christian Classics, vol. 25 (Philadelphia: Westminster Press, 1957), 192.

64. G. R. Potter, *Zwingli* (Cambridge: Cambridge University Press, 1976), 171.

65. Zwingli, "Refutation of the Tricks of the Anabaptists" (1527), in *Huldrych Zwingli,* ed. G. R. Potter (London: Edward Arnold, 1978), 42.

66. While advocates of the practice call it *infant baptism,* its opponents often call it *pedobaptism.* This apparently innocuous label may call up, in the listener's mind, one of the most common of those few English words which begin with the prefix *pedo,* namely *pedophilia* and its cognates. The words may be related only through their prefix; yet even this distant relationships can still produce a negative rhetorical effect.

67. Schrag, *Communicative Praxis* [III/25], 194–95.

68. Perelman and Olbrechts-Tyteca, *The New Rhetoric* [I/55], 296.

69. Vladimir Lossky, "Tradition and Traditions," trans. G. E. H. Palmer and E. Kadloubovsky, in *The Meaning of Icons* (Boston: Boston Book and Art Shop, 1952), 13–24; reprinted in *In the Image and Likeness of God,* ed. John H. Erikson and Thomas E. Bird (Crestwood, N.Y.: St. Vladimir's Seminary Press, 1974), 150–51.

70. Boff, *Theology and Praxis* [II/90], 159–60.

71. Chopp, "Theological Persuasion" [I/88], 29.

72. World Council of Churches, Faith and Order Commission, *Sharing in One Hope: Reports and Documents from the Meeting of the Faith and Order Commission, 15–30 August 1978, Ecumenical Christian Centre, Bangalore, India* (Geneva: Commission on Faith and Order, World Council of Churches, 1978), 201.

73. Donald MacKinnon, "Tillich, Frege, Kittel: Some Reflections on a Dark Theme" (1975), in *Explorations in Theology* 5 (London: SCM Press, 1979), 130.

74. Ibid., 131.

75. The books under discussion are Hannah Tillich, *From Time to Time* (New York: Stein and Day, 1974); and Rollo May, *Paulus: Reminiscences of a Friendship* (New York: Harper and Row, 1973).

76. MacKinnon, "Tillich, Frege, Kittel" [III/73], 133

77. Ibid., 134.

78. Harvey Cox, *New York Times Book Review*, 14 October 1973, p. 31.

79. Ibid., 134.

80. Eberhard Bethge, *Dietrich Bonhoeffer: Man of Vision, Man of Courage* (New York: Harper and Row, 1970), xxiii.

81. In addition to reviews of the two books mentioned in n. 75, above, see Langdon Gilkey, *Gilkey on Tillich* (New York: Crossroad, 1989). Although this book includes a chapter of personal anecdotes and reflections about the life of Paul Tillich, no mention is made of his alleged sexual improprieties.

82. Eberhard Bethge, "The Challenge of Dietrich Bonhoeffer's Life and Theology," in *World Come of Age: A Symposium on Dietrich Bonhoeffer*, ed. Ronald Gregor Smith (London: Collins, 1967), 24.

83. Marjorie O'Rourke Boyle, "A Likely Story: The Autobiographical as Epideictic," *Journal of the American Academy of Religion* 57, no. 1 (Spring 1989): 23–51.

84. Lanham, "The 'Q' Question" [I/39], 692.

4. LOGOS

1. Aristotle *Rh.* 1356a19–21.

2. Here one may apply, *mutatis mutandis*, the general thrust of the argument in Richard Rorty, *Philosophy and the Mirror of Nature* (Princeton, N.J.: Princeton University Press, 1979).

3. Standard works include Michael Polanyi, *Personal Knowledge:*

Towards a Post-Critical Philosophy (1958; reprint, London: Routledge and Kegan Paul, 1973); Thomas S. Kuhn, *The Structure of Scientific Revolutions,* 2nd ed. (Chicago: University of Chicago Press, 1970); Paul Feyerabend, *Against Method: Outline of an Anarchistic Theory of Knowledge* (1975; reprint, London: Verso, 1978); and Mary B. Hesse, *Revolutions and Reconstructions in the Philosophy of Science* (Bloomington: Indiana University Press, 1980).

4. Wittgenstein, *Philosophical Investigations* [I/66], sec. 381, p. 117e.

5. "Not to know of what things one should demand demonstration, and of what things one should not, suggests *apaideusia"* (Aristotle *Met.* 1006a5–8).

6. Wittgenstein, *Philosophical Investigations* [I/66], sec. 1, p. 3e.

7. Aristotle *Eth. Nic.* 1094b25.

8. See the intriguing comments on rhetoric and mathematics in Gregg, *Symbolic Inducement and Knowing* [I/62], 138–39.

9. Cf. Michael Dummett, "The Philosophical Basis of Intuitionistic Logic" (1973), in *Truth and Other Enigmas* (London: Duckworth, 1978), 215–47.

10. T. S. Eliot, "Burnt Norton," in *Four Quartets* (1943; reprint, New York: Harcourt Brace Jovanovich, 1971), lines 1–3, p. 13.

11. Aristotle *An. Pr.* 24b18–22.

12. Toulmin, *The Uses of Argument* [I/63], 154. The same point is made repeatedly in Johnstone, *Validity and Rhetoric* [III/46], *passim.*

13. Richard McKeon, "Introduction," *in The Basic Works of Aristotle* (New York: Random House, 1941), xvii.

14. Booth, *Modern Dogma and the Rhetoric of Assent* [II/94], 144 n. 3.

15. The notion of a subordination of rhetoric to analytic in Aristotle is criticized in a number of recent works, including Arnhart, *Aristotle on Political Reasoning* [I/8]; Grimaldi, *Aristotle, Rhetoric I: A Commentary* [I/25]; and Paolo Valesio, *Novantiqua: Rhetorics as a Contemporary Theory,* Advances in Semiotics, ed. Thomas A. Sebeok (Bloomington: Indiana University Press, 1980). The state of scholarship on Aristotle's *Rhetoric* is discussed in Michael C. Leff, "Recovering Aristotle: Rhetoric, Politics, and the Limits of Rationality," *Quarterly Journal of Speech* 71 (1985): 362–73; and in Rosalind J. Gabin, "Aristotle and the New Rhetoric: Grimaldi and Valesio. A Review Essay," *Philosophy and Rhetoric* 20, no. 3 (1987): 171–82.

16. Olivier Reboul, "Can There Be Non-Rhetorical Argumentation?" trans. Henry W. Johnstone, Jr., *Philosophy and Rhetoric* 21, no. 3 (1988): 226.

17. Anthony Flew and Alasdair MacIntyre, eds., *New Essays in Philosophical Theology* (New York: Macmillian, 1955).

18. Wolfhart Pannenberg, *Theology and the Philosophy of Science*, trans. Francis McDonagh (London: Darton, Longman, and Todd, 1976), ch. 5 *passim*.

19. Dietrich Ritschl, *The Logic of Theology: A Brief Account of the Relationships between Basic Concepts in Theology*, trans. John Bowden (London: SCM Press, 1986).

20. Ibid., xiii.

21. Ibid., 30.

22. Ibid., 72–75.

23. Ibid., 4.

24. Ibid., 86.

25. The attempt to objectify translation, history, and hermeneutics into an empirical reality is as much a rhetorical event as the philosophical objectivism on which it was based. See, *inter alia*, Michel Foucault, *The Order of Things: An Archaeology of the Human Sciences* (New York: Random House, 1970); Gadamer, *Truth and Method* [I/41]; W. V. Quine, *Ontological Relativity and Other Essays* (New York: Columbia University Press, 1969); Douglas Robinson, *The Translator's Turn* (Baltimore: Johns Hopkins University Press, 1991); George Steiner, *After Babel: Aspects of Language and Translation* (Oxford: Oxford University Press, 1975); and Hayden White, *Metahistory: The Historical Imagination in Nineteenth-Century Europe* (Baltimore: Johns Hopkins University Press, 1973).

26. Ritschl, *Logic of Theology* [IV/19], 86.

27. See the work of Michel Foucault, especially *Madness and Civilization: A History of Insanity in the Age of Reason,* trans. Richard Howard (New York: Random House, 1965); *Discipline and Punish: The Birth of the Prison*, trans. Alan Sheridan (New York: Pantheon Books, 1977); and *The History of Sexuality,* trans. Robert Hurley, 3 vols. (1978–86; reprint, New York: Random House, 1980–88).

28. Ritschl, *Logic of Theology* [IV/19], 32–33.

29. Ibid., 65.

30. Ibid., 228.

31. Ibid., 272.

32. Ibid.

33. Ibid., 174–88.

34. Ibid., 68.

35. Ibid., e.g., 68, 90.

36. Ibid., 25.

37. Donald MacKinnon, "The Conflict between Realism and Idealism" (1977), in *Explorations in Theology* 5 [III/73], 164.

38. Scott, "Rhetoric as Epistemic: Ten Years Later" [I/62], 261.

39. Most thoroughly in Grimaldi, *Rhetoric I: A Commentary* [I/25]. Grimaldi's analysis on this point is supported in Leff, "Recovering Aristotle" [IV/15], 365.

40. Aristotle *Rh.* 1355a10.

41. Arnhart, *Aristotle on Political Reasoning* [I/8], 41.

42. Newman, *Grammar of Assent* [I/51], 224.

43. Arnhart, *Aristotle on Political Reasoning* [I/8], 42. Arnhart cites this as Aristotle *Rhet* 1356a19, but the correct reference is 1357a19.

44. Fully developed in Perelman and Olbrechts-Tyteca, *The New Rhetoric* [I/55], 115–20.

45. Perelman, *The Realm of Rhetoric* [I/22], 35.

46. Aristotle *Rh.* 1357b27–30.

47. Toulmin, *The Uses of Argument* [I/63], 122.

48. Karl Rahner, "The Experience of God Today" (1970), in *Theological Investigations,* trans. David Bourke, vol. 11 (London: Darton, Longman, and Todd, 1974), 157–59.

49. Perelman and Olbrechts-Tyteca, *The New Rhetoric* [I/55], 193.

50. Ibid., 197.

51. John Hick, *Evil and the God of Love* (San Francisco: Harper and Row, 1978), 69.

52. Newman, *Grammar of Assent* [I/51], 230.

53. Newman, "The Tamworth Reading Room" [II/96], 294.

54. John Henry Newman, *Apologia Pro Vita Sua* (1864; reprint, Garden City, N.Y.: Doubleday, Image Books, 1956), 264. For a further discussion of Newman's understanding of the "whole man," see Jost, *Rhetorical Thought in Newman* [I/52], 76–84.

55. Cf. Perelman and Olbrechts-Tyteca, *The New Rhetoric* [I/55], 503.

56. Booth, *The Company We Keep* [II/93], 70.

57. Ibid., 72.

58. Ibid., 73.

59. Jost, *Rhetorical Thought in Newman* [I/52], 97.

60. Burke, *A Rhetoric of Motives* [I/6], 77.

61. Burke, *The Rhetoric of Religion* [I/81].

62. Ibid., vi.

63. Ibid., 7–8.

64. Ibid., 13–14.

65. Some of Burke's analogies would probably provoke heated responses, both from philosophers of language and from theologians. For example: "Words are to the non-verbal things they name as Spirit

is to Matter" (p. 16). A full study of this comment would require considerable theological and linguistic unpacking that I am not prepared to undertake here. Nevertheless, a number of Burke's analogies are provocative, and they suggest good reasons for exploring not only the discursive nature of theology, but also the theological nature of discourse.

66. Burke, *The Rhetoric of Religion* [I/81], 18.

67. Ibid., 22.

68. Ibid., 29–33.

69. John Freccero, "Logology: Burke on St. Augustine," in *Representing Kenneth Burke,* ed. Hayden White and Margaret Brose, Selected Papers from the English Institute, New Series, vol. 6 (Baltimore: Johns Hopkins University Press, 1982), 52–53.

70. Ibid., 67.

71. Soskice, *Metaphor and Religious Language* [II/103], 50.

72. Ibid., 57, 88.

73. Gordon H. Clark, "Revealed Religion," in *Fundamentals of the Faith,* ed. Carl F. H. Henry (Grand Rapids, Mich.: Baker Book House, 1975), 28.

74. Dale Moody, *The Word of Truth: A Summary of Christian Doctrine Based on Biblical Revelation* (Grand Rapids, Mich.: William B. Eerdmans, 1981), 40.

75. Edward Schillebeeckx, *Jesus: An Experiment in Christology,* trans. Hubert Hoskins (London: Collins, 1979), 34.

76. John Meyendorff, *Byzantine Theology: Historical Trends and Doctrinal Themes,* 2nd rev. ed. (New York: Fordham University Press, 1983), 79–90.

77. Wainwright, *Doxology* [III/54], 348–49.

78. Macquarrie, *Principles of Christian Theology* [III/61], 71.

79. Ibid., 94.

80. Thomas F. Torrance, *Theological Science* (Oxford: Oxford University Press, 1969), 34.

81. Theodore W. Jennings, Jr., *Introduction to Theology: An Invitation to Reflection upon the Christian Mythos* (London: SPCK, 1977), 3–4.

82. Another good example of this tendency—this time from the Roman Catholic side—is Gerald O'Collins, S.J., *Fundamental Theology* (Ramsey, N.J.: Paulist Press, 1981).

83. Gordon D. Kaufman, *Systematic Theology: A Historicist Perspective* (New York: Charles Scribner's Sons, 1968), 44.

84. Rosemary Radford Ruether, *Sexism and God-Talk: Toward a Feminist Theology* (London: SCM Press, 1983), 15.

85. Ibid., 18–19.

86. For an example of how this sort of analysis might be carried out formally, see Davidson, *Inquiries into Truth and Interpretation* [II/17].

87. Donald Davidson, "Theories of Meaning and Learnable Languages," in *Inquiries into Truth and Interpretation* [II/17], 3–15.

88. Ibid., 8.

89. Perelman and Olbrechts-Tyteca, *The New Rhetoric* [I/55], 116.

90. See Donald Davidson, "The Method of Truth in Metaphysics," in *Inquiries into Truth and Interpretation* [II/17], 199–214.

91. George Lindbeck identifies this traditional vocabulary of theology as its "lexical core" in *The Nature of Doctrine: Religion and Theology in a Postliberal Age* (Philadelphia: Westminster Press; London: SPCK, 1984). While I agree with Lindbeck's advocacy of language as a paradigm for Christian theology, his approach fails to provide the sort of contextual nuances that I am proposing here. I shall return to Lindbeck in chapter 5.

92. Jürgen Moltmann, "Love, Death, Eternal Life: Theology of Hope—the Personal Side," in *Love, the Foundation of Hope: The Theology of Jürgen Moltmann and Elisabeth Moltmann-Wendel,* ed. Frederic B. Burnham, Charles S. McCoy, and M. Douglas Meeks (San Francisco: Harper and Row, 1988), 3–22.

93. Ibid., 12.

94. Soskice, *Metaphor and Religious Language* [II/103], 61.

95. As James Cone describes it, God "undertakes a course of not-so-gentle persuasion for the liberation and restoration of his creatures" (*Black Theology and Black Power* [New York: Seabury Press, 1969; reprint, San Francisco: Harper and Row, 1989], 64).

96. Dalferth, *Theology and Philosophy* [I/77], 40–41.

97. Ibid., 41–44.

98. Ibid., 41.

99. Chopp, *The Power to Speak* [I/80], 103.

5. PRAXIS

1. M. M. Bakhtin, *Problems of Dostoevsky's Poetics*, ed. and trans. Caryl Emerson, with an introduction by Wayne C. Booth, Theory and History of Literature, vol. 8 (Minneapolis: University of Minnesota Press, 1984), 6.

2. Wainwright, *Doxology* [III/54], 9.

3. Barth, *Church Dogmatics* [II/30], I/2:798.

4. Despite the passage of time, the definitive English-language work on the subject remains John Henry Newman, *An Essay on the Development of Christian Doctrine,* 6th ed. (London: Longmans, Green, and Co., 1878; reprint, with a foreword by Ian Ker, Notre Dame: University of Notre Dame Press, 1989). See also Nicholas Lash, *Change in Focus: A Study of Doctrinal Change and Continuity* (London: Sheed and Ward, 1973).

5. Some pertinent reflections may be found in Nicholas Lash, "The Remaking of Doctrine: Which Way Shall We Go?" in *Theology on Dover Beach* [II/32], 109–21.

6. Lindbeck, *The Nature of Doctrine* [IV/91], 16.

7. Ibid., 18.

8. Ibid, 80.

9. Most recently, see Bruce D. Marshall, ed., *Theology and Dialogue: Essays in Conversation with George Lindbeck* (Notre Dame, Ind.: University of Notre Dame Press, 1990).

10. See, for example, Burrell, *Aquinas: God and Action* [II/105]; Fergus Kerr, *Theology after Wittgenstein* (Oxford: Basil Blackwell, 1986); Lash, *Theology on the Way to Emmaus* [II/105].

11. See, for example, the essays gathered by Marshall in *Theology and Dialogue* [V/9]; see also the review essays by William C. Placher, Colman E. O'Neill, O.P., James J. Buckley, and David Tracy in *The Thomist* 49 (July 1985): 392–472.

12. Lindbeck, *The Nature of Doctrine* [IV/91], 84–88.

13. Ibid., 85.

14. Ibid., 93.

15. Cf. the comments on *form* and *substance* in Geoffrey Wainwright, "Ecumenical Dimensions of George Lindbeck's 'Nature of Doctrine,'" *Modern Theology* 4, no. 2 (January 1988): 127–28.

16. The relationship between *res* and *verbum* in Christian theology is explored in John Milbank, "Theology without Substance: Christianity, Signs, Origins. Part One," *Literature and Theology* 2, no. 1 (March 1988): 8–13.

17. Lindbeck, *The Nature of Doctrine* [IV/91], 93.

18. Ibid., 94.

19. Some of the difficulties involved in holding these concepts in tension are discussed—with intelligence and rigor—in Kasper, *The God of Jesus Christ* [II/32], 233–51.

20. Lindbeck, *The Nature of Doctrine* [IV/91], 94.

21. Cf. the comments on "the vast difference that ordinary Christian piety has made to the last two thousand years of history" in Wainwright, *Doxology* [III/54], 433–34.

22. James J. Buckley, "Doctrine in the Diaspora," *The Thomist* 49 (July 1985): 449.

23. Ibid., 449–50.

24. Cf. Alexander Schmemann, *For the Life of the World* [III/54]; and Wainwright, *Doxology* [III/54], 218–19—especially on the development of the *lex orandi lex credendi* principle throughout ch. 7 and 8.

25. Wittgenstein, *Philosophical Investigations* [I/66], sec. 23, p. 11.

26. Ibid., sec. 373, p. 116e.

27. Kerr, *Theology after Wittgenstein* [V/10], 147.

28. I return to the doctrine of the Eucharist in the section below, Luther on the Eucharist.

29. See, for example, the critiques in Rebecca S. Chopp, *The Praxis of Suffering: An Interpretation of Liberation and Political Theologies* (New York: Orbis Books, 1986), 115–17; and Dorothee Soelle, *Suffering*, trans. Everett R. Kalin (Philadelphia: Fortress Press, 1975), 26–27.

30. Cf. the critique offered in Roberto S. Goizueta, *Liberation, Method, and Dialogue: Enrique Dussel and North American Theological Discourse* (Atlanta: Scholars Press, 1988), 131–35.

31. Lee Cormie, review of Michael Novak, *Will It Liberate? Questions about Liberation Theology*, in *Theology Today* 45, no. 3 (October 1988): 372.

32. Jeffrey Stout, review of David Tracy, *Plurality and Ambiguity: Hermeneutics, Religion, Hope*, in *Theology Today* 44, no. 4 (January 1988): 507.

33. Throughout this section, I use the terms *exegesis* and *interpretation* interchangeably. I am fully aware that this goes against common practice, which tends to define *exegesis* as "specifying what the text actually says." The reasons for my usage will, I believe, become apparent in the course of my argument.

34. See the criticisms of this view in Lash, "Performing the Scriptures" [III/54].

35. I would also want to argue that the biblical scholar makes theological choices as well. The arguments for such a claim, however, would extend well beyond the scope of this work.

36. This very brief sketch of biblical hermeneutics cannot do justice to the nuances of each approach—a limitation for which I apologize in advance.

37. David C. Steinmetz, "The Superiority of Pre-Critical Exegesis" (1980), reprinted in *Ex Auditu* 1 (1985): 78.

38. Cf. Thomas Aquinas *Sum. theol.* 1.1.10.

39. Steinmetz, "Superiority" [V/37], 75.

40. See my evaluation of this debate in chapter 3.

41. This has been documented in case studies of Luther's exegesis. See Jaroslav Pelikan, *Luther the Expositor: Companion Volume to Luther's Works* (St. Louis: Concordia, 1959).

42. Friedrich E. D. Schleiermacher, *Hermeneutics: The Handwritten Manuscripts,* ed. Heinz Kimmerle, trans. James Duke and Jack Forstman (Missoula, Mont.: Scholars Press, 1977), esp. 42–44.

43. Benjamin Jowett, "On the Interpretation of Scripture," in *Essays and Reviews*, 7th ed. (London: Longman, Green, Longman, and Roberts, 1861), 330–43; reprinted in part in *Religious Thought in the Nineteenth Century*, ed. B. M. G. Reardon (London: Cambridge University Press, 1966), 315.

44. Dennis Nineham, *Saint Mark* (Philadelphia: Westminster Press, 1963), 52.

45. An argument for this approach can be found in Dennis Nineham, *The Use and Abuse of the Bible* (London: Macmillan, 1976; reprint, London: SPCK, 1978)—where, however, quite exaggerated claims are made on its behalf.

46. Even a sketchy bibliography of this movement would be too long to include here. Good collections of articles may be found in Donald McKim, ed., *A Guide to Contemporary Hermeneutics: Major Trends in Biblical Interpretation* (Grand Rapids, Mich.: William B. Eerdmans, 1986); and in the annual journal *Ex Auditu.*

47. Karl Barth, "The Strange New World within the Bible," in *The Word of God and the Word of Man,* trans. with a foreword by Douglas Horton (1956; reprint, Gloucester, Mass.: Peter Smith, 1978), 35–36.

48. See Peter Stuhlmacher, *Historical Criticism and the Theological Interpretation of Scripture: Toward a Hermeneutics of Consent,* trans. Roy A. Harrisville (Philadelphia: Fortress Press, 1977). The content of a hermeneutics of consent is explored throughout *Ex Auditu* 1 (1985).

49. Similar concerns are voiced in the field of literary theory—for example, in Hirsch, *Validity in Interpretation* [I/67]; and, with somewhat less apocalyptic fervor, in Booth, *The Company We Keep* [II/93].

50. David H. Kelsey, *The Uses of Scripture in Recent Theology* (Philadelphia: Fortress Press; London: SCM Press, 1975), 125–38.

51. This model was developed as a means of making sense of the ambiguities that naturally occur in syllogistic reasoning. Following Toulmin's own practice, it is usually expressed graphically, in this way:

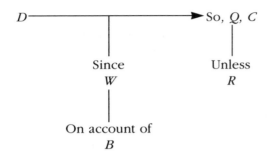

D is the datum with which the argument begins; C is the claim in which it issues. W is the warrant that supports this claim, and B is the backing for that warrant. The remaining letters, Q and R, modify the claim either positively (Q = qualifier) or negatively (R = rebuttal). For a complete description, see Toulmin, *The Uses of Argument* [I/63], ch. 3.

52. Stanley Fish, "Interpreting the *Variorum*," *Critical Inquiry* 2 (Spring 1976): 465–85; reprinted in *Is There a Text* [III/55], 147–73.

53. Jowett, "On the Interpretation of Scripture" [V/43], 315.

54. Edward Farley and Peter C. Hodgson, "Scripture and Tradition," in *Christian Theology: An Introduction to Its Traditions and Tasks*, ed. Peter C. Hodgson and Robert H. King, 2nd ed. (Philadelphia: Fortress Press, 1985), 61.

55. I do not know the precise extent of this influence; however, the book was enlarged and reprinted three years after its original publication.

56. Wainwright, *Doxology* [III/54], 149.

57. Soskice, *Metaphor and Religious Language* [II/103], 160.

58. Bakhtin, *Problems of Dostoevsky's Poetics* [V/1], 8.

59. Ibid., 80.

60. The technical term for this enterprise is *Wirkungsgeschichte*—frequently translated "effective-history."

61. Jerome, *Letter 22*, Ancient Christian Writers (hereafter ACW) 33:154.

62. John Chrysostom *Homily 22*, Nicene and Post-Nicene Fathers (hereafter NPNF), series 2, 10:154.

63. Cyprian *Exhortation to Martyrdom*, Ante-Nicene Fathers (hereafter ANF) 5:535.

64. Jerome, *Letter 14*, ACW 33:63, altered.

65. Augustine *Sermon 50*, NPNF, series 1, 6:420, altered.

66. John Chrysostom *Homily 46*, NPNF, series 1, 10:290.

67. G. E. P. Cox, *The Gospel According to St. Matthew* (London: SCM Press, 1952), 67.

68. Albert Kirk and Robert E. Obach, *A Commentary on the Gospel of Matthew* (Ramsey, N.J.: Paulist Press, 1978), 97.

69. Daniel Patte, *The Gospel According to Matthew* (Philadelphia: Fortress Press, 1987), 119.

70. Cf. Floyd V. Filson, *The Gospel According to St. Matthew* (San Francisco: Harper and Row, 1960), 114; A. W. Argyle, *The Gospel According to Matthew* (Cambridge: Cambridge University Press, 1963), 69.

71. Augustine *Harmony of the Gospels*, NPNF, series 1, 6:102.

72. Martin Luther, "First Sermon on John 4," in *Luther's Works* (hereafter LW), ed. Jaroslav Pelikan, vol. 22 (St. Louis: Concordia, 1957), 504–5.

73. Barth, *Church Dogmatics* [II/30], IV/1:166.

74. Homily 9, in NPNF, series 1, 10:59, altered.

75. Barth, *Church Dogmatics* [II/30], IV/2:167.

76. Tertullian *On Idolatry*, ANF 3:72–73.

77. Now collected in John Chrysostom, *On Wealth and Poverty*, trans. Catherine P. Roth (Crestwood, N.Y.: St. Vladimir's Seminary Press, 1984).

78. John Chrysostom, *Homily against Marcionites and Manicheans*, NPNF, series 2, 9:206, altered.

79. Thomas Aquinas *Sum. theol.* 3.40.3.

80. Ibid.

81. Ibid., quoting Jerome, *In Matt. I (PL* 26:53).

82. Ibid., quoting Jerome, *In Matt. I (PL* 26:62).

83. John Calvin, *Commentaries,* vol. 1: *A Harmony of the Gospels,* trans. A. W. Morrison, ed. David W. Torrance and Thomas F. Torrance (Grand Rapids, Mich.: William B. Eerdmans, 1972), 254.

84. Martin Luther, "Commentary on Psalm 45," LW 12:259.

85. Martin Luther, "Commentary on Psalm 110," LW 13:345–46.

86. Martin Luther, "Commentary on Galatians" (1535), LW 27:122.

87. "Dans le cas du Seigneur, c'est en ce sens figuré qu'il convient d'interpréter l'expression «pas de lieu où reposer la tête». Il est exclu de lui donner son sense strict: pas d'habitation. Car, on sait, par l'Ev. lui-même, que le Maître des Douze avait bien un domicile légal, un logement à lui ou un pied-à-terre. C'était à Capernaüm" (Georges Gander, *L'Evangile de l'église: Commentaire de l'Evangile selon Matthieu*, vol. 1 [Aix-en-Provence: Faculté Libre de Theologie Protestante, 1967], 56 [my translation]).

88. R. T. France, *The Gospel According to Matthew* (Grand Rapids,

Michigan: William B. Eerdmans; Leicester, England: Inter-Varsity Press, 1985), 160.

89. J. C. Fenton, *Saint Matthew*, Westminster Pelican Commentaries (London: Penguin, 1963; reprint, Philadelphia: Westminster Press, 1977), 128.

90. H. Benedict Green, *The Gospel According to Matthew*, New Clarendon Bible, ed. H. F. D. Sparks (Oxford: Oxford University Press, 1975), 101.

91. Plutarch *Tib. Grac.* 9. Cited, for example (in this instance in reference to the parallel passage in Luke), in Alfred Plummer, *A Critical and Exegetical Commentary on the Gospel According to St. Luke*, International Critical Commentary (Edinburgh: T. and T. Clark, 1922), 266.

92. One may apply here, *mutatis mutandis*, the insights of writers such as Kenneth Burke, Michel Foucault, and Hayden White, who have sought to describe the hidden agendas operative within traditional historiography.

93. Steven Mailloux, "Rhetorical Hermeneutics," *Critical Inquiry* 11 (June 1985): 631.

94. Rhetorical history in this sense owes its genesis to a short but highly influential article: Leland M. Griffin, "The Rhetoric of Historical Movements," *Quarterly Journal of Speech* 38 (1952): 184–88.

95. Mailloux, "Rhetorical Hermeneutics" [V/93], 631.

96. Bourdieu, *Homo Academicus* [II/29]; Foucault, *Discipline and Punish;* idem, *Madness and Civilization* [IV/27]; idem, *The History of Sexuality* [IV/27]; Mailloux, *Rhetorical Power* [II/83].

97. Heinrich Bornkamm, *Luther and the Old Testament*, trans. Eric W. Gritsch and Ruth C. Gritsch (Philadelphia: Fortress Press, 1969), 247.

98. Mark Ellingsen, "Luther as Narrative Exegete," *Journal of Religion* 63, no. 4 (October 1983): 408.

99. Bainton, *Here I Stand* [II/34], 41.

100. Ibid., 42.

101. Martin Luther, "Disputation against Scholastic Theology," in *Luther: Early Theological Works*, ed. and trans. James Atkinson, Library of Christian Classics, vol. 16 (Philadelphia: Westminster Press, 1962), 267.

102. Ibid., 269.

103. Martin Luther, "The Heidelberg Disputation," in *Early Theological Works* [V/101], 276.

104. Paul Althaus, *The Theology of Martin Luther*, trans. Robert C. Schultz (Philadelphia: Fortress Press, 1966), 156.

105. David C. Steinmetz, *Luther in Context* (Bloomington: Indiana University Press, 1986), 96.

106. Luther, "Disputation against Scholastic Theology" [V/101], 273.

107. C. K. Brampton, ed., *The* De Imperatorum et Pontificum Potestate *of William of Ockham* (Oxford, 1927), quoted in Ernest A. Moody, s.v. "William of Ockham," in *The Encyclopedia of Philosophy* (New York: Macmillan, 1967), 8:317.

108. Pelikan, *Luther the Expositor* [V/41], 71.

109. Ibid., 76.

110. Desiderius Erasmus, "On the Freedom of the Will" (1524), ed. and trans. E. Gordon Rupp and A. N. Marlow, in *Luther and Erasmus: Free Will and Salvation,* Library of Christian Classics, vol. 17 (Philadelphia: Westminster Press, 1969), 38–41.

111. Martin Luther, "On the Bondage of the Will" (1525), ed. and trans. Philip S. Watson and B. Drewery, in *Luther and Erasmus: Free Will and Salvation* [V/110], 110.

112. Ibid., 159. See Klaas Runia, "The Hermeneutics of the Reformers," *Calvin Theological Journal* 19, nos. 2–4 (April-November 1984): 132.

113. Althaus, *Theology of Martin Luther* [V/104], 76.

114. Martin Luther, "Answer to Latomus," in *Early Theological Works* [V/101], 331.

115. Ibid., 337.

116. David Lotz, "*Sola Scriptura:* Luther on Biblical Authority," *Interpretation* 35, no. 3 (July 1981): 272–73.

117. Pelikan, *Luther the Expositor* [V/41], 174.

118. Martin Luther, *The Babylonian Captivity of the Church* (1520), in *Three Treatises,* 2nd rev. ed. (Philadelphia: Fortress Press, 1970), 132–33.

119. Ibid., 133.

120. Martin Luther, "The Sacrament of the Body and Blood of Christ, against the Fanatics" (1526).

121. Martin Luther, "That These Words of Christ, 'This is my Body,' etc., Still Stand Firm against the Fanatics," LW 37:13–150.

122. Ibid., 100.

123. Cf. Perelman, *The Realm of Rhetoric* [I/22], 126–37.

124. Luther, "That These Words of Christ" [V/121], 79.

125. Ibid., 118.

126. Ibid, 120–24.

127. Ibid., 134.

128. Zwingli's list of Lutheran errors are summarized by Robert H. Fischer in LW 37:155.

129. Martin Luther, "Confession Concerning Christ's Supper," LW 37:161–372.

130. Ibid., 360.

131. Ibid., 303–60.

132. "The Marburg Colloquy and the Marburg Articles," LW 38:20.

133. See, for example, Hedio's report on the colloquy in LW 38.

134. Martin Luther, "Brief Confession Concerning the Holy Sacrament," LW 38:315.

135. Torrance, *Theological Science* [IV/80], 75.

136. Gadamer, "Scope and Function" [I/68], 24.

137. Steinmetz, *Luther in Context* [V/105], 96.

138. Augustine *Conf.* 1.1.

UNCONCLUDING RHETORICAL POSTSCRIPT

1. Lash, *Easter in Ordinary* [I/90], 296.

2. T. S. Eliot, "Little Gidding," in *Four Quartets*, lines 240–42.

3. St. Gregory of Nazianzus, "Fifth Theological Oration," in *Christology of the Later Fathers* [Intro./2], 214, altered (emphasis mine).

Index of Names

Adam, Andrew, xv
Adam, Margaret, xv
Agrippa, King, 50
Althaus, Paul, 291–92n
Ameringer, T. E., 266n
Anselm of Canterbury, St., 51, 93, 105
Aquinas: *See* Thomas Aquinas, St.
Argyle, A. W., 290n
Aristotle (Aristotelian), 9, 15–18, 25,
    27, 30, 32–34, 39, 42–46, 69, 82–83,
    98–99, 101–2, 112–13, 115–17,
    126–28, 131–33, 139, 148–49, 153,
    155–56, 164–71, 174, 176, 213, 234,
    242, 261–62n, 265n, 268n, 275n,
    277–78n, 280–81n, 283n
Arius (Arian), 33
Arnhart, Larry, 83, 166, 261–62n,
    273n, 281n, 283n
Atkinson, Gary, xv
Augustine of Hippo, St., 33–34, 37,
    39, 51–52, 105, 177, 179, 222,
    231–32, 243, 249, 266–68n, 284n,
    289n, 290n, 293n

Bacon, Francis, 22, 276n
Bainton, Roland, 241, 269n, 291n
Bakhtin, Mikhail, 74, 205, 229, 268n,
    272n, 285n, 289n

Baldwin, Charles Sears, 262n
Balthasar, Hans Urs von, 269n
Barilli, Renato, 260n, 262–63n
Barth, Karl, 54–55, 60–61, 72,
    135–36, 138, 192, 206, 233–34,
    265n, 269n, 272n, 279n, 285n,
    288n, 290n
Basil the Great, St., 34, 266n
Bauer, Walter, 39
Beardsley, Monroe C., 276n
Beeck, Frans Josef van, 265–66n
Bellah, Robert, 269–70n
Benjamin, Walter, 277n
Berger, Teresa, xv
Berkeley, George, 22
Bernstein, Richard J., 19–20, 25,
    263–64n, 269n
Berquist, Goodwin F., 260n
Bethge, Eberhard, 145, 280n
Bitzer, Lloyd, 261n
Black, Edwin, 261n, 265n
Blair, Hugh, 14
Bloom, Allan, 268n, 277n
Boff, Clodovis, 271n, 273n, 276n,
    279n
Boff, Leonardo, 276n
Bonhoeffer, Dietrich, 144–45

295

Index of Subjects

abbreviated enthymemes and syllogisms, 166–68

abominations, as "devil–term," 137, 236

abstract(ion), 8, 21, 28, 40, 42, 57, 61–62, 64, 67, 73, 76–77, 83, 102, 113, 116–17, 129, 131, 133, 148, 171, 182, 188, 214, 218, 239, 253

academy, as "public" of theology, 64–66, 94, 96, 129

actions, 86–87, 93, 100, 106, 114, 127, 139–45, 151, 250. *See also* discursive and nondiscursive communication

"adequate to the occasion," 69, 72–75, 82, 96–97

adoration: *See* worship

agonistic structures, 74, 76

agreeing, agreement, xiii, 13, 15, 46, 48, 50, 55, 61, 72, 102, 112, 115, 131, 151–55, 168–70, 182, 193–94, 204, 208, 211–13, 250–51

alētheia: *See* truth

allegory, allegorical interpretation, 85–86, 221

alliances: *See* audience; community; scope

amoralism in rhetoric, 11

amore: *See* "arguing with love"

anabaptism: *See* baptism; radical Reformation

anagogical sense of scripture, 221

anakephalaiōsis, 255

analogy: of context, 116; of doctrine to rules (Lindbeck), 211; linguistic, 193, 200, 205, 208; as theological approach, 85–86, 176, 178–79, 283–84n

analytic method, 15–16, 28, 34–37, 82, 155–59, 166–67, 170, 172, 212, 225, 281n

anastaurountas: *See* crucifixion

Anfechtung, 241

anonymous and/or pseudonymous works, 13, 120–21

anti-Semitism, 143

antistrophē, 16–17

apaideusia, 153–55

apodeixis, 155

apostolicity, 199

appearances, 9, 14, 40, 99, 132, 144

application, 9, 27, 30, 156–57, 170, 219–21

aretē, 127. *See also* actions; virtue

"arguing with love" (Johnstone), 126, 139, 208

Index of Scriptural Citations